THE·ORDEAL OF
AMERICAN
ENGLISH

HOUGHTON MIFFLIN RESEARCH SERIES

Number 9

HOUGHTON MIFFLIN RESEARCH SERIES

THE ORDEAL OF
AMERICAN
ENGLISH

Edited by

C. MERTON BABCOCK

Michigan State University

HOUGHTON MIFFLIN COMPANY · BOSTON

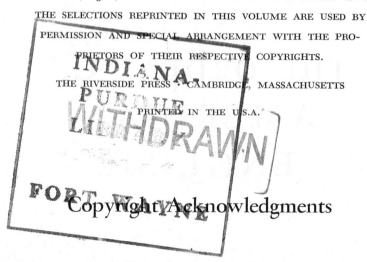

Copyright Acknowledgments

"Concerning the American Language" from *The Stolen White Elephant* by Mark Twain, reprinted by permission of Harper & Brothers.

"The Myth of an American Language" by J. St. Loe Strachey, reprinted from the May 15, 1926, issue *of The Independent*, by permission of The Rt. Hon. John Strachey, M.P.

"Speaking of Books" by Ivor Brown, reprinted from *The New York Times Book Review*, May 4, 1952, by permission of the author and *The New York Times*.

The following articles are reprinted by permission from *The Nation:* "Do Americans Speak English?" by John Erskine, in the April 15, 1925, issue, and "Language by Legislation" in the April 11, 1923, issue.

"American English and English English" by Randolph Quirk, professor of English Language in the University of London. Reprinted from *The New York Times Magazine*, December 2, 1956, by special permission of the author and *The New York Times*.

"Caun't Speak the Language" from *Walking Stick Papers* by Robert Cortes Holliday. Copyright 1918 by George H. Doran Company. Reprinted by permission of Doubleday & Company, Inc.

"The Characteristics of American English and Their Origin" by John W. Clark in *British and American English Since 1900* by Eric Partridge and John W. Clark. Copyright 1951 by Philosophical Library. Reprinted by permission of the publisher.

"American Speech: An Indictment" by S. F. Markham, in *The New York Times Magazine*, February 26, 1939. Reprinted by permission of the author and *The New York Times*.

"Our Living Language: A Defense" reprinted by permission of Dodd, Mead & Company from *How to Write* by Stephen Leacock. Copyright 1943 by Dodd, Mead & Company, Inc.

"The Conquering Tongue" by D. W. Brogan from the February 5, 1943, issue of *The Spectator*. Reprinted by permission of *The Spectator*.

"The American Language" by H. L. Mencken, from *The Yale Review*, copyright Yale University Press. By permission of the managing editor of *The Yale Review*.

In Memory of

LOUISE POUND

Publisher's Note

The use of selected research materials no longer needs justification — if indeed it ever did. That they ease the strain on overtaxed libraries and aid the instructor in teaching the heart of the research method by giving him control of material which all his class is using, there is no dispute. But there are other advantages worth noting.

A genuine grasp of research method is of life-long value. The habit of sifting evidence, weighing bias, winnowing fact from opinion, assessing the judgments of others, and reaching an opinion of one's own with due regard for the possibility that new-found evidence may change it tomorrow — this is far more than a means to better grades and better papers; it is a way of mature and responsible thinking which can affect one's competence in every aspect of living. It is the aim of this book, and of the others in the Houghton Mifflin Research Series, to help the student take a stride in this direction.

The aim has been to pack into these pages enough central documentary material to give useful practice in choosing a limited topic within a broader area, scanning a large body of material, and hence in learning to reject that which is not immediately relevant and to select that which is. The major emphasis is thus placed, as it should be, on the selection, evaluation, organization, and synthesis of materials. The mechanics of notetaking, outlining, and footnote and bibliographical form are treated in every handbook and rhetoric and are not discussed here. For accurate documentation, however, the page numbers of original sources are given in heavy type immediately *after* the material from the page.

Within the limits of these broad aims the book can be used in many ways: (a) for short practice papers stressing the mechanics of research technique; (b) for full-length research papers using only materials here provided; and (c) as a springboard for papers which involve use of the library and additional reading, either historical or literary. Literature as such has been excluded, partly for reasons of length and of general student interest, and partly because only the gifted or the specially trained student can at this stage competently handle the very different problems of research and of criticism at the same time. For such students thre is ample opportunity to step from the present materials into the relevant literature of special interest to him.

The editor has appended a list of suggested topics for longer papers, some demanding the use of only the materials in this collection, some leading to further reading and research. He has also included questions for writing and discussion which give both practice and example to encourage the kinds of reading and thinking essential to competent research in any field and which will suggest many topics that may be treated in shorter papers. The Selected Bibliography may serve as a basis for extended investigation.

Introduction

British visitors to the United States have been, for the most part, hypercritical of the language habits of the American people. A London journalist, commenting on America's use of English, once asked: "Will they ever learn the English language, which was the best thing imported in the Mayflower?" In 1839, Frederick Marryat was shocked at "how very debased the language has become in a short period in America." A century later, the British magazine *Punch* referred to the language of the United States as "a form of verbal expectoration that is most profane and most detestable." Nor was that the last word on the subject. Just three years ago a British lord sent us a *billet-doux* entitled "You Americans are Murdering the Language."

This kind of criticism, of course, is not restricted to the English people. Anglomaniacs on this side of the Atlantic have spared no effort to defend the virgin chastity of the Queen's English against the various intrepidations of Mrs. Malaprop, the Spelling Demons, and the Seven Deadly Sins of Syntax. Linguistic royalists in the time-honored tradition of Benjamin Franklin, John Quincy Adams, and John Pickering have deplored any innovations in our speechways. One educator has called our "abuse" of the Mother tongue "the modern crime of linguacide."

From the time of the American Revolution, the Anglo-American atmosphere has been right for a linguistic war between the two countries. Literary men and philologists, politicians and statesmen, pedants and schoolma'ams, have volunteered on one side or the other in the battle over words. Noah Webster, in 1789, penned what might appropriately be called a "Declaration of Linguistic Independence," and his patriotism has been fervently supported by such men as Timothy Dwight, Thomas Jefferson, Ralph Waldo Emerson, Herman Melville, James Russell Lowell, and Walt Whitman. The history of American English up to the present day has been punctuated with the well-aimed fussilades of both factions. At about the time of World War I, it seemed more than likely that a truce could be reached, but, when in 1919 Mencken trained his howitzers on England, in the form of *The American Language*, all hope of an armistice was forfeited, and hostilities were renewed with increased vigor. To this day, the smoke of battle clouds the important issues in any discussion of the two principal streams of the English language.

The forces that have made the language spoken in the United States differ from that spoken in England are the same forces that have molded American culture and American civilization; for the American language owes its very character to the circumstances of our country's development. Social, racial, religious, economic, and geographic factors have influenced the idiom of democracy. The spirit which founded the Republic, the early struggle with Great Britain, the New England theocracy, the conquest of the wilderness, the taming of the frontier, the open-door policy to foreigners, the distrust of aristocratic "virtues," the concept of progress, the will to succeed, the open-endedness of American planning, have made indelible impressions on the words and phrases which have become the currency of American speech. Mr. Dooley was right when he said that "when we Americans are done with the English language it will look as if it had been run over by a musical comedy."

Through the generations since the founding of Jamestown and the landing of the Pilgrims, the language of America has undergone tremendous transformations. New words have been coined, old words have acquired new meanings, spellings have been altered, and the very sounds of English have been changed. The Massachusetts School Law of 1647 would be all but incomprehensible to a schoolboy of today. The people of Great Britain have watched with considerable consternation the Americans outstrip them in population, prestige, wealth and power. It has been increasingly difficult for the Mother Country, under the circumstances, to maintain linguistic control of her wayward stepchild in the New World. More and more Americanisms are becoming part of the vocabulary of England, what with increased facilities for transportation, and communication between the two countries. The time may yet come when the linguistic differences will cancel themselves out and the philological hatchet be buried once and for all.

The principal purpose of this volume of readings in American English is to supply materials for documentary papers in the broad field of the American language. Three types of exercises have been planned: (1) short papers based on specific essays included in the collection; (2) longer papers which synthesize ideas from many of the essays included in the volume; and (3) papers which reach outward to materials not included in this collection. The documents have been chosen so as to favor no one point of view in a controversial issue. They were selected primarily for their appropriateness to the subject, although lucidity and readability have also been considered. The documents have been arranged in topical rather than chronological order, and there is some overlapping, so that certain essays classified in one section of the book comment significantly on topics treated specifically in other sections. The bibliography is highly selective and by no means complete.

It is hoped that the readings and exercises will help students to become better acquainted with the forces that have shaped American civilization and the American language, and to acquire open-minded attitudes toward the problems of composition and communication.

— C. Merton Babcock

East Lansing, Michigan

Contents

1
THE AMERICAN LANGUAGE: MYTH OR REALITY

from *The Stolen White Elephant*
by Mark Twain
London: George Newnes, Ltd., n.d.

Concerning the American Language

Mark Twain

There was an Englishman in our compartment, and he complimented me on — on what? But you would never guess. He complimented me on my English. He said Americans in general did not speak the English language as correctly as I did. I said I was obliged to him for his compliment, since I knew he meant it for one, but that I was not fairly entitled to it, for I didn't speak English at all — I only spoke American.

He laughed, and said it was a distinction without a difference. I said no, the difference was not prodigious, but still it was considerable. We fell into a friendly dispute over the matter. I put my case as well as I could, and said:

"The languages were identical several generations ago, but our changed conditions and the spread of our people far to the south and far to the west have made many alterations in our pronunciation, and have introduced new words among us and changed the meanings of many old ones. English people talk through their noses; we do not. We say *know*, English people say não; we say *cow*, the Briton says *kãow* we — "

"Oh, come! that is pure Yankee; everybody knows that."

"Yes, it is pure Yankee; that is true. One cannot **page 219/** hear it in America outside of the little corner called New England, which is Yankee land. The English themselves planted it there two hundred and fifty years ago, and there

1

it remains; it has never spread. But England talks through her nose yet; the
Londoner and the backwoods New Englander pronounces 'know' and 'cow' alike,
and then the Briton unconsciously satirizes himself by making fun of the Yankee's
pronunciation."

We argued this point at some length; nobody won; but no matter, the fact remains — Englishmen say *nāo* and *kāow* for "know" and "cow," and that is what the
rustic inhabitant of a very small section of America does.

"You conferred your *a* upon New England too, and there it remains; it has not
travelled out of the narrow limits of those six little States in all these two hundred
and fifty years. All England uses it, New England's small population — say four
millions — use it, but we have forty-five millions who do not use it. You say
'glahs of wawtah,' so does New England; at least, New England says *glahs*.
America at large flattens the *a*, and says "glass of water.' These sounds are
pleasanter than yours; you may think they are not right — well, in English they
are *not* right, but in 'American' they are. You say *flahsk*, and *bahsket*, and *jackahss*;
we say 'flask,' 'basket,' 'jackass' — sounding the *a* as it is in 'tallow,' 'fallow,' and
so on. Up to as late as 1847 Mr Webster's dictionary had the impudence to still
pronounce 'basket' *bahsket*, when he knew that outside of his little New England
all America shortened the *a* and paid no attention to his English broadening of it.
However, it called itself an English Dictionary, so it was proper enough that it
should stick to English forms, perhaps. It still calls itself an English Dictionary
to-day, but it has quietly   page 220/   ceased to pronounce 'basket' as if it were
spelt *bahsket*. In the American language the *h* is respected; the *h* is not dropped
or added improperly."

"The same is the case in England — I mean among the educated classes, of
course."

"Yes, that is true; but a nation's language is a very large matter. It is not simply
a matter of speech obtaining among the educated handful; the manner obtaining
among the vast uneducated multitude must be considered also. Your uneducated
masses speak English, you will not deny that; our uneducated masses speak
American — it won't be fair for you to deny that, for you can see yourself that
when your stable-boy says, 'It isn't the 'unting that 'urts the 'orse, but the 'ammer,
'ammer, 'ammer on the 'ard 'ighway,' and our stable-boy makes the same remark
without suffocating a single *h*, these two people are manifestly talking two different languages. But if the signs are to be trusted, even your educated classes used
to drop the *h*. They say *humble* now, and *heroic*, and *historic*, etc., but I judge
that they used to drop those *h*'s because your writers still keep up the fashion of
putting *an* before those words, instead of *a*. This is what Mr. Darwin might call a
'rudimentary' sign that that *an* was justifiable once, and useful — when your
educated classes used to say *'umble*, and *'eroic*, and *'istorical*. Correct writers
of the American language do not put *an* before those words."

The English gentleman had something to say upon this matter, but never mind
what he said — I'm not arguing his case. I have him at a disadvantage now. I
proceeded.

"In England you encourage an orator by exclaiming 'H'yaah! h'yaah!' We pronounce it *heer* in some sections, *'h'yer'* in others, and so on; but our whites do not

say 'h'yaah,' pronouncing the **page 221/** *a's* like the *a* in *ah*. I have heard English ladies say 'don't you' — making two separate and distinct words of it; your Mr Burnand has satirized it. But we always say 'dontchu.' This is much better. Your ladies say, 'Oh, its *o*ful nice!' Ours say, 'Oh, it's *aw*ful nice!' We say '*Four* hundred,' You say '*For*' — as in the word *or*. Your clergymen speak of the 'Lawd,' ours of 'the Lord'; yours speak of 'the gawds of the heathen,' ours of 'the gods of the heathen.' When you are exhausted you say you are 'knocked up.' We don't. When you say you will do a thing 'directly,' you mean 'immediately'; in the American language — generally speaking — the word signifies 'after a little.' When you say 'clever' you mean 'capable'; with us the word used to mean 'accommodating,' but I don't know what it means now. Your word 'stout' means 'fleshy'; our word 'stout' usually means 'strong.' Your words 'gentleman' and 'lady' have a very restricted meaning; with us they include the barmaid, butcher, burglar, harlot, and horsethief. You say, 'I haven't *got* any stockings on,' 'I haven't *got* any memory,' 'I haven't *got* any money in my purse'; we usually say, 'I haven't any stockings on,' 'I haven't any memory,' 'I haven't any money in my purse.' You say 'out of window'; we always put in a *the*. If one asks 'How old is that man?' the Briton answers, 'He will be about forty'; in the American language we should say, 'He *is* about forty.' However, I won't tire you, sir; but if I wanted to, I could pile up differences here until I not only convinced you that English and American are separate languages, but that when I speak my native tongue in its utmost purity an Englishman can't understand me at all."

"I don't wish to flatter you, but it is about all I can do to understand you *now*." **page 222/**

That was a very pretty compliment, and it put us on the pleasantest terms directly — I use the word in the English sense. . . . **page 223/**

from *The Independent*, Vol. CXVI
May 15, 1926

The Myth of an American Language

J. St. Loe Strachey

In all probability, more nonsense is talked about what is termed the American language than about any other subject. In America I noticed a distinct tendency among the more conservative classes to bewail the vulgarization or, at any rate, the alteration of the language. Some people even went so far as to say they supposed that the current writing and talking was often almost unintelligible to an Englishman. I hope I was able to reassure them on that point. There are changes in the language going on both here and in America, and one ought to be thankful that this is so, for when languages cease to grow and develop the end is near.

So far from my being unable to follow the American language, I was distinctly disappointed at not adding as much as I had hoped to my knowledge of transatlantic slang. Ever since as a boy I ardently admired Artemus Ward, I have loved the vividness of American slang and the intense ingenuity with which new words are coined and old words given new significance. Still, I gathered something into my granary. For example, though I do not know how old the phrase is in America, I had never till last autumn heard, "You said a mouthful!" The expression is distinctly forceful and picturesque, even though a certain amount of intricacy is involved in explaining it. There seems to be some mystery as to whether the mouthful belongs to the auditor or is the prerogative of the speaker. Indeed, I often used to take pleasure in puzzling over this, as Sir Thomas Browne tells us he enjoyed puzzling out some of the paradoxical and mystical propositions of the scholastic theologians. I am told that a civic lady who received a fascinating queen upon her visit to America used it most effectively. The queen in question expressed in glowing terms all the delightful things that every tourist, except one with the hide of an elephant and the heart of an iceberg, feels on landing in New York. The New York lady replied, "Say, queen, you said a mouthful!" I must leave my mystery at that — and after all, mysteries were meant to be enjoyed, not to be anatomized.

Another expression which, though not quite new to me, since I am a reader of *Life*, was the word "Attaboy!" When the thing is explained to you, you see it in a moment; but up to that time you keep wondering whence came this strange verbal anomaly. I used to think that it was a negro or an Asiatic word that had somehow been seized by an American, just as the immortal Mr. Pinkerton swooped down on words like "hebdomadal" and in the twinkling of an eye had them in his advertisements, as he put it, in letters as big as themselves. But in reality "Attaboy" had no Persian or Tartar origin. It is as simple a perverted colloquialism as you could imagine. An old fan is at a baseball or a football match. In the course of the game he sees with delight his kinsman, his fellow citizen, or some member of his old university perform a special act of skill or daring. Instantly he calls out, "That's the boy! That's the boy for me!" Now, if you say that phrase very fast and cut off your words at the beginning and at the end, "Ah, that's the boy for me!" soon becomes "Attaboy!" If I were younger and bolder I should use that expression as a commendation for men of politics or men of letters, hitherto obscure, who suddenly do a good thing. But alas! I have not quite the pluck to put "Attaboy!" in solitary grandeur at the end of a description of Mr. Jones' new book or Mr. Smith's fiery oration on currency in the House of Commons.

In the United States I met with an almost universal sense of love and reverence for that English language which is as much America's heritage and possession as ours. But, since the great principle of the exception proving the rule should not be broken, I found in this connection one — though only one — immovably defeatist lady. She tried her very best to convince me that the American and British languages have practically nothing in common, so greatly and so fundamentally have they diverged, and she intimated that I was either a foolish flatterer or else an insidious enemy when I refused to admit that I found any difficulty in understanding what I read and heard in America. It was useless to declare that I often found better and purer language in American newspapers than even in English books. I was not believed. So eloquent was the lady, and so determined to show me that I must not claim any share in the American language, that I was quite depressed. I drove back from my dinner party with a nightmarish conviction that I   page 579/   had not only failed to understand the things that had been said to me, but that I might feel equally sure that no American could have understood what I myself said. In this devitalized condition I reached home and prepared for bed; but as I was undressing my eyes alighted upon a little book which my wife had brought home that day after some investigation into the matter of children's courts. It was a reprint of some of the more recent statutes of the State of New York, empowering and enlarging laws administered in the State courts. I began to read, and within three or four minutes all my doubts were gone. The conversation of the depressing lady had vanished like a dream.

I am generally rather a condemner of the literary style that parliamentary draftsmen affect, with its verbiage, its ambiguity, and its refusal to say a plain thing in a plain way; but I cannot exaggerate my comfort in finding that here was the State of New York, in the year 1925, legislating with all the worst tricks of the legislative trade as I knew it in England. Such words as "An Act to amend the Twenty-fourth Statute of such and such a year" warmed my heart. The act itself began in the fearless old fashion legislating by reference. Previous statutes were dealt with in such a way that no human being could possibly understand them. "Be it enacted by and with the consent of . . . , that so much of Clause 6, Subsection 3, which refers to the female child delinquent, shall be repealed" — going on to say that "in Clause 8 all the words from 'By' to 'through' shall be   page 587/   repealed and the following words substituted therefor." Then came scraps of language as doubtful and ambiguous as a Greek oracle, and yet clothed in exactly the legal phraseology which had enriched my youthful efforts as a law student. To me these words now seemed blessed. They were like "the shadow of a great rock in a weary land." So long as Parliaments carry on in this fine style, I have no fear that the two branches of the language will become "mutually unintelligible." The *liaison* of technical jargon was complete. Since I have been a little hard on legal jargon, I ought to say that I am by no means oblivious to the magnificent help which has been given by the lawyers on both sides of the Atlantic in maintaining the unity of the English-speaking race. Read any report of proceedings, not merely in the Supreme Court, but in any court in which a legal argument is being heard, and you will find that a high strain of vigorous and polished English is employed in the speeches of counsel and in the decisions of the judges.

The fact is that the English language is as secure in America as it is in England and is as much the language of Shakespeare and of the Bible, of Bacon, of Burke, of Walter Scott, and of Jane Austen as it is in England. My only fear in the matter is that the Americans, being at bottom a very conservative people, may, especially in the legal, political, theological, and philosophic worlds, tend to be too much bound — may forget, in fact, Dryden's glorious outburst: "I trade both with the living and the dead for the enrichment of our tongue."   page 588/

 from *The New York Times Book Review*
May 4, 1952

American Language Myth

Ivor Brown

There is no such thing as the American Language any more than there is such a thing as the English Language. There are half a dozen species of each and some of them are more or less identical. I have, for example, just been reading through some editorials in *The New York Times* and *The London Times.* As far as style and vocabulary are concerned you could slip the writing of one into the columns of the other without anybody noticing any difference in their excellence.

There is, indeed, in the case of these two countries, a unified, editorial-writer's language, which has its own formalities on both sides of the ocean. For example, both in Times Square and in Printing House Square the builders of opinion are apt to observe that "It is incumbent on us all" or "To vote is an obligation and privilege of citizenship." Yet nobody supposes that when they are setting out in the afternoon to write their evening pieces of grave counsel for the morrow they say, on parting from the ever-loving wife, "It is an obligation and privilege to ask the Simpsons back to dinner and it is incumbent on you to see that the dinner is a good one."

I am not decrying the formalities. It is a particular pleasure to a conservative Englishman to discover how much of his language's old leisured stateliness has been preserved in America. The "gotten" of U.S.A. is still preferred by an Englishman of literary taste to the snappy English "got," and all lovers of the eighteenth century and its classical elevation of style must like to hear of an elevator operated and not of a lift worked; there is more distinction in the aloofness of an apartment than in the levelness of the curt, undignified flat.

Shakespeare and Milton, if their shades revisited a Hollywood film, might recognize many words which were the English of their time and some of which have been lost. Christopher Morley has reminded me that Shakespeare wrote of a "deck" of cards and not a pack. Milton's use of "homely" is preserved in America, having changed its meaning in England, and he would have called a sidewalk just that, whereas this simple and precisely explanatory term has been lost by the English, who use the vague "pavement" instead. So it is pleasant for one who has had pleasant hours among the minds of the seventeenth century to meet their vocabulary still alive in another continent.

Where the languages might naturally fall apart is in their slang; but are they so far sundered? The Englishman who cannot grasp and enjoy the vivacity and pungency and metaphorical richness of the various American slangs is either a prig or a fool. In his introduction to a collection of Damon Runyon stories, which shares place of honor with the Sherlock Holmes collection at my bedside, E. C. Bentley has very properly denounced the feeble English habit of asking for glossaries of American slang. Good American speech of the people declares its meaning by its force and picturesqueness of imagery and he who cannot understand it must, in my view as well as Bentley's and in Runyon's idiom, be such a guy as is more than somewhat dumb.

There may be some words spoken at Lindy's that are strange to our eyes and ears, but Runyon is ready to explain them. Fink, for example. Joe the Blow Fly is a fink, a fink being "such a guy as is extra nothing" — and also "a character who is lower than a mud-cat's vest pocket." Yet even in my Runyon I find, among the conversations of such as Hot-Horse Herbie and Regret the Horseplayer the use of dast for darest; and that at once sets the bells of the seventeenth century ringing in the ears, just as such a grave, admonitory name as Regret reminds one of the old moralists. Here Runyon and Bunyan commingle.

Few in England would now call a hammer a "mawl," yet this old word for the mallet used in the game of Pall Mall (and so giving London one of its most august street names) turns up when Rusty Charley enters Nathan Detroit's crapgame. The players "are packed so close you cannot get a needle between two guys with a mawl."

The formal and the fresh, the classic cadence and the invention of the last minute — America retains them so fondly and creates so fruitfully. At one time the American language is still strolling with the silken ladies of Pomander Walk; at another it is the utterance of guys and dolls. Guys? Yes, they are older than Guy Fawkes and one stalks majestic in Scottish Dunbar's famous praise of London. Of London's Lord Mayor that fifteenth-century balladist wrote that "No Lord of Parys, Venyce, or Floraunce" was the equal in dignity of this civic "exampler, lode-star, and guye." Great guy indeed!

Guys and dolls, not to mention molls, are familiar in American fiction and "musicals." Yet here is the guye in the London of Henry VII, while Doll or Doll-Common was Ben Jonson's name for a woman of the town and Molls or Moll-Commons were of the same low company in that high period of comedy. Incidentally, Ben Jonson used "beat it" for go. Continually the lingo of new Broadway is linked with that of old Bankside. How can any word-lover resist such a language? page 2/

from *The Nation*, Vol. CXX
April 15, 1925

Do Americans Speak English?

John Erskine

In a sense, it is of little importance whether we do or not. Some of our neighbors like to say we do, but when we hear an Englishman speak he seems not to be an American. Yet we get the gist of what he says. Others try to convince us that we speak an American language, and they prove their case by citing all the words and phrases which some of us use and no Englishman uses, and by ignoring the far larger group of words and phrases which we and the Englishman use in common. Yet there are also expressions familiar to Englishmen and not to us; are they alone what constitutes the English language? In the United States as in England every large district or city has at least a few expressions not used elsewhere. It is a harmless but comparatively unilluminating pastime to study a language exclusively in its fringes, as Mr. Mencken likes to do; and a fine poet like William Barnes has the right, doubtless, to bury his talent in a dialect, if he wishes that kind of obscurity. Mr. John Weaver is going the same path through the local and personal slang which to him, when he writes, is the American language. But Mr. Mencken and Mr. Weaver do not, I believe, talk the language they call American; they speak a very good — as we careless folk would say — English. It's the language we speak that counts, in life and in literature — so much so that the great men in literature have usually tried to bring the written word into harmony with the spoken, instead of encouraging an exclusive language to write in.

For the average person the important thing is to speak as well as he can the best language he and his hearers know. The philosophical person may also find it important to compare his speech with that of others presumably in the same tongue, to discover if his own usage might be improved. I assume that we Americans speak English, and I concede that we do not speak it as the English do, not even in those parts of our vocabulary which are common to both peoples. I should like to note some of the differences, and to ask what they mean.

Not the differences in words, I repeat. No two of us in New York, no two in London, use an identical vocabulary. Words, anyway, are the last things the civilized will attend to. Perhaps we ought to notice them, but we rarely do. When we are learning to talk, as babies in our own language or as adults in a foreign tongue, we have to work our way syllable by syllable, but when we have a mastery of speech we express ourselves and understand others largely through the tune, the accent, the rising and falling of the voice. When we call out a question to someone in another room, we can tell the answer if we can hear the tune of it; the words don't matter. How embarrassing it is to try our knowledge of a foreign language in the land where it belongs, and to discover that the natives seem not to be saying any of the individual words we got out of the dictionary. Our impression is correct; the man who speaks his own tongue is talking less in words than in a tune. But since the tune can't be written down, we can't find it outside of the spoken word.

Though they use the same words, the Englishman and the American do not speak the same tune. Why they don't, I haven't the faintest idea. But again I am disposed not to worry about it, for though the English tune is pretty to my ear, it often brings the accent of the sentence into conflict with the logic of it, and in an ideal language I should think the accent and the logic would coincide. "Household," "housekeeper," "housewife" — in such classes of words the distinguishing part ought logically to be accented. In Greek — not a bad language — we should say "househóld," "housekeéper," not "hóusehold," "hóusekeeper." In so far as the American accent moves in a logical direction, we may be reconciled to our ignorance of the English tune. There is the same conflict between logic and tune in longer phrases, in whole sentences. When an Englishman wishes to give the effect of a strong negative, he emphasizes the positive **page 410/** element in the sentence. The Irish, who seem to the English illogical, emphasize the negative. "Is Mrs. Smith at home?" "She is *not*," says the Irish maid. "She *isn't*," says the English one. To English ears the Irish tune, in that case, sounds abrupt, and it says not a negative but a discourtesy. I fear we Americans shall always have some difficulty in understanding the English — not when they write, but when they speak; for many of the cadences which mean to them friendly solicitude are the very tunes we are accustomed to use to express superciliousness and contempt.

Coleridge pointed out that logic sometimes gets the better of an Englishman, when he is off his guard, and spoils his tune, and even makes a serious statement seem ridiculous. In church, he said in his "Table Talk," he had often heard clergymen read the first chapters of Genesis with an intonation prompted by logic but giving the effect of incredulity. "And God said, let there be light. And there *was* light" — strange to say! The proper English tune would suppress the important verb, and emphasize the noun, "God said, let there be light. And there was *light*."

If we have observed the strange effect that the English tune makes upon our ears, we can understand why some of the younger generation find it hard to appreciate the music of great English verse. As a matter of fact, they haven't heard it. They read their Tennyson or their Keats, their Byron or their Shelley, set to an American tune. It is not surprising, after all, that Shakespeare rarely fares well on our stage, since our actors and actresses, no matter how beautifully they pronounce his words (of course, not as he pronounced them), are almost completely at sea as to the larger melody of the verse. It is not surprising that thoughtful American poets should be consciously trying to write in the American tune, in the shorter cadences most of us use. For that reason I've thought that the free-verse movement of a few years ago was chiefly important as disclosing our taste in speech, our positive, declarative sentences laid down line by line, our neglect of qualifying clauses, the monotony of our tune. For in the matter of the tune we have departed not only from the English but from our earlier selves. To my ears the tune of Walt Whitman, the long-phrased, varied, sinuous tune, is the tune of Lincoln in the Gettysburg Address. The tune of Miss Lowell's verse seems to me the tune of Roosevelt's prose.

The first complaint I should make against our speech is that it is horribly monotonous — it hasn't tune enough. Perhaps you might say that the immigrant races other than English have mastered the words, but have wiped out the tune altogether. That theory doesn't account for the awful level on which the New England voice can move in its purest moments of tradition. Are we losing our ear? Is language for us an appeal only to the eye? After a century of silent drama on the films, shall we be able to hear anything?   **page 411/**   . . .

2

DIVERGENCE OF AMERICAN FROM ENGLISH

from *More Fables*
by George Ade
Chicago and New York: Herbert S. Stone,
1900

The Fable of the Michigan Counterfeit Who Wasn't One Thing or the Other

George Ade

Two Travelers sat in a Sleeping Car that was fixed up with Plush and Curly-Cues until it resembled a Chambermaid's Dream of Paradise. They were talking about the Man who sat across the Aisle.

"I think he is an Englishman," said the First Traveler.

"Why do you think so?" queried his Companion.

"Well, in the first place his Clothes don't fit him," replied the First Traveler. "I observe, also, that he has piled all his Luggage on Another Man's page 91/ Seat, that he has opened several Windows without asking Permission, that he has expected the Porter to pay Attention to him and nobody else, and that he has Kicked at something every Thirty Seconds since we left Buffalo."

"You make out a Strong Case," said the Second Traveler, nodding. "I will admit that the Suit is Fierce. Still, I maintain that he is not an Englishman. I notice that he seems somewhat Ashamed of his Clothes. Now, if he were an Englishman, he would Glory in the Misfit."

"Perhaps he is a Canadian," suggested the First Traveler.

"Impossible," said the other. "He may be English, but he is not sufficiently British to be a Canadian. If he were a Canadian he would now be singing page 92/ 'Britannia Rules the Wave!' No, I insist that he is an American traveling Incog. I suspect that I have Caught him with the Goods. While sitting here, I have had my Sherlock Holmes System at work. A few Moments ago he read a Joke in a Comic Paper, and the Light of Appreciation kindled in his Eye before a full Minute had elapsed."

"Perhaps it was not a Comic Paper at all," said the First Traveler. "It may have been Punch. Very often an Englishman will Get Next almost immediately if the Explanation is put in Parentheses. You have to Hand it to him with a Diagram and a Map and then give him a little Time, and then he Drops. This man is certainly an Englishman. Notice the Expression page 94/ of Disapproval. He does not fancy our Farm Scenery. Get onto the Shoes, too. They are shaped like Muffins. Then if you are still in Doubt, pay attention to the Accent. Didn't you hear him just now when he was complaining to the Porter because the Sun was on the wrong side of the Car?"

"Yes, but did you hear him use 'Cahn't and 'Glass' both in the same Sentence? When a Man Plays it Both Ways, it is a Sign that he was born in Wisconsin and attended Harvard. I am convinced that he is not an Englishman at all. He is probably an American who takes a Bahth in a Bath-Tub."

But the First Traveler persisted that surely the Man across the aisle was an Englishman, so they Jawed back and page 95/ forth and finally made a Bet. Then the First Traveler stepped over and begged the Stranger's Pardon and asked him as a personal favor, to Identify himself. Was he an Englishman or an American?

"Really, that is a Hard Question to answer," said the Surprised Stranger. "I confess with some Mortification that Father was an American, but he wore Detachable Cuffs and talked about Live Stock at the Table, so the Heirs are trying to Forget him. As nearly as we can learn, one of my Ancestors came to this Country from Yorkshire early in the Eighteenth Century and founded a Tannery in Massachusetts, so I feel that I can claim an English Birthright, regardless of the intervening Ancestors. My Claim is strengthened by the Fact that our Family has a Regular Coat-of- page 96/ Arms. Everybody had forgotten about it for over Seven Hundred Years until Sister and I hired a Man to find it. Sister is now Lady Frost-Simpson and lives on the Other Side. When she discovered his Lordship he was down to his last Dickey. She took him out of Hock, and he is so Grateful that sometimes he lets me come and Visit them. I have seen the Prince."

"Then you are an Englishman?" queried the Traveler who had Bet that way.

"It is not admitted in London," was the sorrowful Reply. "Sometimes if Frost-Simpson has to come Home for Money while I am visiting Sister, he puts me up at the Clubs and all the Chaps seem to think I am an American. I try to be exactly like them but page 98/ I fail. They say I have an Accent, although I have been working all my Life to overcome it. I have not used the word 'Guess' for many Years."

"Yours is a Sad Case," remarked the Second Traveler. "Why do you ever come back?"

"To collect my Income," was the Reply. "Isn't it a Bore? Rents and all that sort of Rot, you know."

"But you have not settled the Bet," said one of the Persistent Travelers. "Are you a Yankee?"

"I have never Admitted it, and I cannot do so now," said the Brother-in-Law of Lord Frost-Simpson. "At the same time, it is on the Record that I was born at Pontiac, Michigan. Of course, you know What I am Striving to be. But there must be a Handicap some- **page 99/** where. During the Two Hundred Years in which my Ancestors temporarily resided in the States, they must have absorbed some of the Characteristics of this Uncouth and Vulgar People, and as a Result the Sins of the Father are visited upon the Child even to the third and fourth Generations, and I cannot hold a Monocle in my Eye to save my Life. I live Abroad, and strive to Forget, and work hard to be just like the other Fellows, but I do not seem to Arrive. Even in this Beastly Country, where the Imitation Article usually passes current as the Real Thing, there seems to be some Doubt as to my Case, seeing that you two Persons have made this Bet. Concerning the Bet, I fear that I am unable to Decide it. I do not know What I am." **page 100/**

"I know What you are," said the First Traveler, "but I do not dare to tell you right here in the Car, because the Pullman Company has a Rule against the use of such Language."

So they declared the Bet off and went forward and sat in the Day Coach.

Moral: *Be Something.* **page 101/**

 • from *The New York Times Magazine*
December 2, 1956

American English and English English

Randolph Quirk

London.

In speaking (impeccably) of the English spoken in the United States, Professor Higgins-Harrison, of "My Fair Lady," notes nightly: "In America, they haven't used it for years." I suppose all of us, fair ladies or flower girls, are touchy about our English, some of us more so than others. Since Colonial days, Americans have been aware, sometimes nervously, of the difference between their speech and that of the British Isles. In Britain there has been a corresponding readiness not only to spot such differences but to dub them uncultured, outlandish and slangy.

British travelers in the New World since the eighteenth century have returned home with lurid tales of the "barbarous" English used there. This description was in fact used by an Englishman in the Seventeen Thirties of the word "bluff," which he had heard in the sense of "steep bank." A century later we find Dickens in "Martin Chuzzlewit" making sarcastic comments on words like "location" and pronunciations like "prod-ooce" and "terri-tory." During the same period American can visitors in Britain returned with jeers about the Englishman's overfrequent use of "you know," his "wery" for "very," "anythink" for "anything" and his clipped words like "lib'ry" and "secret'ry." An early nineteenth-century American farce burlesqued British speech also with lines like "Halbert, did you 'ear 'im?" And, in the face of British accusations about neologisms in American English, a Yale professor about 1820 collected a list of British neologisms which included "absenteeism," "dupery" and "ill-timed," which have, of course, long since ceased to be purely British.

But, despite spirited American counterattacks of this kind, the undeniable historical priority of British English, as well as the still enduring prestige of the English Court, have left most Britons and many Americans with the belief that British English is somehow purer, more refined, less slangy than the New World variety. A typically nineteenth-century British attitude is illustrated in the story of a visit to England about 1850 by a young American lady of high social standing. At a party she got talking to a British officer who could not disguise his admiration for the way she was able to make herself understood. Unconscious of the implied insult, he took it upon himself to compliment her on her English; he even asked her if she were not remarkable among her compatriots. The girl answered, "Oh, yes, but then I had unusual advantages; there was an English missionary stationed near my tribe."

It is hard to imagine a similar exchange today. The growth of American prestige and other factors, such as the development of more sophisticated and tolerant attitudes to variations in speech (probably more prominently displayed today in Britain than in the United States), have contributed to a recognition of the right of American English (together with Australian English and other varieties) to be different from British English and yet be equally acceptable socially.

As for the extent of actual differences, there still remain serious misconceptions. These can be largely attributed to sensationalism and oversimplification on the part of most writers who offer commentaries on the regional variations within English. It is much easier to attract attention by concentrating on the differences that exist than on the broad area of agreement. It is engaging to read of what outlandish names others give to familiar objects; it is amusing to hear quips like "divided by a common language" and to read the largely invented stories of how Britons and Americans can misunderstand each other.

Take the story, for instance, of the American who is supposed to have asked an Englishman, "Do you have many chil- page 132/ dren?" and to have got the reply, "Oh no, only one every couple of years." This is based on the slender fact that educated people in the south of England tend not to use the auxiliary "do" with "have" except with reference to habitual action. ("Have you any cigarettes?" but "Do you always have eggs for breakfast?") The inventor of the story ignores the fact that southern Englishmen have plenty of opportunity of hearing "do you have" in other contexts from North-country folks, Irishmen and others — to say nothing of Americans — so that they understand such departures from their own usage without difficulty. It is a failure to distinguish between recognition and reproduction in language knowledge that permits such stories to have an air of validity about them. We understand large numbers of words and expressions that we never ourselves use.

There are popular lists of British and American variants arranged in double mutually exclusive columns which give a truly frightening impression of the degree of divergence between the major members of the English-speaking family. The British say "car," Americans, "automobile" at that, and that "automobile" is readily understood in England, being found in the titles of the two motoring organizations, the Royal Automobile Club and the Automobile Association.

The British word "tap," we are told, corresponds to the American "faucet." Again there is truth in this so far as it goes; but it is dangerously incomplete — unless we know that many Americans use "spigot" instead; that both "spigot" and "faucet" have some currency in British dialects, and that having filled a glass from his faucet or tap, the American is likely to call it "tapwater." What Americans call "quotation marks" the British call "inverted commas." But there are many Britons who call them "quotation marks," too.

When the American says "sick," he means what the Englishman calls "ill," but throughout the British armed forces one "reports sick" at the "sick bay," and if lucky gets sent home on "sick leave," and, needless to say, this is seldom on account of nausea. In fact there are parts of the United Kingdom where "sick" is the normal word and "ill" is regarded as highfalutin.

The American "mad" and British "angry" are another pair; people tend to ignore both the frequency of "mad" in this sense in Britain and also the sub-standard flavor attached to its usage in the United States. "Mail" and "post," "sidewalk" and "pavement" are not absolute divergences. "Pavement" is used in the sense of "sidewalk" not only in Britain but in Philadelphia and elsewhere. The "post" is often called "mail" in Britain and is carried in red mail vans, on mail trains, and on Royal Mail steamers; in America, mail is sorted at the post office, often takes the form of a postcard, bearing a stamp saying "United States Postage" and is delivered by a man who is often described as a postman.

And so one could go on. The long and imposing lists of so-called distinctively British and American words and usages are 75 per cent misleading; it turns out either that both the words so neatly separated are used in one or the other country, or that both are found in both countries but are used in slightly different contexts or in different proportions. At their best, such lists draw attention to differences in preferred usage in the two areas; they are certainly no index of mutual intelligibility. There is sufficient variety of speech on both sides of the Atlantic to familiarise us with most of the forms actually used by any native speaker of English.

Indeed, even in matters of pronunciation, it is difficult to find many absolute British and American distinctions. The broad "a" in the southern British "dance" is not unlike that heard in Boston. Nasalized vowels, so often regarded as solely American, are found in Liverpool and London; the Cockney, like the New Yorker, is apt to say "noo toon" for "new tune," and "lieutenant" is pronounced "lootenant" in the Royal Navy.

In some cases, an archaic form, once standard in both areas, has ceased to be standard in one only. This is the case with "r" after a vowel (as in "far"), still general in standard American usage but not in Britain, where, however, it is widespread in dialects such as the West Country and in Scotland. This phenomenon is to be seen in grammar and vocabulary, too. American English retaining "gotten," "I guess," and "fall," which have disappeared from standard British English. But Chaucer and Shakespeare had a word play with "fall" meaning autumn: "A green plum that ***falls *** before the fall should be."

Thus, in the historical and contemporary fabric of our common language it is important to look below the surface of these apparent divergences in usage. Even where they are real and important they often point not to cleavages between Britain as a whole and America as a whole but to cleavages between Briton and Briton, American and American, or (more subtle) to the existence of an intricate pattern of ties between some Britons and some Americans, between small groups of the English-speaking peoples across national frontiers.

Quite apart from the tremendous linguistic influence of America upon Britain at present, Americans and Britons are united over the long years of physical separation by a network in literature and life of individual threads which often have never operated to unite Britons as a whole or Americans as a whole.

In the last war our leaders not only communicated on strategy but each heartened the other by exchanging poems in our common language. But the unity of the English-speaking world is not just a political necessity and a social boon; it is also a linguistic fact. It is obvious linguistically as well as politically, to exaggerate divergences or to talk (like H. L. Mencken, but blessedly few others) of the "American Language." Noah Webster spent years trying, largely in vain, to create a linguistic gulf by encouraging Americans to say things like "ax" for "ask," "deef" and "heerd" for "deaf" and "heard." But in his maturity, he came to recognize that in all essentials Britons and Americans spoke the same language and that (as he said) it was highly "desirable to perpetuate the sameness." There is no reason to believe that history will prove false to his wish.   page 140/

from *American Speech*, Vol. I
June, 1926

American and English

Claude de Crespigny

. . . The American traveling in England, or the Englishman traveling in America, finds borne upon him, with startling suddenness, the fact that he is indeed in a foreign country. He makes the dumbfounding discovery that the vast difference in language is not so much that the words he hears are unfamiliar, but that the familiar words themselves are vested with unfamiliarity. They contain meanings that are meaningless; significances that are insignificant.

All reasons underlying such a change in language are purely psychological. Mr. G. K. Chesterton has admirably outlined the difference between the two psychologies of England and America, respectively, in his book, "What I saw in America." He finds a simple key to the solution of the puzzle in the expressions used by each nation to signify a dilemma. The English expression is 'in a hole.' This bespeaks fatalism. The American expression is 'up a tree,' which indicates a wild flight of fancy, in that the American is not without eventual hope of soaring into the clouds, thus escaping from his predicament.

An American gentleman in London once inquired of me the way to go 'downtown.' I explained that it was impossible to go 'downtown,' but that he could go to 'the City.' "But," he protested, "I am in the city." I carefully explained to him that the difference was one of a capital letter. 'Downtown' districts in England are called 'the City,' because the metropolitan areas take their cue from London. Now London originally consisted of a square-mile of ground enclosed by a wall and fortifications. The heterogeneous cosmopolis that has supplanted the former stronghold is called, legally, the County of London. Hence, the only distinction between that which was and that which is, is a distinction that is implied by the use of the definite article and a capital letter. Thus 'downtown' is 'the City.' Now while a person leaving the metropolis for the provinces travels 'down' (even while he may make an evident ascent), one traveling toward the metropolis invariably travels 'up,' even though he comes from a place that is considerably below sea-level. It needs quite a lecture to be explicit even in the simple matter of giving a direction. My American will no longer be lost, for he not only understands the term for 'downtown,' but he understands that there are no such things as 'blocks' in a tortuous maze of streets and boroughs, in each of page 149/ which the main theme of planning is represented by the hub and spokes of a wheel. One must, in England, take 'the first to the left, the second to the right, go round the square and then take the fourth to the left again.' This is quite incomprehensible to the American even as 'two blocks over,' or 'a block south of City Hall' is to an Englishman, who always calls his city hall a 'town hall,' a 'guild-hall,' or, in the case of the London County Council, a 'Spring Gardens.'

While an American cannot understand, at first, that a 'store,' in England, becomes a 'shop' (not 'shoppe'), a moment's reflection will remind him that Americans do go shopping. 'Clerk' (pronounced 'clark') is a word by which stenographers and scriveners, bank-tellers and book-keepers are known, but which the American will discover is entirely inadequate if he requires the services of a 'shoe-clerk' or a 'dry-goods clerk.' He must ask for a 'boot-maker's assistant' or a 'draper's assistant.'

A false rumor is circulated. The Englishman investigates the case, turns it upside down — and finds that there is 'nothing *in* it.' The American looks at the proposition, finds it lacks substance and concludes that there is 'nothing *to* it.' The one deals with the hollowness of a 'tinkling cymbal,' and the other with intangibility, a vast difference.

Now a 'barber-shop,' in England, is a place to which only the most proletarian of the proletariat may repair. The best institution of this kind (which is, after all, but a sorry apology for the American temple of face-worship) is known as a 'hair-dresser's,' possibly because to be thoroughly professionally English one must be thoroughly terminologically French. All French barbers are 'coiffeurs,' apparently because they will never learn to be barbers.

Our American may desire to purchase 'candy.' If he should be successful in discovering that candy is sold only in 'sweet-stuff shops,' or more snobbishly, 'confectioners,' he will find, upon asking for candy, that he will be handed a callous-looking, uninspiring boiled-sugar concoction, which alone has retained the old-fashioned appellation. He must ask for 'chocolates,' 'chocolate creams,' or even 'coffee creams.' Department stores sport the classic term of 'emporiums,' 'dry-goods' stores are 'drapers'; 'draperies' are 'hangings'; 'men's furnishings' are 'haberdashery.' The traveler's wife will experience less difficulty, for feminine fashions follow French phraseology, as 'robes, millinery, lingerie' (although a Frenchman would hardly understand the English 'linger-E' any more than he would understand the American 'lonjeray').

A 'drug-store' ceases to exist when the shores of Merrie England are reached. The 'chemist's shop' comes into being. It matters not that the druggist is not a chemist, but merely an apothecary, or a pharmacist. The most peculiar thing about the English druggist is that he sells only drugs, or sundries appertaining to them. It is true that one or two enterprising 'chemists' are fashioned on the American plan of a drug-store, but these are merely the exceptions that prove the rule.

It is difficult to determine the subtle differences that compel an American to admonish a friend by saying 'Now don't get hard (or sore)' — and an Englishman to say 'Keep your 'air on.' It is impossible to say why a 'human-fly' should be considered in America as having 'lots of nerve' and in England as having 'no nerves at all.'

Many of the good old-fashioned phrases and words have been retained in American, where they have given way to   **page 492/**   Latinized versions in English. Perhaps the word 'crazy' is the most outstanding example of this difference. 'Lunatic' has most effectively displaced 'crazy man' in English parlance, with its colloquialisms of 'looney,' 'balmy' and 'a bit off.' It has several variations in the terms 'loopey,' 'lossy,' 'up-the-loop' and 'up-the-pole.' Of the entire collection I prefer 'balmy' as it endows the crazy with the irresponsibility that belongs to the 'balmy breezes' or zephyrs. It is the most rational of English idiomatic colloquialisms, and its cogency may be remarked in comparing the following expressions: "Hey! 'Red,' you're crazy," "Hey! 'Red,' you're all wet," "Ho! Ginger, you're balmy."

One bright and sunny day, I stood at the geometrically paradoxical location known in London as the 'corner of Oxford Circus' at a time when the drains (sewers) were in process of repair. An obnoxious effluvium pervaded the atmosphere. Two young men paused. One was evidently the scion of the idle rich, the other was a hardy son of toil. The first spoke first.

"Pretty priceless niff, what?"

"I don't 'arf um," admitted the other.

Soon two Americans paused.

"Say, that smell's got teeth in it," observed one.

"Sure thing," answered his companion, "if they put the Stockyards here it'd be so jealous it'd go out of business."

In the first instance there is a glimpse of the English expressional motive — hesitancy, unwillingness to concede too much. Any superlative degree he expresses by admitting that it is less than a moiety of its actual substance, that is, it is 'not half.' It seems to convey the idea of enormity by negation rather than by direct statement.

But in the case of the Americans there is no hesitancy. There is the pluperfection of positivism, enhanced by extravagant exaggeration and the momentousness of metaphor in that the smell has such substance, such tangibility, that it has 'teeth.'

The difference is the difference between W. W. Jacobs and Mark Twain.

The American feels impelled to attend a certain function. He is 'bound to go.' The Englishman would be highly indignant at the idea of anybody being forced to go anywhere against his will, and, although he may be as determined as the American to be present, he prefers to express his positivism by negation. 'Nothing would make him miss going.'

An English lady, without any pretence to being versed in ornithology, may refer to her American friend's baby eulogistically as 'a perfect duck.' Should, however, the American attempt to assent by affirming that the child was 'cute,' the Englishwoman would depart with the impression that the child was a prodigy of perspicacity, in other words, a smart Aleck.

The American is permitted to 'laugh himself sick' but the Englishman may 'simply roar.' The American, after a long 'hike' may have enjoyed the 'tramp' as well as his English friend. Yet while the American may be 'all in' the Englishman finds that he is 'knocked up.' It is easy to see that there are pitfalls in America for the slangy Englishman.

'Bum,' in America, may be 'bad,' or 'unsatisfactory,' or a son of the free, generally termed a 'hobo.' In England it is merely the portion of the anatomy that comes in contact with the chair during the action of sitting.

'Is that so?' becomes 'Really' (pronounced 'rahly'). The word 'so' is always an adverb in England, 'I did *so*' becomes 'I did.'

An American will feel flattered if re- page 493/ ferred to as a 'regular guy.' To call an Englishman such, is to criticize his clothes, or taunt his taste. The parallel phrase is 'a ripper,' or a 'corker.' Curious terms of address permissible in England are 'old bean,' 'old pippin,' 'old fruit,' or, in the lower classes, 'old cock.'

There are very few 'Judges' in England. While it would be perfectly correct to refer to County Court Judge Cluer, as Judge Cluer, it would be very bad taste to refer to Mr. Justice Avery as Judge Avery, or the Lord Chief Justice as Chief Justice So-and-so. Municipal Court judges are all magistrates and are entitled to no title. It is correct to speak simply of Mr. Fordham, or Mr. d'Eyncourt, magistrate of the West London Police Court.

The American expletive 'Hell!' becomes 'Blimey' when applied to things English by the English. As an illustration, the emphatic assent of an American expressed in 'Hell! Sure' becomes 'Blimey, not 'arf' in the Cockney tongue.

There was once an American lady traveling in a London 'bus. She nursed an extremely ugly (homely) child, that proved to be a most hypnotic attraction for an old gentleman seated opposite her. The American lady was naturally indignant.

"Rubber!" she said.

The gentleman appeared vastly relieved.

"Thank God!" he said, "I thought it was real."

In order to have made herself understood, slangily, the lady should have said "Go on, boss at me." As it was, she merely indicated that the baby was a rubber counterfeit of a human.

In this connection it may be stated that 'rubbers' are always called 'galoshes' in England.

'I guess so,' that good old standby of American speech, is not 'I suppose so' in English, but 'Of course.'

It may be instructive to close with two selections from colloquial usage, the first American (for which I am indebted to Mr. W. R. Bowlin of the *Chicago Daily News*) and the second English.

"I'm going to shoot the bull to this baby, and maybe I'll make him come across."

"I'm going to spoof this bloke and perhaps I'll make him part up."

Again, the English for 'kid somebody' is 'pull somebody's leg.' 'Go chase yourself' may be understood in England, but it will be more significant if the exhortation takes the form of 'Go and eat coke' or 'Go and fry your face.'

It is, in truth, in the popular parlance that language differences develop. The only safe and sane way for travelers to avoid misunderstandings is to practice the principles of the purist. England and America both have a heritage in Shakespeare, but it is certainly cogent to observe that any American or Englishman who attempted to express himself in the language of Shakespeare would find himself lodged in an institution for the insane.   **page 494/**

from *Walking-Stick Papers*
by Robert Cortes Holliday
New York: George H. Doran Company, 1918

Caun't Speak the Language

Robert Cortes Holliday

Whenever we go to England we learn that we "caun't" speak the language. We are told very frankly that we can't. And we very quickly perceive that, whatever it is that we speak, it certainly is not "the language."

Let us consider this matter. A somewhat clever and amusingly ill-natured English journalist, T. W. H. Crosland, not long ago wrote a book "knocking" us, in which he says "that having inherited, borrowed or stolen a beautiful language, they [that is, we Americans] wilfully and of set purpose distort and misspell it." Crosland's ignorance of all things American, ingeniously revealed in this lively bit of writing, is interesting in a person of, presumably, ordinary intelligence, and his credulity in the matter of what he has heard about us is apparently boundless.

However, he does not much concern us. Well- page 201/ behaved Englishmen would doubtless consider as impolite his manner of expression regarding the "best thing imported in the *Mayflower*." But however unamiably, he does voice a feeling very general, if not universal, in England. You never get around — an Englishman would say "round" — the fact over there that we do not speak the English language.

Well, to use an Americanism, they — the English — certainly do have the drop on us in the matter of beauty. Mr. Chesterton somewhere says that a thing always to be borne in mind in considering England is that it is an island, that its people are insulated. An excellent thing to remember, too, in this connection, is that England is a flower garden. In ordinary times, after an Englishman is provided with a roof and four meals a day, the next thing he must have is a garden, even if it is but a flowerpot. They are continually talking about loveliness over there: it is a lovely day; it is lovely on the river now; it is a lovely spot. And so there are primroses in their speech. And then they have inherited over there, or borrowed or stolen, a beautiful literary language, worn soft in colour, like their black-streaked, grey-stone buildings, by time; page 202/ and, as Whistler's Greeks did their drinking vessels, they use it because, perforce, they have no other. The humblest Londoner will innocently shame you by talking perpetually like a storybook.

One day on an omnibus I asked the conductor where I should get off to reach a certain place. "Oh, that's the journey's end, sir," he replied. Now that is poetry. It sounds like Christina Rosetti. What would an American car conductor have said? "Why, that's the end of the line." "Could you spare me a trifle, sir?" asks the London beggar. A pretty manner of requesting alms. Little boys in England are very fond of cigarette pictures, little cards there reproducing "old English flowers." I used to save them to give to children. Once I gave a number to the ringleader of a group. I was about to tell him to divide them up. "Oh, we'll share them, sir," he said. At home such a boy might have said to the others: "G'wan, these're fer me." Again, when I inquired my way of a tiny, ragged mite, he directed me to "go as straight as ever you can go, sir, across the cricket field; then take your first right; go straight through the copse, sir," he called after me. The copse? Perhaps page 203/ I was thinking of the "cops" of New York. Then I understood that the urchin was speaking of a small wood.

Of course he, this small boy, sang his sentences, with the rising and falling inflection of the lower classes. "Top of the street, bottom of the road, over the way" — so it goes. And, by the way, how does an Englishman know which is the top and which is the bottom of every street?

Naturally, the English caun't understand us. "When is it that you are going 'ome?" asked my friend, the policeman in King's Road.

"Oh, some time in the fall," I told him.

"In the fall?" he inquired, puzzled.

"Yes, September or October."

"Oh!" he exclaimed, "in the autumn, yes, yes. At the fall of the leaves," I heard him murmur meditatively. Meeting him later in the company of another policeman, "He," he said to his friend, nodding at me, "is going back in the fall." Deliciously humorous to him was my speech. Now it may be mentioned as an interesting point that many of the words imported in the *Mayflower*, or in ships following it, have been quite forgotten in England. Fall, as in the fall of the year, I   page 204/   think, was among them. Quite so, quite so, as they say in England.

Yes, in the King's Road. For, it is an odd thing, Charles Scribner's Sons are on Fifth Avenue, but Selfridge's is in Oxford Street. Here we meet a man *on* the street; we kick him *into* it. And in England it is a very different thing, indeed, whether you meet a lady in the street or on the street. You, for instance, wouldn't meet a lady on the street at all. In fact, in England, to our mind, things are so turned around that it is as good as being in China. Just as traffic there keeps to the left kerb, instead of to the right curb, so whereas here I call you up on the telephone, there you phone me down. It would be awkward, wouldn't it, for me to say to you that I called you down?

England is an island; and though the British government controls one fifth, or something like that, of the habitable globe, England is a very small place. Most of the things there are small. A freight car is a goods van, and it certainly is a goods van and not a freight car. So when you ask what little stream this is, you are told that that is the river Lea, or the river Arun, as the case may be, although they look, indeed, except   page 205/   that they are far more lovely, like what we call "cricks" in our country. And the Englishman is fond of speaking in diminutives. He calls for a "drop of ale," to receive a pint tankard. He asks for a "bite of bread," when he wants half a loaf. His "bit of green" is a bowl of cabbage. He likes a "bit of cheese," in the way of a hearty slice, now and then. One overhearing him from another room might think that his copious repast was a microscopic meal. About this peculiarity in the homely use of the language there was a joke in *Punch* not long ago. Said the village worthy in the picture: "Ah, I used to be as fond of a drop o' beer as any one, but nowadays if I do take two or dree gallons it do knock I over!"

Into the matter of the quaint features of the speech of the English countryside, or the wonders of the Cockney dialect, the unlearned foreigner hardly dare venture. It is sufficient for us to wonder why a railroad should be a railway. When it becomes a "rilewie" we are inclined, in our speculation, "to pass," as we say over here. And ale, when it is "ile," brings to mind a pleasant story. A humble Londoner, speaking of an   page 206/   oil painting of an island, referred to it as "a painting in ile of an oil."

An American friend of mine, resident in London, insists that where there is an English word for a thing other than the American word for it, the English word is in every case better because it is shorter. He points to tram, for surface-car; and to lift, for elevator. Still though it may be a finer word, hoarding is not shorter than billboard; nor is "dailybreader" shorter than commuter. I think we break about even on that score.

This, however, would seem to be true: where the same words are employed in a somewhat different way the English are usually closer to the original meaning of the word. Saloon bar, for instance, is intended to designate a rather aristocratic place, above the public bar; while the lowest "gin mill" in the United States would be called a "saloon." I know an American youth who has thought all the while that Piccadilly Circus was a show, like Barnum and Bailey's. With every thing that is round in London called a circus, he must have imagined it a rather hilarious place.

The English "go on" a good deal about our   page 207/   slang. They used to be fond of quoting in superior derision in their papers our, to them, utterly unintelligible baseball news. Mr. Crosland, to drag him in again, to illustrate our abuse of "the language," quotes from some tenth-rate American author — which is a way they have had in England of judging our literature — with the comment that "that is not the way John Milton wrote." Not long ago Mr. Crosland became involved in a trial in the courts in connection with Oscar Wilde, Lord Alfred Douglas and Robert Ross. He defended himself with much spirit and considerable cleverness. Among other things he said, as reported in the press: "What is this game? This gang are trying to do me down. Here I am a poor man up against two hundred quid (or some such amount) of counsel." Well, that wasn't the way John Milton talked, either.

The English slang for money is a pleasant thing: thick'uns and thin'uns; two quid, five bob; tanners and coppers. And they have a good body of expressive and colourful speech. "On the rocks" is a neat and poetic way of saying "down and out." It is really not necessary to add the word "resources" to the expression "on his own."   page 208/   A "tripper" is a well-defined character, and so is a "flapper," a "nipper," and a "bounder." There had to be some word for the English "nut," as no amount of the language of John Milton would describe him; and while the connotation of this word as humour is different with us, the appellation of the English, when you have come to see it in their light, hits off the personage very crisply. To say that such a one "talks like a ha'penny book" is, as the English say, "a jolly good job." And a hotel certainly is presented as full when it is pronounced "full up." A "topper" would be only one kind of a hat. Very well, then it is quite possible, we see, to be "all fed up," as they say in England, with English slang.

Humorous Englishmen sometimes rather fancy our slang; and make naïve attempts at the use of it. In England, for instance, a man "gets the sack" when he is "bounced" from his job. So I heard a lively Englishman attracted by the word say that so and so should "get the bounce."

In writing, the Englishman usually employs "the language." He has his yellow journals, indeed, which he calls "Americanised" newspapers. But crude and slovenly writing certainly is not a   page 209/   thing that sticks out on him. What a gentlemanly book reviewer he is always! We have here in the United

States perhaps a half dozen gentlemen who review books. Is it not true that you would get tired counting up the young English novelists who are as accomplished writers as our few men of letters? The Englishman has a basketful of excellent periodicals to every one of ours. And in passing it is interesting to note this. When we are literary we become a little dull. See our high-brow journals! When we frolic we are a little, well, rough. The Englishman can be funny, even hilarious, and unconsciously, confoundedly well bred at the same time. But he does have a rotten lot of popular illustrated magazines over there compared to ours.

When you return from a sojourn of several months in the land of "the language" you are immediately struck very forcibly by the vast number of Americanisms, by the richness of our popular speech, by the "punch" it has, and by the place it holds in the printed page at home. In a journey from New York I turned over in the smoking-car a number of papers I had not seen for some time, among them the New York *Evening Post, Collier's, Harper's, Puck,* and the Indianapolis *News.* Here, generally without quotation marks and frequently in the editorial pages, I came across these among innumerable racy phrases: nothing doing, hot stuff, Right O! strong-arm work, some celebration, has 'em all skinned, mad at him, this got him in bad, scared of, skiddoo, beat it, a peach of a place, get away with the job, been stung by the party, got by on his bluff, sore at that fact, and always on the job. I learned that the weather man had put over his first frost last night, that a town we passed had come across with a sixteen-year-old burglar, and that a discredited politician was attempting to get out from under. Perhaps it is not to be wondered at that the Englishman frequently fails to get us.

You note a change in the whole atmosphere of language. A pronounced instance of this difference is found in public signs. You have been seeing in English conveyances the placards in neat type posted about which kindly request the traveller not to expectorate upon the floor of this vehicle, as to do so may cause inconvenience to other passengers or spread disease, and so forth and so on. Over here: page 211/

Don't Spit
This means You!

This is about the way our signs of this kind go. Now what about all this? I used to think many persons just returned from England ridiculously affected in their speech. And many of them are — those who say caun't when they can't do it unconsciously. That is, over here. In Britain, perhaps, it is just as well to make a stagger at speaking the way the Britains do. When you accidentally step on an Englishman's toe, it is better to say "I'm sorry! or simply "sorry," than to beg his pardon or ask him to excuse you. This makes you less conspicuous, and so more comfortable. And when you stay any length of time you fall naturally into English ways. Then when you come back you seem to us, to use one of the Englishman's most delightful words, to "swank" dreadfully. And in that is the whole story.

Mr. James declares that in the work of two equally good writers you could still tell by the writing which was that of the Englishman and which that of the American. The assumption of course is that where they differed the Ameri-

page 212/ can would be the inferior writer. Mr. James prefers the English atmosphere. And the Englishman is inclined to regard us in our deviation as a sort of imperfect reproduction of himself. What is his is ours, it is true; but what's ours is our own. That is, we have inherited a noble literature in common. But we write less and less like the Englishman all the while. Our legacy of language brought over in the *Mayflower* has become adapted to our own environment, been fused in the "melting-pot," and quickened by our own life to-day. Whether for better or for worse — it may be either — the literary touch is rapidly going by the board in modern American writing. One of the newer English writers remarks: "A few carefully selected American phrases can very swiftly kill a great deal of dignity and tradition."

Why should we speak the very excellent language spoken in the tight little isle across the sea? In Surrey they speak of the "broad Sussex" of their neighbours in the adjoining county. Is it exactly that we caun't? Or that we just don't? Because we have an article more to our purpose, made largely from English material, but made in the United States? page 213/

from *British and American English Since 1900*
by Eric Partridge and John W. Clark
New York: Philosophical Library, 1951

The Characteristics of American English

John W. Clark

A language is a part of a culture (not in the women's-club sense, but in the anthropologist's), and reflects that culture in considerable detail. The most important event of the last hundred and fifty years of Western culture — in some ways, it might be argued, the most important event in human history — is the rapid transformation of an agrarian society (one in which the great majority of men are almost exclusively occupied with the direct production of food — chiefly their own) into a technological one (one in which the application of technology to agriculture liberates from that employment large masses of the population, who are then deflected into the occupation of tending the machines that represent the application of technology to the production of other than agricultural goods). Two peasants out of three leave the plow for the factory.

Largely because a factory takes less space and costs more money than a farm, the application of technology to producing non-agricultural goods leads to increasingly numerous and populous cities, and of this, one important result is the urbanization of culture.

Applied science and the growth of cities, then, have profoundly affected modern Western society and culture and all aspects of that culture, including language. But there is a third influence of more or less equal power, namely, democracy, or the rise of the masses, of which the essential quality is, almost by definition, the heightened influence of the many on almost every aspect of the culture of their society. Democracy is of course complexly related to technology and urbanization, and they are related to each other both as cause and as effect; the order in which I have for convenience introduced the three terms into this discussion is not chronological, but neither would any other order be.

Almost all the changes that have come about, within the last hundred and fifty years and especially within the last fifty, in   page 204/   Western society, culture, and specifically language, and more specifically in the English, and yet more specifically in American English (by which I mean, here and elsewhere, the language of the United States), are, I think, chargeable to the direct or indirect influence of one or more of these three forces, with the single qualification that we should include pure science — philosophical science, so to speak — along with technology or applied science, as being partly its parent and partly its child, and as operating on culture sometimes conjointly with technology and sometimes separately.

Of the three forces, at least two, science and democracy, work with less restraint in the United States than in Great Britain; and it is to this fact that I should attribute many of the leading differences between British and American English, especially in the last half century.

I say "especially in the last half century" because even if science and democracy had not advanced beyond the point they had reached in 1900 — or in 1800 — American English would doubtless differ now, as it differed then, from British English. The chief reasons for such difference as existed in 1900, and still more in 1800, were the difference in physical environment, for example, in climate, terrain, flora and fauna, and density of population; the difference in dominant background and temperament between the British and the American peoples; and the different social and economic and — secondarily and derivatively — political and educational organization.

The first point hardly needs illustration: one need only think of the different senses in which Englishmen and Americans use such words as *robin, daisy, corn, creek, barn,* and *to hunt,* and of the early British immigrants' adoption of a considerable number of American Indian names (and later, Spanish ones) for things unknown in Great Britain. The second point perhaps requires a little more discussion. In the first place, early British immigrants to America were predominantly of the lower and lower-middle classes; their language differed from that of their social betters partly because of the social difference itself, partly because of ignorance, and partly because of jealousy, which can   page 205/   lead to (usually imperfect) imitation, but which can just as well lead to perversely deliberate divagation. In the second place, immigrants are typically misfits, or enterprising, or (commonly) both, and consequently tend to be sturdily self-reliant, opinionated to the point of surliness, and given to innovation, partly from eccentricity, partly from ignorance of old ways, and partly from the irrelevance or insufficiency of those ways under new conditions. The third point is even more familiar than the first; but I will mention one illustration. Some years ago I used to ask college freshmen who had been reading Macaulay's great "third chapter" to write themes comparing some aspect of England in 1685 with the corresponding aspect of America in the 1930's. One of the favorite topics was the country gentleman; and of many — too many — scores of themes that I have read on the subject, not one ever showed any comprehension of the essential differences between the seventeenth-century English squire and the twentieth-century Middle Western American farmer — whose real opposite number was of course the prosperous yeoman.

Here then are six leading influences to which I should attribute the principal differences between British and American English. But there are several more influences, some of them more or less independent. The first of these is the conservatism of most transplanted languages. This is illustrated not only by the English of the United States, but also by that of Ireland, as well as by the Norse of Iceland, the French of Quebec, and in some ways the Spanish of Latin America. Its coexistence with the contrary tendency to innovation may seem paradoxical, but is undeniable. Further influences are (2) the influence of business and advertising and "efficiency"; (3) the universality, if not of literacy, then at any rate of what we may call quasi-literacy; (4) the somewhat paradoxical bookishness of American culture — its dependence, more than in England, on the printed word; (5) social climbing, proceeding mainly from the exceptional fluidity of American social classes; (6) what I will call, for the want of a better name, puritanism; and (7) the influence of non-British immigrants. To these we might add an eighth, chauvin- page 206/ ism, which displays itself in two forms: Anglophobia, and xenophobia generally. Anglophobia — conscious and specific Anglophobia — has greatly decreased since *American Notes* and *Martin Chuzzlewit*, and, so far as it still exists among the populace, tends now to blend with inverted snobbishness. Xenophobia of the more general kind expresses itself, at least in the sphere of language, mainly on a low social and educational plane, in such utterances as "Why don't you talk American?" muttered at UN delegates on trains plying between Pennsylvania Station in New York and Lake Success.

The characteristics of American English throughout its history, and especially in the last fifty years, may, I think, be explained almost entirely in terms of the action and interaction of these dozen or more factors. page 207/ . . . .

3

AMERICAN ENGLISH ON TRIAL

from *A Vocabulary, or Collection of Words and Phrases which have been Supposed to be Peculiar to the United States of America*
by **John Pickering**
Boston: Cummings and Hilliard, 1816

An Essay on the Present State of the English Language in the United States

John Pickering

The preservation of the *English Language* in its purity throughout the United States is an object deserving the attention of every American who is a friend to the literature and science of his country. It is in a particular manner entitled to the consideration of the Academy; for, though subjects, which are usually ranked under the head of *Physical Science*, were doubtless chiefly in view with the founders of the Academy, yet, our *language* also, which is to be the instrument of communicating to the public the speculations and discoveries of our countrymen, seems necessarily "to fall within the design of the institution"; because, unless that language is well settled, and can be read with ease by all to whom it is addressed, our authors will write and publish, certainly under many disadvantages, though perhaps not altogether in vain.

It is true, indeed, that our countrymen may speak and write in a *dialect* of English, which will be understood in the *United States;* but if they are ambitious of having their works read by Englishmen as well as by Americans, they must write in a language that Englishmen can read with pleasure. And if for some time to come it should not be the lot of many Americans to publish works, which will be read out of their own country, yet all, who have the least tincture of learning, will continue to feel an ardent desire to acquaint themselves with *English* authors. Let us then for a moment imagine the time to have arrived   **page 9/** when *Americans* shall no longer be able to understand the works of Milton, Pope, Swift, Addison, and other English authors, justly styled classic, without the aid of *translation* into a language, that is to be called at some future day the *American* tongue! By such a change, it is true, our loss would not be so great in works purely scientific, as in those which are usually termed works of taste; for the obvious reason, that the design of the former is merely to communicate information, without regard to elegance of language or the force and beauty of the sentiments. But the excellencies of works of taste cannot be felt even in the best translations; — a truth, which, without resorting to the example of the matchless ancients, will be acknowledged by every man, who is acquainted with the admirable works extant in various living languages. Nor is this the only view in which a radical change of language would be an evil. To say nothing of the facilities afforded by a *common language* in the ordinary intercourse of business, it should not be forgotten, that our religion and our laws are studied in the language of the nation, from which we are descended; and, with the loss of the language, we should finally suffer the loss of those peculiar advantages which we now derive from the investigations of the jurists and divines of that country.

But, it is often asked among us, do not the people of this country now speak and write the English language with purity? A brief consideration of the subject will furnish a satisfactory answer to this question; it will also enable us to correct the erroneous opinions entertained by some Americans on this point, and at the same time to defend our countrymen against the charge made by some English writers, of a *design* to effect an entire change in the language.

As the inquiry before us is a simple question of fact, it   **page 10/**   is to be determined, like every other question of this nature, by proper evidence. What evidence then have we, that the English language is not spoken and written in America, with the same degree of purity that is to be found in the writers and orators of England?

In the first place, although it is agreed, that there is greater uniformity of dialect throughout the United States (in consequence of the frequent removals of people from one part of our country to another) than is to be found throughout England; yet none of our countrymen, not even those, who are the most zealous in supporting what they imagine to be the honour of the *American* character, will contend, that we have not in some instances departed from the standard of the language. We have formed some *new* words; and to some *old* ones, that are still used in England, we have affixed *new significations:* while others, which have long been *obsolete* in England, are still retained *in common use* with us. If then, in addition to these acknowledgments of our *own countrymen,* we allow any weight to the opinions of *Englishmen,* (who must be competent judges in this case,) it cannot be denied, that we have in several instances deviated from the standard of the language, as *spoken and written in England at the present day.* By this, however, I do not mean, that so great a deviation has taken place, as to have rendered any considerable part of our language unintelligible to Englishmen; but merely, that so many corruptions have crept into *our English,* as to have become the subject of much animadversion and regret with the learned of Great Britain. And as we are hardly aware of the opinion entertained by them of the extent of these corruptions, it may be useful, if it should not be very flattering to our pride, to hear their remarks on this subject in their own words. We shall find that these corruptions are censured, not by mere pretenders   page 11/   to learning, but, (so far as the fact is to be ascertained from English publications,) by all the scholars of that country, who take an interest in American literature. In proof of this, I request the attention of the Academy to the following extracts from several of the British Reviews . . .

The *British Critic* (for February 1810) in a review of the Rev. Mr. *Bancroft's* Life of Washington, says — "In the style we observe, with regret rather than with astonishment, the introduction of several *new* words, or *old* words in a new sense; a deviation from the rules of the English language, which, if it continues to be practised by good writers in America, will introduce confusion into the medium of intercourse, and render it a subject of regret that the people of that continent should not have an entirely separate language as well as government of their own. Instances occur at almost every page; without pains in selecting, the following may be taken as specimens," &c. The Reviewers then mention several words, all of which are inserted in the following Vocabulary.   page 12/   . . . .

The *Critical Review* (for September 1809) in remarks upon *Travels through France, by Col. Pinckney,* says — "He falls into occasional inaccuracies . . . but the instances are rare, and by no means so striking as we have *frequent* occasions of remarking in *most American* writers." . . . .

The *Monthly Reviewers* (in May 1808) in their account of a little work, entitled *A Political Sketch of America,* cite with approbation, the following passage — "The national *language* should be sedulously cultivated; and this is to be page 13/   accomplished by means of schools. This circumstance demands particular attention, for the language of *conversation* is becoming incorrect; and even in America *authors* are to be found, who make use of *new* or *obsolete* words, which no good writer in this country would enploy."   page 14/   . . . .

Upon an impartial consideration of the subject, therefore, it seems impossible to resist the conclusion, that, although the language of the United States has, perhaps, changed less than might have been expected, when we consider how many years have elapsed since our ancestors brought it from England; yet it has in so many instances departed from the English standard, that our scholars should lose no time in endeavouring to restore it to its purity, and to prevent future corruption.   page 17/   . . . .

from *Travels in New-England and New-York*, Vol. IV
by Timothy Dwight
New-Haven: Timothy Dwight, 1822

Language of New-England

Timothy Dwight

Letter I

Dear Sir,

Among the things for which the people of the United States, particularly of New-England, have been censured, and ridiculed, by your countrymen, our language, in a variety of respects, has come in for its share. We have been accused of an erroneous pronunciation; of retaining ancient words, which you have discarded; of annexing to others an unwarranted meaning; of coining new ones; and of thus contributing to render the language perplexed, unsettled, and imperfect. As I have never seen this subject examined, except on one side, I shall take the liberty to give you a few thoughts concerning it; and flatter myself that you will willingly accompany me through the investigation.

I shall not, I believe, offend against either truth or propriety, if I say, that the English language is in this country pronounced more correctly than in England. I am not, indeed, sanguine enough to expect that you will credit the assertion, nor that you will believe me to be a competent judge of the subject. Still, I am satisfied that the assertion is true. That you may not mistake my meaning, I observe, that by a correct pronunciation I intend that of London; and, if you please, that of well-bred people in London. You may, perhaps, be inclined to ask how I can even know what this pronunciation is. I know it in two ways: from hearing a considerable number of Englishmen of this description converse extensively; and from information which enlightened Amer- **page 277/** icans have given me concerning the subject, who have resided in London. In both ways my information has been so extensive, as to forbid every reasonable doubt, in my own mind concerning its sufficiency.

When I say that the language is pronounced here more correctly than in England, I do not intend that it is pronounced more correctly, or even as much so, as by some Englishmen; although in this respect I have good reason to believe the difference to be scarcely perceptible. This I was taught before the revolutionary war, by an English gentleman; an inhabitant of London: who resided in New-Haven a considerable time, and who was several years in the service of the

British government. Since that period I have been often told the same thing by respectable Englishmen, travelling, or residing on this side of the Atlantic. I have also found the observation verified by the pronunciation of these very Englishmen, and of others.

My meaning is, that the inhabitants at large speak English with a nearer accordance to your standard of pronunciation, than the inhabitants of England. Of this the proof is complete. I have seen a dramatic performance, written in the West Country dialect: the words being spelt according to the local pronunciation; of which I was scarcely able to understand a sentence. I have also seen a volume of poems, professedly written in the dialect of Yorkshire, in which, independently of some local phraseology, the distorted pronunciation required a glossary to explain the meaning of many sentences, even to an English reader. Now, sir, it is no exaggeration to say, that from Machias to St. Mary's, and from the Atlantic to the Mississippi, every American, descended from English ancestors, understands every other, as readily as if he had been bred in the same neighbourhood. I have continually, and long, had under my own instruction youths from almost all American States; and am ordinarily unable to conjecture page 278/ from their pronunciation, the part of the country which gave them birth. There is nothing here which can be called without an abuse of language, *dialectic*. This, it is believed, cannot be said of an equal number of people in any country of Europe. The differences of pronunciation, here, are of no moment, unless that of the vowel U deserves to be excepted. page 279/ ....

Among the reasons, which here contribute to a general propriety both in the use, and the pronunciation, of language, the following are not without their influence.

A great multitude of the parochial schools are taught to a considerable extent by young men, educated in Colleges; and in this manner derive their pronunciation immediately from the common standard, in a good degree.

The great body of our people are regularly at church; and thus imbibe their pronunciation in a considerable degree from the clergy.

All those, who are liberally educated, and polished, converse, as I have heretofore observed, more freely, and universally, with their plain neighbours than probably was ever done in any other country: and some persons of the former character are found in almost every village.

As there are here no distinct orders in society, all men endeavour to copy the manners of those, who have acquired superiour importance and reputation; and that in their pronunciation, as well as in their dress and manners. To acquire this resemblance is an object of direct design, and active ambition.

Our countrymen, as has been observed, read: and that in such numbers, that it may be justly said to be the general character. Hence they obtain the intelligence, necessary to comprehend the importance of this object; and that attentive observation, which secures the attainment.

Many of them also, are to a considerable extent, present at courts, and there acquire an additional conformity to the standard pronunciation. From these, and doubtless from other causes, some of which may have escaped my attention, we have derived a pronunciation; probably more uniform than has ever prevailed in any other country in the world.

From an observation in the Eclectic Review, I am ready to believe, that the writer supposed the peculiarities of Mr. Web- **page 282/** ster's pronunciation to be generally adopted in this country. The opinion, if it exist, is erroneous. These peculiarities have spread very little. The friends of Mr. Webster, of whom I am one, regret that his learning, and labours, should be rendered less useful by his departure, in several instances, from the common standard.

I am, Sir, yours, &c. **page 283/**

Letter II

Dear Sir,

We are accused, also, of *retaining ancient words*, brought by our ancestors from their native country, and since that period left by the English out of their vocabulary. The charge undoubtedly, is to some extent well-founded. That bodies of men, speaking originally the same language, should, when separated from each other to the distance of three thousand miles, retain, at the end of two centuries, precisely the same words, may, I think, be justly regarded as an absolute impossibility. Certainly no instance of this nature has been hitherto known: of course it ought not to have been expected here. Men always have such words, as will express the ideas, which they have occasion to communicate to each other. Nothing is more natural than that we should retain some ideas, and have occasion to communicate them, which you have not retained. Both you and we unquestionably retain some part of the manners of our ancestors; but it is scarcely credible, that we should both retain, we shall severally have occasion to converse; and each must have words, expressing the ideas, out of which the conversation is made. These, so far as they were in the possession of our ancestors, we naturally retain. This you have done as well as we; and to as great an extent. Nay, I believe you have many more words, which are not considered as classical by yourselves, than we have. **page 284/** . . . On what principles are you justified in retaining these words, which will not justify us in retaining ours.

But we are censured, also for *making new words*. The charge is undoubtedly just. Wherever we find occasion for the use of words, and have them not, we like you and all other nations, make them. In the State of Connecticut a number of men are chosen annually by each town, to receive from each inhabitant a list of the taxable property in his possession. This list is required by law; and is made up by the proprietor. The men, who receive it, are from their employment styled *Listers*. If the proprietor gives in a false list, he is punished by having the falsified article increased on the list four-fold. Englishmen on both sides of the Atlantic, have no fondness for circumlocution. We therefore, style this punishment *Four-folding*. These are terms, confined to this State: and, although sufficiently remote from elegance, yet serve to convey ideas of some importance in our state of society, which otherwise could not be conveyed without a periphrasis. A few others, local also, may be found in other parts of our country; and a small number have had a more extensive currency. Among these, *immigrate, immigration* and *immigrant,* hold a conspicuous place. The stream of population flows *out* of Great Britain; but a part of it flows *into* the United States. You, therefore, have no use for these words; but we have at least as much, as you have for *emigrate*, and its derivatives. page 285 / . . . .

from *The New York Times Magazine*
February 26, 1939

American Speech: An Indictment

S. F. Markham

London.

Recently I had the honor to second the address in the House of Commons in reply to the King on the occasion (to use the formal phrase) of the Most Gracious Speech from the Throne. During the course of my speech I said that their Majesties' forthcoming visit to the United States would be welcomed on all sides of the House and that

> Their Majesties would take with them a great message of affection and admiration from us to those two great countries of North America who have the same ideals as we have. It has been said that the English-speaking countries can agree upon everything except how to speak English. It is certain that the tongue which Shakespeare and Milton spake has had some strange twists put upon it by our trans-Atlantic cousins in the last few years.
>
> Now, through the radio and films, we are acquiring in this country what might almost be described as a mid-Atlantic accent. Certain it is that many American idioms are being adopted over here. I see that in a recent American grammar that great phrase "Sez you" is now lifted to the dignity of "a doubting affirmative," while another phrase, "Include me out," is defined as an "unqualified negative." It may be that the First Commissioner of Works, in his zest for bringing the House up-to-date, will now label the "Aye" Lobby the "Sez you" Lobby, and the other the "Include me out" Lobby.

This part of my speech, meant as a light quip on the reforming activities of our First Commissioner of Works, brought me an indignant protest from a distinguished American, who, in a 100-word cable said that my remarks on American English were "uncalled for," and that "more than 1,000 Americanisms are habitually used by the best English writers, such as 'annex,' 'bluff,' 'to belittle,' 'radio,' 'to figure,' 'to grill,' 'chain-store,' 'movie,' 'film,' 'reliable,' 'talented,' 'influential,' 'lengthy,'" etc.

I might of course have replied that the word "annex" can be found in English documents as far back as the year 1405, and that many other so-called "American" terms are to be found in Shakespeare or even earlier writers.

But let me continue with the cable. "Please bear in mind," it went on, regardless of expense, "that two-thirds, or 130,000,000, of the English-speaking peoples speak American. It is not impossible that the future will find American English the language of the English-speaking races."

How preposterous! In 200 years America has done no more than add about 1,000 words (many of which are already obsolete) to the English tongue. She has altered neither its grammar, nor (save in a score or so of cases) its spelling. "American English" is English save for a decimal percentage of new accretions.

This hectic cable was followed by a letter from quite another gentleman in South Main Street, Nevada, Mo., who jeers at the English language as "the most inconsistent, impractical, cumbersome jumble of dark-age idioms." But it is this language which has given the world its greatest literary treasures, and among these are those masterpieces of American literature whose authors would have been shocked to learn that they wrote anything but English — plain, simple English.

When I talk about the tongue of Shakespeare and Milton, I mean also the tongue of Lincoln and Walt Whitman — the tongue of the most educated people on both sides of the Atlantic. The only difference between cultured American and cultured English speech is one of accent and not of idiom, one of intonation and not of verbal felicity.

During my frequent visits to the United States I have noticed that most educated Americans deprecate those slang utterances belched forth by the tabloid press, the gangster films, and such writers as Damon Runyon. But youth — extreme youth, on both sides of the Atlantic revels in them. The English schoolboy joyously uses not only the archaic "O. K. Chief" and the pre-war "sez You," but can even "talk turkey" and "boondoggle" his "buddy" with "boloney."

Naturally such expressions as these enrich a language in the same way that too much salt enriches an egg. But a selective pinch is better, and for my part I would as soon speak the hyper-urban Runyonese or Bowery as I would speak Cockney or Lancashire. And the sins of American speech, therefore, in my eyes, are those sins due to illiteracy, ignorance or a willful desire to acquire a reputation for "pep" or "smartness" otherwise lacking in one's character.

I have recently read Damon Runyon's latest book "Take It Easy," and if ever an American of unblemished lineage and character speaks as Runyon's characters speak I will cheerfully admit that American English is a separate language — and rejoice that it is so. A defeated boxer, for example, is alluded to as "a big umbrella," while a successful one has "a pair of scrambled ears to prove it." A "dame" with a jealous husband is "cemetery bait," and so on.

But on the other hand, when this author breaks away from the "historical present," he uses an English that is direct, facile and masterly, and I confess that I like reading him for his sheer page 8/ mastery of succinct English. His irony, heartlessness and humor demand a better vehicle than that which he sometimes drives. As it is he gives us what he would call the "old hoovus-goovus."

It is, however, a fallacy to think that these idioms are in some way crisper than the equivalent English expression. Take, for example, the following, which is, I believe, a fairly good illustration of the type of American spoken by the criminal section of your great nation: "He was taken for a ride, put on the spot, and bumped off." The English (i.e., good American) for this would be "He was abducted, condemned and killed." Nearly a 50 per cent saving in words!

You in America during this past century have had a great task of teaching English to 20,000,000 non-English-speaking immigrants. Some of these acquired English rapidly — others did not — and it is these latter who have created the slipshod utterance that endeavors to call itself American. The Central European immigrant found it difficult to say a "sausage sandwich" but easy to say a "hot dog," and many words of German, Mexican or even Italian origin drifted into the speech of the lower American because their users could not speak English properly.

These bastardizers of the finest tongue in the world show their manners in their speech — for it is full of "scrams," "skip it's" and "quit stalling's." Many of these expressions were sired by Illiteracy out of Rudeness, and the progeny is like a mule — evil-tempered and impotent. And yet how good some of this slang is! I myself have been a "carpet bagger," possibly a "mugwump," but I've never "gerrymandered" an election.

There remains, of course, the question of accent or pronunciation. And here I am with America nearly all the way. I love your well-open vowels, and I deplore the English mumble, plum in mouth. I love your way of giving every syllable its due share of emphasis — and hate the English way of clippin' our words and making a bi-syllable out of such words as "literary."

In short, therefore, the sins of American speech in my eyes are that it welcomes too eagerly new immigrant forms from "molls" and "saps" and "hoodlums," "hobos" and "gangsters." Terms that have their origin on the race track, or in the ring, that are the verbal currency of gamblers, bootleggers and gunmen, may safely be left to take care of themselves — for their dissolution is writ within them.

But when America wants new terms to describe modern industrial processes or scientific advances she does not turn to her blighted areas but rather (even if unconsciously) to the home of the most widely spoken language the world has ever heard or read. America's greatest intellectual heritage is the King's English, which has been used with sublime mastery by leading Americans since the Declaration of Independence. To that language you have given a crispness of utterance, a cheerful virility, that many of us envy. But none of us, save immature youths and our own criminal classes, envy you your slang, nor have we the slightest desire to become more familiar with it. page 22/

from *How to Write*
by Stephen Leacock
New York: Dodd, Mead & Company,
1943

Our Living Language: A Defense

Stephen Leacock

. . . To what extent are we to think of our language as a moving current, never the same except in its identity, and to what extent should we wish to check the flow of the current, so that stiller waters may run deeper! Obviously there is a limit in each direction. A current totally arrested means stagnation. Waters that run too fast end in the sand. Somewhere there may be a happy mean between the two.

Now this question arises for all languages. But it has **page 118/** a very peculiar importance for the English language since here the current flows in two parts, the American and the British; and many people are inclined to think that one tends to run too fast and the other tends to slacken. In other words we have here the problem of the American language and American slang. Every now and then controversy breaks out in regard to British English and American English — or it used to before the war stilled all babble — and it sometimes had a rather nasty edge to it. It carried in it one of the last faint survivals of the Stamp Act and the Boston Tea Party. Great quarrels die away to leave only generous memories; little quarrels live on. Hence the question of "slang" as between England and America (England, not Scotland; the Scots are not worrying) keeps its edge; all the more so, in that a lot of Americans think in their hearts, that the reason why the English don't use much slang is that they can't make it up, and a lot of English people think that the Americans use slang because they weren't brought up properly — or, no, they don't think it, they know it. That's the provoking thing about the English (say the Americans); they don't think things, they know them. They did all their thinking years and years ago.

I can write on this controversy with the friendly neutrality of a Canadian. In Canada we have enough to do keeping up with two spoken languages without trying to invent slang, so we just go right ahead and use English for literature, Scotch for sermons and American for conversation.

Perhaps the highest point of controversy is reached in the discussion whether there is, whether there ought **page 119/** to be, whether it is a shame that there isn't, an "American" language. Some people feel very strongly on this point. They think that having your own language is a mark of independence like owning your own house, driving your own car and having your own shaving mug in the barber shop. Gangs of boys make themselves up a "language" and revel in its obscurity. The leading boys in this respect are the Irish, so anxious to have their own language that they are trying to learn Gaelic. If they are not careful, first thing they know they'll get to talk it and then they'll be sorry.

On the other hand, some people feel just the other way about it. A most interesting article appeared a little while ago in one of the leading British Quarterlies, written by an American, and deprecating all idea of the creation of an American language as dangerous to our mutual dependence and kinship.

My own feeling about this, if I may put it in slang, is "I should worry." Or, in other words, there is not the faintest chance of there ever being an American language as apart from English. The daily intercommunication of telegraph, telephone, literature and the press, fuses all forms of "English" toward one and the broadcast and the talking pictures even fuse the toned voice. In the world of today languages cannot separate. That process belonged to epochs of distance and silence unknown now. Even then it was long. It took Latin a thousand years to turn into French.

The situation in the world today is this: There is a language called "English." It is too bad, if you like, that one country should seem to have stolen or to monopolize the claim to the name. But if the English   page 120/   stole the name of a language, the "Americans" stole the whole of two continents. Humble people, like the Canadians, and the Eskimos, have to live in "America" and speak "English," without fretting about it.

English is spoken by the people in England; is also spoken by the Scots, by the unredeemed Irish, the Australians — a lot of other people than Americans. Who speaks it best, no one knows; it's a matter of taste. Personally I think I like best the speech of a cultivated Scot, and perhaps least a certain high-grade English which calls a railroad a "wailwoad." I myself talk Ontario English; I don't admire it, but it's all I can do; anything is better than affectation.

Now by slang is meant the unceasing introduction into language of new phrases, and especially new nouns as names for things. There is no doubt that this peculiar fermentation of language has reached in America higher proportions than ever known anywhere else. For example — and my authority here is Mr. Eric Partridge, who cannot be wrong — a test was taken not long ago in a Wisconsin high school to see how many different words the boys and girls employed to express a low opinion of a person. Their list read, *mutt, bonehead, guy, carp, highbrow, tightwad, grafter, hayseed, hot-air artist, rube, tough-nut, chump* and *peanut*. Perhaps they thought of more after they got home; these no doubt were only some of the things they called their teachers.

Many people, without being students of language, have observed the extraordinary number of ways in which American slang can indicate that a man has had too much drink. The chief authority on the subject (I   page 121/   refer to American slang and don't want to be ambiguous), H. L. Mencken, gives a partial list, brought up to 1923, and including *piffled, fiddled, spiflicated, tanked, snooted, stewed, ossified, slopped, jiggered, edged, loaded, het up, frazzled, jugged, soused, cornered* and *jagged*.

Slang passes as it comes. It lives only when it deserves to live, when the word has something about it that does a real service. In the Wisconsin students' list above I can detect only two words that look permanent, *guy* and *highbrow*. *Guy* is a word with a history; it comes down to us from poor Guy Fawkes (Guido Faukes), tortured and executed for trying to blow up the English Parliament. His "Fifth of November" crime was kept alive in memory — still is — by toting around a tattered figure on a stick in a procession with the cry, "Oh, please to remember the fifth of November, with gunpowder, treason and plot." So the word came to mean a tattered-looking person and then just a queer-looking person, like a professor. From that it began to mean just a person: *I was out with another guy last night.*

The fact is we are always hard up for neutral words to mean "just a person"; each new one gets spoiled and has to be replaced. Be careful how you call a "woman" a "woman," and a "lady" is apt to be worse; don't call a Frenchman an "individual," or an Englishman a "fellow." Hence the need for "guy," which will gradually rise from ridicule to respectability . . . At some future British coronation the Archbishop of Canterbury will say to the Queen, "Will you take this guy to be your   page 122/   husband?" And for all we know the Queen will answer, "Sez-you."

The other word, *highbrow*, will live for another reason. We need it. It is a little different from *intellectual, learned, cultivated.* It started like most slang as a brilliant image, or metaphor, taken from the sweeping forehead, smooth as an egg, of a Shakespeare or a Hall Caine. But, with perhaps a change of spelling, the thought of brow will disappear and we shall use the term naturally and effectively — a *highbrow audience; the opinion of highbrows*, etc.

The making of slang is, as I say, a sort of living process of language like the scum on wine. Without it there is no wine, no life, no fermentation. Later on, the scum passes as dust and dregs and leaves behind the rich fluid of the wine. A language that has ceased to throw off slang has ceased to live. Thus came all our language. Every syllable of it since the dawn of speech has been rolled over and over in endless renewal. Our oldest words, our oldest names, were once bright with the colours of the morning, striking some new metaphor that brought into full relief the image of the thing seen. Centuries ago some Roman called his fellow-Roman's head a "pot" and put the word *testa* (tête) into the French language. His genius for seeing resemblances was no greater than that of his American successor who perceived that the human head was a *bean.*

Now, the process of creating slang is not confined to America. But I think the fermenting, slang-making process is livelier far in America than in England. This would seem to be the consequence of setting a language   page 123/   in a new country — with new lives, new scenes to turn it to, and with the débris of other languages jostling beside it. Under the wide canopy of heaven above the prairies a preacher became a *sky-pilot.* In England he remained, among other things, an *incumbent,* still sitting there. A newcomer in the West was a *tenderfoot* or a *greenhorn,* a locomotive an *iron horse,* and so on. Little snips of foreign *idiom* like the *something else again* of German, and the *I should worry* of Yiddish, came snuggling into the language. *Yes, we have no bananas* carries with it the whole Mediterranean migration.

This process of change, like invention itself, became more conscious in America than in England. What the English did for lazy convenience or by accident, the Americans did on purpose. Hence American slang contains a much greater percentage of cleverness than English. A lot of English slang words are just abbreviations. To call a professional at cricket a *pro*, or breakfast *brekker*, or political economy *pol. econ.*, saves time but that is all. To call a pair of trousers *bags*, is a step up; there is a distinct intellectual glow of comparison. But it is only twilight as compared with such American effects as *lounge-lizard, rubber-neck, sugar-daddy, tanglefoot* and *piece of calico*.

It is, moreover, a peculiar merit of American slang that a lot of it has the quality of vitality — vital force of renewed life. Take such words as a *hide-out* and *frame-up*, or a *tie-up* (on a railway). To make these involves the process of *starting over again*, forming language from the beginning. Compare *sob-stuff, fade-out, send-off, side-track* and a host of others.　**page 124/**

Everything, as the French say, has the defects of its merits. American slang forces the pace, and hence a lot of it *is* forced, pointless, of no literary or linguistic value. Especially tiresome is the supposed slang of the criminal class, as used in crime novels to heighten the reader's terror. Every one recognizes such language as *See here, pal, if the narks grab you for doing in that moll, the beak will send you up, see, and you'll burn.* I don't know whether any people really use this stuff. I hope not. If they must be criminals, they might at least talk like gentlemen. But in any case English crime stories often run to the same kind of stuff; indeed I am not sure just where the words above belong.

But no one need be afraid that slang will really hurt our language, here or in England. It cannot. There is no dictatorship behind it. Words and phrases live only on their worth; they survive only on their merits. Nor does slang tend to separate America and England. As a matter of fact, the rising generation in England reach out eagerly for American slang. If that means they're not rising but sinking, it's too bad. But anyway we'll sink together.　**page 125/**

from *The Dial*, Vol XIV
April 16, 1893

The Future of American Speech

. . . The degradation of the American language from the high standard still measurably preserved in the parent country is a phenomenon of the gravest significance. We are not now concerned with the quibbling about "Americanisms" and "Briticisms" that has supplied amusement to many ingenious controversialists. There is about as much to say upon one side of that question as upon the other, and the game appears to be drawn. The question now before us is not that of certain objectionable locutions — whether their origin be English or American;

it is the far more serious question of how far the American language has become an inferior dialect of the English. Those of our writers who resent any imputation of this sort usually ignore the real question altogether. They seek to divert attention from it either by childish *tu quoque* arguments, or by resort to vague generalizations upon the fluctuations to which all living languages are subject. They eloquently oppose "the wild flowers of speech, plucked betimes with the dew still on them, humble and homely and touching," to "the waxen petals of rhetoric as a schoolmaster arranges them." To the writer who has arrayed for us these touchingly contrasted figures "the grammarian, the purist, the pernicketty stickler for trifles, is the deadly foe of good English, rich in idioms and racy of the soil." That American English is, on the whole, as good as any other, that its peculiarities are but the evidences of a healthy vitality, is the sum of the plea urged by these zealous linguistic patriots.

But the question is not to be thus flippantly disposed of. Dr. Fitzedward Hall, who is, we must remember, an American, although he has lived in England for many years, replies to the sort of apologists above cited in the following emphatic terms: "With those who, either from denseness of ignorance or from aesthetic insensibility, deliver themselves in this uncritical fashion, it would be squandering words to argue: they must be left to perish in their pravity." And he goes on to say: "More or less as much as the language of Scotland, American English, as a whole has already come to be a dialect; and day by day it entitles itself more and more to that designation." These quotations are taken from an article published by Dr. Hall in the London "Academy" after it had been declined by "two American periodicals." The greater part of the article is devoted to a list of "locutions which go far to realize finished debasement," taken from a book by one of our better American writers. Although exception may be taken to some of Dr. Hall's illustrations, the majority of them are clearly examples of bad English. That it is difficult for an American to avoid writing bad English he freely admits, and the passage in which the admission is made, although somewhat long, is of so great interest that it deserves to be reproduced here in full. "If egotism for a moment is pardonable, no false shame deters me from avowing that, though I have lived away from America upwards of forty-six years, I feel, to this hour, in writing English that I am writing a foreign language, and that, if not incessantly on my guard, I am in peril of stumbling. Nor will it be amiss for any American, when experimenting like myself, to feel as I do, and never to relax his vigilance, if he would not, every now and then reveal himself, needlessly and to his prejudice, as an exotic. Not for five minutes can he listen to the conversation of his fellow-countrymen, or for that length of time read one of their newspapers, or one of such books as they usually write, **page 234/** without exposure to the influence of some expression which is not standard English. Try as he will to resist this influence, successful resistance to it is well-nigh impossible. On the other hand, if he is indifferent about resisting it, his fancied English will, a thousand to one, be chequered with solecisms, crudenesses, and piebald jargon, of the sort which the pages of Mrs. Stowe, Mr. E. P. Roe, and Mr. Howells have rendered familiar. In short, the language of an American is, all but inevitably, more or less dialectal." That Dr. Hall speaks with authority few will be bold enough to dispute. And, although he does not suggest any definite remedy for the insidious disease that has attacked our language, he clearly believes that remedies are yet available. A century from now, he says, our population will be several times that of Great Britain. "Circumstances generated by unprecedented combinations have entailed on us a recognizable dialect, and one which is rapidly developing. Whether it is fated to remain a dialect is a hazardous speculation. Yet, unless we chance to breed a matter of half a dozen Shakespeares and Miltons, it will hardly, without great purification, reach the dignity of a substantive language. But, be its eventual status what it may, that which should especially weigh with us is its unquestionable destiny to serve as the mother-tongue of hundreds of millions. Towards the shaping of it, so that our successors shall do us credit, we can contribute consciously. Most surely it behoves us, therefore, to take measures, and take them promptly, to the end that, so far as may prove feasible, its evolution be controlled by proficients in knowledge and taste, and not by sciolists and vulgarians."

What these measures should be, we are left to determine. Half a century ago, writing, *mutatis mutandis,* upon the same subject, Schopenhauer proposed in all seriousness that the State should take a hand in the matter, and establish a system of linguistic censorship of the press, with penalties for the misuse of words, for syntactical errors, and for "impudent mockery of grammar." "Is the German language outlawed?" he exclaimed, "too insignificant to deserve the legal protection enjoyed by every dung-hill?" So heroic a remedy as this is hardly within our reach, and we must look for aid to educational systems rather than to legislatures. By wisely directed education, and by that alone, may we hope to come once more into secure possession of the rich heritage, so nearly lost, of the speech of Shakespeare and of Tennyson. To accomplish this we must improve the methods of our elementary education, and must make our higher education higher still. We must strengthen at all points the study of the English language and literature; we must insist upon the acquaintance, from childhood up, with only good models of style; we must make the proper expression of thought, in every department of work, an aim concurrent with that of acquiring the special subject-matter of the study pursued.   page 235/

from *The Spectator* **CLXX**
February 5, 1943

The Conquering Tongue

D. W. Brogan

Every few years someone sounds the clarion and fills the fife, calling on us to man the breeches and repel the assailing hordes of Americanisms that threaten the chastity of the pure well of English undefiled. Sometimes the invaders intend to clip off the strong verbs, sometimes they threaten to enrich our language with new and horrid words. Whatever they do, or threaten to do, it must be resisted. But despite all the rallying battle-cries, the battle, when it is delivered so far forward, is always lost. We may regret that the battle is so ill-conducted, but we should not hide the truth. "Even our newspapers, hitherto regarded as models of correct literary style, are many of them following in their wake; and, both in matter and phraseology, are lending countenance to what at first sight appears a monstrously crude and imbecile jargon; while others, fearful of a direct plunge, modestly introduce the uncouth bantlings with a saving clause." So wrote John Farmer in 1899. So, with very slight modifications, could our contemporary viewers-with-alarm write today. In vain they belittle the merits of the importations from America ("belittle" is one of them). In vain they forbid Americanisms to darken our doors (and "darken our doors" is another). However talented as controversialists the defenders of the old English tongue may be, they will find facts too much for them, such facts for example as the American origin of "talented."

There is nothing surprising in the constant reinforcement or, if you like, corruption of English by American. And there is every reason to believe that it has increased, is increasing and will not be diminished. If American could influence English a century ago when the predominance of the Mother Country in wealth, population and prestige was secure, and when most educated Americans were reverentially colonial in their attitude to English culture, how can it be prevented from influencing English today when every change has been a change of weight to the American side? That the balance of linguistic power is upset is hard to doubt. Of the two hundred million people speaking English nearly seven-tenths live in the United States, and another tenth in the British Dominions are as much influenced by American as by English English. Nor is this all. As an international language, it is American that the world increasingly learns. The grammatical simplicity of English, its hospitality to new words, its freedom from the purist fetish that afflicts modern German for instance, make it a good international language. Its handicaps are its spelling and its pronunciation — and American is in some degree less erratic in spelling and less troublesome in pronunciation than is standard English. It is easier to learn to speak like Raymond Gram Swing than like Alvar Liddell. Whether it be true or not that Pius XI said he could understand spoken American but not spoken English, it is *ben trovato.*

To understand what is happening to the language in whose ownership and control we are now only minority shareholders is an object of curiosity worthy of serious persons. It is also an object worthy of less serious persons, for the study of American is rich in delights and surprises. And this is especially true when we begin by slang. It was Mr. Dooley who said that when the Americans were done with English it would look as if it had been run over by a musical comedy. Today, we should substitute the talkies for the musical comedy, for it is the latest of the arts that most affects English speech and, in America itself, is the main vehicle for the spread of general slang, as apart from the trade slang of special groups or crafts, such as tramps or railroadmen. It is an error, it is true, to think of "American" as merely a regularised form of slang; it has other roots than the luxuriant undergrowth of slang. But slang not only plays a great part in the growth of any language, it plays an especial part in the growth of a language like American, where the pressure of a uniformly accepted standard speech is less than it is with us and where such standard literary speech as there is, is further divorced from the living tongue than it is with us. . . . page 120/

4

TOWARD LINGUISTIC FREEDOM

from *Dissertions on the English Language with Notes, Historical and Critical*
by Noah Webster, Jun. Esquire
Boston: Isaiah Thomas and Company, 1789

Declaration of Linguistic Independence

Noah Webster

As an independent nation, our honor requires us to have a system of our own, in language as well as government. Great Britain, whose children we are, and whose language we speak, should no longer be our standard; for the taste of her writers is already corrupted, and her language on the decline. But if it were not so, she is   **page 20/**   at too great a distance to be our model, and to instruct us in the principles of our own tongue.

It must be considered further, that the English is the common root or stock from which our national language will be derived. All others will gradually waste away — and within a century and a half, North America will be peopled with a hundred millions of men, *all speaking the same language*. Place this idea in comparison with the present and possible future bounds of the language in Europe — consider the Eastern Continent as inhabited by nations, whose knowledge and intercourse are embarrassed by differences of language; then anticipate the period when the people of one quarter of the world, will be able to associate and converse together like children of the same family. Compare this prospect, which is not visionary, with the state of the English language in Europe, almost confined to an Island and to a few millions of people; then let   **page 21/**   reason

NOAH WEBSTER

and reputation decide, how far America should be dependent on a transatlantic nation, for her standard and improvements in language.

Let me add, that whatever predilection the Americans may have for their native European tongues, and particularly the British descendants for the English, yet several circumstances render a future separation of the American tongue from the English, necessary and unavoidable. The vicinity of the European nations, with the uninterrupted communication in peace, and the changes of dominion in war, are gradually assimilating their respective languages. The English with others is suffering continual alterations. America, placed at a distance from those nations, will feel, in a much less degree, the influence of the assimilating causes; at the same time, numerous local causes, such as a new country, new associations of people, new combinations of ideas in arts and science, and some intercourse with tribes wholly unknown in Europe, will introduce new words into the American tongue. These causes will produce, in a course of time, a language in North America, as different from the future language of Eng- page 22/ land, as the modern Dutch, Danish and Swedish are from the German, or from one another: like remote branches of a tree springing from the same stock; or rays of light, shot from the same center, and diverging from each other, in proportion to their distance from the point of separation. page 23/ . . . .

We have therefore the fairest opportunity of establishing a national language, and of giving it uniformity and perspicuity, in North America, that ever presented itself to mankind. Now is the time to begin the plan. The minds of the Americans are roused by the events of a revolution; the necessity of organizing the political body and of forming constitutions of government that shall secure freedom and property, has called all the faculties of the mind into exertion; and the danger of losing the benefits of independence, has disposed every man to embrace any scheme that shall tend, in its future operation, to reconcile the people of America to each other, and weaken the prejudices which oppose a cordial union. page 36/ . . . .

from **The Works of John Adams, Vol. VII**
by **Charles Francis Adams**
Boston: Little, Brown and Company, 1852

A Letter to the President of Congress

John Adams

Amsterdam, 5 September, 1780.

Sir, — As eloquence is cultivated with more care in free republics than in other governments, it has been found by constant experience that such republics have produced the greatest purity, copiousness, and perfection of language. It is not to be disputed that the form of government has an influence upon language, and language in its turn influences not only the form of government, but the temper, the sentiments, and manners of the people. The admirable models which have been transmitted through the world, and continued down to these days, so as to form an essential part of the education of mankind from generation to generation, by those two ancient towns, Athens and Rome, would be sufficient, without any other argument, to show the United States the importance to their liberty, prosperity, and glory, of an early attention to the subject of eloquence and language.

Most of the nations of Europe have thought it necessary to establish by public authority institutions for fixing and improving their proper languages. I need not mention the academies in France, Spain, and Italy, their learned labors, nor their great success. But it is very remarkable, that although many learned and ingenious men in England have from age to age projected similar institutions for correcting and improving the English tongue, yet the government have never found time to interpose in any manner; so that to this day there is no grammar nor dictionary extant of the English language which has the least public authority; and it is only very lately, that a tolerable dictionary has been published, even by a private person, and there is not yet a passable grammar enterprised by any individual.

The honor of forming the first public institution for refining, correcting, improving, and ascertaining the English language, I hope is reserved for congress; they have every motive that can possibly influence a public assembly to undertake it. It will have a happy effect upon the union of the States to have a pub-
page 249/ lic standard for all persons in every part of the continent to appeal to, both for the signification and pronunciation of the language. The constitutions of all the States in the Union are so democratical that eloquence will become

the instrument for recommending men to their fellow-citizens, and the principal means of advancement through the various ranks and offices of society.

In the last century, Latin was the universal language of Europe. Correspondence among the learned, and indeed among merchants and men of business, and the conversation of strangers and travellers, was generally carried on in that dead language. In the present century, Latin has been generally laid aside, and French has been substituted in its place, but has not yet become universally established, and, according to present appearances, it is not probable that it will. English is destined to be in the next and succeeding centuries more generally the language of the world than Latin was in the last or French is in the present age. The reason of this is obvious, because the increasing population in America, and their universal connection and correspondence with all nations will, aided by the influence of England in the world, whether great or small, force their language into general use, in spite of all the obstacles that may be thrown in their way, if any such there should be.

It is not necessary to enlarge further, to show the motives which the people of America have to turn their thoughts early to this subject; they will naturally occur to congress in a much greater detail than I have time to hint at. I would therefore submit to the consideration of congress the expediency and policy of erecting by their authority a society under the name of "the American Academy for refining, improving, and ascertaining the English Language." The authority of congress is necessary to give such a society reputation, influence, and authority through all the States and with other nations. The number of members of which it shall consist, the manner of appointing those members, whether each State shall have a certain number of members and the power of appointing them, or whether congress shall appoint them, whether after the first appointment the society itself shall fill up vacancies, these and other questions will easily be determined by congress.

It will be necessary that the society should have a library con- page 250/ sisting of a complete collection of all writings concerning languages of every sort, ancient and modern. They must have some officers and some other expenses which will make some small funds indispensably necessary. Upon a recommendation from congress, there is no doubt but the legislature of every State in the confederation would readily pass a law making such a society a body politic, enable it to sue and be sued, and to hold an estate, real or personal, of a limited value in that State. I have the honor to submit these hints to the consideration of congress, and to be, &c.

page 251/
John Adams.

from *The North American Review,*
Vol. X

April, 1820 (A review of *An appeal from
the judgments of Great Britain respecting
the United States of America.* By Robert
Walsh, jr. Second edition. Philadelphia,
Mitchell, Ames, & White, 1819, 8vo. pp.
512).

Resolutions Regarding the American Language

. . . The English language corrupted in America! What are the Columbiads, or Webster's Dictionaries, or any other name of American innovation, compared with the lucubrations of Jeremy Bentham! We cannot here forebear to present our readers with a passage from a *jeu d'esprit,* which has fallen in our way, under the name of 'Report of Resolutions to be proposed in the House of Representatives.' These proposed resolutions are intended to return the compliment paid to us by the Marquis of Lansdowne, in the session of 1819, in moving for an inquiry into the conduct of Gen. Jackson. In order to show that we are as willing to aid our brethren, in the British Parliament, in inquiring into their affairs, as they to aid our representatives, in inquiring into ours, these proposed resolutions go **page 364/** over most of the points in the British policy and condition, which appear to us here to need a little revision. That to which we now allude, is as follows:

'Whereas the House of Representatives, in common with the people of America, is justly proud of its admirable native tongue, and regards this most expressive and energetic language as one of the best of its birthrights, Resolved that the House acknowledge with gratitude the zeal, which several respectable writers and critics in England have shown for the preservation of the purity of the language in America; and, although these writers and critics, misled by the reports of illiterate English travellers, whose breeding and education confined them to the society of the more ignorant part of our community, have indiscriminately stigmatized, as Americanisms, words, which may be vulgarisms, or individual or provincial peculiarities, but are in no way adopted at large, by the well-educated people of America; and although the aforesaid critics and writers, being but imperfectly read in the early English writers, the great masters and standards of the language, have also denounced as Americanisms certain other words, such as *to progress, to advocate,* &c. which be, nevertheless, words of approved use and authority in the Augustan age of English literature; nevertheless, the House is grateful to these writers and critics, for their kind efforts abovementioned, and particularly for the *amiable spirit* and *courteous tone,* in which they have been made: and whereas the House of Representatives of the United States of America will ever feel it a duty to watch, with jealousy, over the preservation of the English tongue, in its original purity, and it is a matter of great interest to the House and to the American people, that their native language should not degenerate in the parent state, and it would afflict the American people to find their brethren in England gradually contracting the habit of a mixed and barbarous jargon; therefore resolved, that the House of Representatives of the United States of America regard with unfeigned sorrow the continued prevalence of five or six languages or dialects, within the narrow compass of the British isles, as a circumstance which menaces, at no remote period, the radical corruption of the English tongue; that it is a matter of high astonishment to the House, that no measures have been employed to exterminate the native dialects of the Celtic, still spoken in Cornwall, in Wales, in Ireland, in the Isle of Man, and in Scotland, with the corrupt French in the isles of Jersey and Guernsey; dialects mutually different from each other, and from the English, and which cannot continue to be spoken, without disastrous consequences to the English language and literature; that the page 365/ House, moreover, looks with still greater anxiety on the utterly corrupt and barbarous state, to which the English language has already sunk, in most of the counties of England, to the degree that various dialects which prevail, such as those in Yorkshire, Somersetshire, and Cumberland, at the same time that they are in themselves utterly uncouth and hideous, are unintelligible to any one, but a person born and educated in these counties respectively; and though the House views with more respect the lowland dialect of Scotland, as having been ennobled by the writings of some admirable original authors, particularly in the last and present centuries, yet the House still trembles at the deleterious effect, which this very ennobling of a subordinate and provincial dialect may have on the pure English tongue, and regards it as a symptom of the approaching degeneracy of that tongue, that writings in said provincial dialect are eagerly sought and familiarly read; that the House further regards, as still more pernicious either than the prevalence of the Cornish, Welsh, Erse, Mankish, or Gaelic, or of the provincial corruptions of the English, that barbarity which from various causes is fast creeping into the language of the highest and best educated classes of society in England, a corruption which, in some respects, the House thinks to have been much promoted by the leading critical journals of the day; an affectation, at one time, of forgotten old words, and at another of pedantic new ones, each equally unauthorized in a pure and chaste style of writing and speaking; the perpetual recurrence of the plural number, instead of the singular, as *charities, sympathies, tendencies,* &c., a phraseology which tends in a high degree to weaken a language, by leading writers and speakers to place that emphasis in the grammatical plurality, which ought to reside in the term itself; an unwise attempt to ennoble such words as *clever, you know, vastly,* &c. which are pardonable only in a colloquial use, and unworthy the dignity of grave and sustained discourse; an adoption by noblemen, gentlemen, and clergymen, of the terms of horse-jockeys, boxers, and shooters, to the degree, that a great number of vulgar and cant terms are heard in what are called the best circles, which the House has reason to apprehend are often the worst, in which the human blood, drawn by the clenched fist of a ruffian, is unrighteously called "claret," and shooting two dozen of birds, "bagging 12 pair of cocks"; lastly an alarming prevalence of profane and obscene language, in the highest and best bred circles, which, though liable to high moral objections, the House is willing to regard here merely as another agent of brutalizing the English tongue, and which, though it is unhappily a vice too common in all countries, the House has unquestioned information prevails in   **page 366/**   England to an unparalleled and odious extent, reaching into the societies which consider themselves the most polite and best bred. In view of these facts, Resolved, that the House of Representatives of the United States of America is apprehensive, that the genuine purity of the English tongue is already fatally assailed, and is threatened with being wholly destroyed at no remote period; that the possibility of such an event is to be considered by the American people as a just ground of national alarm and apprehension, and that it is their duty to provide, if it may be, against its occurrence; and inasmuch as the circumstances, that this country was at first in general settled by Englishmen of good education, by aggrieved gentlemen and ejected clergymen, and has continued to this day, remarkably free from all those classes of men, which most corrupt a language, such as an accumulation of miners, manufacturers, and beggars, and is blessed, to an extent elsewhere unknown, with the means of popular education, so much so, that in more than one of the American states, it is supposed that there is not a native citizen unable to read and write; inasmuch as from these and other circumstances easy to be deduced from the previous enumeration of some of the causes of the corruption of the language in England, the English language has been preserved in a state of admirable purity, in the United States of America, a purity so great, that in the most remote and unfavoured portions of our country, the popular dialect is far purer than in some counties in the heart of England, while the style of speaking and writing is, by the blessing of God, quite untainted with most of the above mentioned vulgarities prevalent in the high English circles, and but partially infected with any of them: Resolved, therefore farther, in consideration of these premises, that the nobility and gentry of England be courteously invited to send their elder sons, and such others as may be destined to appear as public speakers in church or state, to America, for their education; that the president of the United States be requested to concert measures with the presidents and heads of our colleges and schools, for the prompt reception and gratuitous instruction of such young persons, and to furnish them, after the expiration of a term of —————— years, certificates of their proficiency in the English tongue.' pp.12—15.

We look upon the above as a fair piece of good natured insolence, quite excusable in the way of retaliation, and fraught, moreover, with a very large portion of truth. . . .   **page 367/**

from *The Nation*, Vol. CXVI
April 11, 1923

Language by Legislation

Who that is a patriot can hear without a thrill what the Honorable Washington Jay McCormick, Republican member of the House of Representatives from Montana, urges upon the national legislature for the sake of the national language and literature? It is no less than the passage of a bill, which the Honorable Mr. McCormick himself has prepared, to make constitutional and statutory the "flowing, growing, and glowing" lingo of the real American.

This is the way he tells the world what he has on his chest:

> I might say I would supplement the political emancipation of '76 by the mental emancipation of '23. America has lost much in literature by not thinking its own thoughts and speaking them boldly in a language unadorned with gold braid. It was only when Cooper, Irving, Mark Twain, Whitman, and O. Henry dropped the Order of the Garter and began to write American that their wings of immortality sprouted. Had Noah Webster, instead of styling his monumental work the "American Dictionary of the English Language," written a "Dictionary of the American Language," he would have become a founder instead of a compiler. Let our writers drop their top-coats, spats, and swagger-sticks, and assume occasionally their buckskin, moccasins, and tomahawks.

Sure! Maybe the Honorable McCormick let his foot slip when he pulled that one about Cooper and Irving, for those guys certainly wrote what the poor boobs thought was English and either one of them would have thrown a fit if he thought he was doing anything to the good old mama-tongue. But that bird McCormick's heart is in the right place, and we have to hand it to him for being the first Congressman since the Johnstown flood to make a noise about it. The trouble with this country is these here foreigners coming in and learning English out of grammar books instead of picking up American on the vacant lots where the boys would give them the merry-ha-ha if they pulled any of the high-and-mighty. We got to shake the real Americans out of the feathers and make them get behind a line of patter that doesn't sound as if it came through a nose with a monocle sitting just off to starboard. It is time to tell these here foreigners and high-brows where they get off.

It's not so easy, we will say that. You got to go some to make people use their Watermans the way they talk. The preachers get into one-way ruts, and so do the school-teachers and the editors, and they won't try new tricks for fear of skidding. The best hunch for Congress is to set up that Academy of the American Language that the Honorable McCormick has doped out. Make Mencken president of the outfit, put George Ade, Ring Lardner, Warren Harding, and

Billy Sunday on the executive committee, and tell them to go to it. They could fix it so the Supreme Court umpired in a language a man could get without wearing out his finger-nails on the dictionary. They could can all the printers of the *Congressional Record,* and hand a straight tip to the newspapers to follow suit, and jazz up, or reach their necks out for the ax. Billy Sunday could pass the high sign to the sky-pilots and bring them down to green grass. If Mencken could have a mandate, as the fellow says, for Harvard, that would help some. Sure it can be done. Anyhow, we got to get behind and boost.   page 408/

from *The Yale Review*, Vol. XXV
March, 1936

The American Language

H. L. Mencken

The first Englishman to notice an Americanism sneered at it aloofly, thus setting a fashion that many of his countrymen have been following ever since. He was one Francis Moore, a ruffian who came out to Georgia with Oglethorpe in 1735, and the word that upset him was *bluff*, in the sense of "a cliff or headland with a broad precipitous face." He did not deign to argue against it; he simply dismissed it as "barbarous," apparently assuming that all Englishmen of decent instincts would agree with him. For nearly a century they seem to have done so, and *bluff* lingered sadly below the salt. When it was printed at all in Great Britain it was set off by sanitary quotation marks, or accompanied by other hints of deprecation, as *rubberneck, hot spot* and *nerts* are accompanied today. But then, in 1830, the eminent Sir Charles Lyell used it shamelessly in the first volume of his monumental "Principles of Geology," and from that day to this it has been a perfectly respectable if somewhat unfamiliar word in England, with a place in every dictionary.

Its history is the history of almost countless other Americanisms. They have been edging their way into English since early colonial times, and, for more than a century past, in constantly increasing volume, but I can't recall one that didn't have to run a gauntlet of opposition in the motherland, at times verging upon the frantic. After the Revolution, that opposition took on the proportions of a holy war. Never an American book came out that the English reviewers did not belabor its vocabulary violently. The brunt of the attack, of course, had to be borne by the poetasters of the era — for example, Joel Barlow, whose "Co- page 538/ lumbiad" (1807) loosed a really terrifying geyser of abuse. But even the most serious writers got their share — among them, Jefferson, John Marshall, Noah Webster, and John Quincy Adams. Jefferson's crime was that he had invented the verb *to belittle*. It was, one may argue plausibly, a very logical, useful, and perhaps even nifty word, and seventy-five years later the prissy Anthony Trollope was employing it without apology. But when Jefferson ventured to use it in his "Notes on Virginia" (1787) "The London Review" tossed and raged in a manner befitting the discovery of a brace of duelling pistols beneath the cope of the Archbishop of Canterbury, and for several years following its dudgeon was supported virtuously by most of the other reviews. "What an expression!" roared the "London." "It may be an elegant one in Virginia, but for our part, all we can do is to *guess* at its meaning. For shame, Mr. Jefferson! Freely, good sir, will we forgive all your attacks, impotent as they are illiberal, upon our national character; but for the future spare — O spare, we beseech you, our mother-tongue!" **page 539/** . . . .

. . . Every British traveller who came to these shores between the War of 1812 and the Civil War had something to say about the neologisms his ears and eyes encountered on his tour, and nearly all were constrained to deplore them. Captain Basil Hall, who was here in 1827 and 1828, went about in a palpitating daze, confounded and outraged by the signs on American places of business. *Clothing Store* he interpreted after long thought, and *Flour and Feed Store* after prayer and soul-searching, but what on earth was a *Leather and Finding Store?* Captain Thomas Hamilton, who followed five years later, found it impossible to penetrate to "the precise import" of *Dry-Goods Store,* and when he encountered an establishment offering *Hollow Ware, Spiders,* and *Fire-Dogs* he gave up in despair.

Hall was not one to take it lying down. He decided to **page 541/** call upon Noah Webster, whose American Dictionary of the English Language had just come out, to find out what the Yankees meant by using the mother tongue so cruelly. Webster shocked him by arguing stoutly that "his countrymen had not only a right to adopt new words, but were obliged to modify the language to suit the novelty of the circumstances, geographical and political, in which they were placed." The great lexicographer "who taught millions to spell but not one to sin" went on to observe judicially that it was "quite impossible to stop the progress of language — it is like the course of the Mississippi, the motion of which, at times, is scarcely perceptible; yet even then it possesses a momentum quite irresistible. Words and expressions will be forced into use in spite of all the exertions of all the writers in the world."

"But surely," persisted Hall, "such innovations are to be deprecated?"

"I don't think that," replied old Noah. "If a word becomes universally current in America, where English is spoken, why should it not take its station in the language?"

"Because," declared Hall with magnificent pertinacity, "there are words enough already."

This heroic dogma is still heard in England, where even native novelties are commonly opposed violently, and not infrequently strangled at birth. There seems to be, in the modern Englishman, very little of that ecstasy in word-making which so prodigiously engrossed his Elizabethan forebears. Shakespeare alone probably put more new words into circulation than all the English writers since Carlyle, and they were much better ones. The ideal over there today is not picturesque and exhilarating utterance, but correct and reassuring utterance, and one of its inevitable fruits is that bow-wow jargon which Sir Arthur Quiller-Couch describes in "On the Art of Writing" as "the medium through which boards of government, county councils, syndicates, committees, commercial firms, express the   page 542/   processes as well as the conclusions of their thought, and so voice the reason of their being." It is, at its worst, at least in accord with what are taken to be the principles of English grammar, and at its best it shows excellent manners and even a kind of mellifluous elegance; indeed, the English, taking one with another, may be said to write much better than we do — at all events by the standards of the schoolmaster. But what they write is seldom animated by anything properly describable as bounce. It lacks novelty, variety, audacity. There is little juice in it. The reader confronted by it is treated politely and lulled pleasantly, but he seldom enjoys the enchantment of surprise. That diligent search for new and racy locutions which occupied so much of the work day of Walt Whitman and William Dean Howells alike, and is practised so assiduously by scores of saucy Andersons and Hemingways, Sandburgs and Saroyans today, is carried on across the ocean by only a few extravagant eccentrics, virtually all of whom — for example, James Joyce and Ezra Pound — are non- and even anti-Englishmen. The hundred-per-cent English writers, save when they stoop to conscious wickedness, seldom depart very far from the jargon of Quiller-Couch. It is by no means a monopoly of the classes he named, nor is it reserved for solemn occasions. I find it also in my favorite English weekly, the "News of the World," which is devoted principally to sports, the theatres, and the more scabrous varieties of crime, and is probably a far better mirror of England than the "Times." When the "News of the World" reports the downfall of a rural dean or a raid on a Mayfair night club, the thing is done in a style so tight and brittle that nothing to match it is discoverable in this country, at least outside the pages of "The Homiletic Review." "When we want to freshen our speech," Mrs. Virginia Woolf was lately saying, "we borrow from American — *poppycock, rambunctious, flip-flop, booster, good mixer.* All the expressive, ugly, vigorous slang which creeps into   page 543/   use among us, first in talk, later in writing, comes from across the Atlantic."   page 544/   . . . .

One finds in current American all the characters and tendencies that marked the rich English of Shakespeare's time — an eager borrowing of neologisms from other languages, a bold and often very ingenious use of metaphor, and a fine disdain of the barricades separating the parts of speech. The making of new words is not carried on only, or even principally, to fill gaps in the vocabulary; indeed, one may well agree with Captain Hall that "there are words enough already." It is carried on because there survives in the American something that seems to have faded out of the Englishman: an innocent joy in word-making for its own sake, a voluptuous delight in the vigor and elasticity of the language. The search for the *mot juste* is an enterprise that is altogether too pedantic for him; he much prefers to solve his problem by non-Euclidian devices. *Hoosegow* was certainly not necessary when it appeared, for we already had a large repertory of synonyms for *jail*. But   page 549/   when the word precipitated itself from the Spanish *juzgado* somewhere along the Rio Grande it won quick currency, and in a little while it was on the march through the country, and soon or late, I suppose, it will produce its inevitable clipped forms, *hoose* and *gow*, and its attendant adjective and verb. *Corral*, which entered by the same route in the Forties of the last century, had hatched a verb before the Civil War, and that verb, according to Webster's New International (1934), now has four separate and distinct meanings. *Bummer*, coming in from the German, is now clipped to *bum*, and is not only noun, verb, and adjective but also adverb. *Buncombe*, borrowed by the English as *bunkum*, has bred *bunco* and *bunk* at home, both of which rove the parts of speech in a loose and easy way, and the last of which has issue in the harsh verb to *debunk*, still under heavy fire in England.

The impact of such lawless novelties upon the more staid English of the motherland is terrific. The more they are denounced as heathen and outlandish, the quicker they get into circulation. Nor do they prosper only on the level of the vulgate, and among careless speakers. There are constant complaints in the English newspapers about their appearance in the parliamentary debates, and even in discourses from the sacred desk, and they begin to show themselves also in *belles-lettres*, despite the English dislike of new ways of writing. Their progress, in fact, is so widespread and so insidious that they often pop up in the diatribes that revile them; the Englishman, conquered at last, can no longer protest against Americanisms without using them. Moreover, they are now supported actively by a definitely pro-American party of writers and scholars, and though it is still small in numbers, at least compared to the patriot band, it shows some distinguished names. The late Robert Bridges, Poet Laureate, was an active member of it, and among its other adherents are Wyndham Lewis, Edward Shanks, Richard Aldington, and Sir John Foster   page 550/   Fraser. Sir William Craigie, perhaps the first of living lexicographers, is so greatly interested in the American form of English that he has spent the years since 1925 in a scientific examination of it, and will presently begin the publication of an elaborate dictionary. If only because of the greater weight of the population behind it, it seems destined to usurp the natural leadership of British English, and to determine the general course of the language hereafter. But its chief advantage in this struggle is really not the numerical one, but the fact that its daring experiments and iconoclasms lie in the grand tradition of English, and are signs of its incurable normalcy and abounding vigor.

How far it will move away from the theorizing of grammarians and the policing of schoolmarms remains to be seen. They still make valiant efforts to curb its wayward spirit, but with gradually diminishing success. When, a few years ago, the late Sterling A. Leonard of the University of Wisconsin submitted a long series of their admonitions to a committee of educated Americans, including many philologians, he found that opinion was against them on that high level almost as decidedly as it was on lower ones. His judges favored scores of forms that the school grammars and popular handbooks of usage still condemn. Since then a more direct attack upon the conservative position has been made by Dr. Robert

C. Pooley of the same university. He shows that some of the rules laid down with most assurance by pedants have no support in either history or logic, and are constantly violated by writers of unquestionable authority. There have even been rumblings of revolt in the conservative camp. The late George Philip Krapp of Columbia, who was surely anything but a radical, was of the opinion that English would undergo profound changes in the United States, and that many of them would be of such a character that its very grammatical structure would be shaken. Dr. George O. Curme of Northwestern University is another eminent grammarian who warns his **page 551/** colleagues that the rules they cherish have no genuine authority, and must be overhauled from time to time. Once they steel themselves to that sacrifice of their professional dignity, he says, "it will give a thrill to English-speaking students to discover that the English language does not belong to the schoolteacher but belongs to them, and that its future destiny will soon rest entirely in their hands."

Dr. Curme is always careful to think and speak of American as no more than a variation of English. But it must be obvious that, in late years, the tail has begun a vigorous wagging of the dog. "The facts that we ought to realize," says Edward Shanks to his fellow Britons, "and that we ignore when we talk loftily about Americanisms, are that America is making a formidable contribution to the development of our language, and that all our attempts to reject that contribution will in the long run be vain." **page 552/**

from *The English Journal*, Vol. XXXI
February, 1942

One People, One Language

Robert C. Pooley

. . . In a day when names hitherto innocent become overnight objects of shame and derision or are used as the rally-cries of bigoted partisans, it is unfortunate that our language has to bear a name not distinctly our own. The name "English" is the honored token of a debt we owe to a great and rich culture, the source and wellspring of much of our own today. But the name English also implies a dependency, it carries a connotation of something borrowed or secondhand, at variance with our rather complete freedom from the development of English in England or elsewhere. Mr. Mencken, perhaps justly objecting to the implications of the name English, boldly calls our language the "American language." While I do not go with him all the way in casting off our obligations to the land from which our language sprang or in exaggerating the differences, real or imagined, between our English and that of England, I do share his feeling that the official speech of a land of one hundred and thirty millions of people should bear a name characteristic of our unique and independent culture. But new names lead to misunderstanding, they exaggerate differences, and appear to create the kind of rally-cry of bigotry to which I referred a moment before. For that reason we shall undoubtedly continue to call our language English, but we shall keep before us a lively sense of our own English, the English of the United States of America. From many races, with many cultures and languages our people came, but today we stand before the world one people with one language. The historical accident which gave it the name English does not carry with it any sense of subordination or dependence.

We can be justly proud of our language. Consider, first, its spread and uniformity. From Maine to California, from Washington State to Florida, from Minnesota to Texas, the same American English is spoken. Nowhere else in the world can one find such an enormous geographical territory or so vast a population united in one common tongue. And in speaking of a common tongue I do not mean only the language of the cultured, educated minority. I mean that the humblest citizens of Bangor, Pullman, San Diego, and Tallahassee could meet in St. Louis and there converse with one another and with page 111/ residents of Missouri without perceptible barriers to complete communication. This fact is not only an achievement of such magnitude as to be scarcely grasped, so accustomed to it are we; it is, indeed, a defense second to none against the malignant forces in the world today which are openly striving to rend us apart as a people, to set us against each other by creating artificial lines of race, culture, or region. As long as we remain a people of one language — of a truly common language — the enemy can be held at bay.

Consider next the enormous size and flexibility of our vocabulary. Upon the original stock of Anglo-Saxon grammar and basic vocabulary, we have borrowed from the world over to enrich our speech with words for every purpose, from the common affairs of life to the exacting demands of modern science or the delicate subtleties of fine literature. It is remarkable to note that all this borrowing has not resulted in a polyglot tongue of garbled words. English does more than borrow; it absorbs. If a word, no matter what its source, is useful to us, it becomes our own and is part of English. Just as "macaroni," "sauerkraut," "banana," "chile," and "vanilla" have become a part of our national diet, so too have the words become ingested in the common tongue. The new word of today becomes the familiar word of tomorrow. It is a sad commentary on the state of the world that the larger part of our recent borrowings have to do with warfare.

One sign of the vitality of a speech is its readiness to make new words. American English may be derided by conservative critics for the readiness with which neologisms become accepted and flash overnight to all parts of our land, but the fact itself is a sign of health. The purpose of a language is to communicate; if a new word or a new phrase carries with it a freshness of meaning, a short cut to communication, it is a desirable addition to our tongue, no matter how low its source or how questionable its etymology. We need not fear word creation as harmful to our language; what we must fear is crystallization, the preservation of a conventional vocabulary by a limited minority who resent the normal steady changes which inevitably must take place within a language.

Consider again the simplicity of our grammar. We are indeed fortunate that the system of inflections characteristic of a language **page 112/** in the earlier stages of its development has been largely discarded by English. A thousand years ago the speakers of English, in using an adjective, had to choose between a weak and a strong declension and, within that declension, whether the nouns to be modified were masculine, feminine, or neuter, singular or plural. Only after all these factors were considered could the correct adjective be used. We have entirely discarded that lumbering machinery. One word, like "good," can be used in every sense required in modern English. To a greater or less degree a similar simplification has taken place in the other inflectional systems of English. This process of simplification should go on unhindered. We still have much machinery which could be profitable discarded. The forms of the verb "to be" could be further simplified without loss; apostrophes — relics of a discarded genitive — could be dispensed with without loss; and what is left of our subjunctive shows signs of completely disappearing. I do not imply here that it is our duty to teach these simplified forms or even to hasten the change; I stress, rather, an attitude of mind which can look upon these simplifications as improvements which strengthen our language rather than deplore them as corruptions. There is a crying need also to have our grammar completely re-written, to bring it in line with theories of language of the twentieth century, rather than to rest upon the ideologies of the eighteeenth cenutry, as it does now. In some less troubled times it may be a task for the National Council of Teachers of English to undertake to appoint a commission of the leading scholars of the land to re-write completely the grammar of English.

We may be proud of the fact that English has always been a free language, untrammeled by an academy or other governing body. From time to time efforts have been initiated to control the language, to place it under restraints, but always these efforts proved abortive, and the language went its own way. I take this fact to be the token of a certain quality of independence of those who speak English. I take it also as an indication of the democratic nature of English in America, that, while aristocratic and conservative elements in our population may decry change in language, and deplore the creation of new words, new idioms, and new forms of syntax, the American people as a whole have resisted efforts to set arbitrary standards. **page 113/** We are a youthful nation, exuberant and perhaps sometimes a little rowdy. But there is promise and hope in the exuberance of youth; we see in our language a lively imagination, a picturesque freshness, and a readiness to accept change, which are characteristics of youth. We need not fear exuberance. What we must fear and guard against is senility, the complacency of old age, which is content with things as they are and mockingly derisive of change. Let foreigners mock if they will; we can be proud and happy in the possession of a free, lively, and even racy speech. **page 114/** . . . .

5

FOREIGN COMMENTS

from *Travels in North America*, Vol.
II.
by Captain Basil Hall
Edinburgh: Cadell and Co., 1829

Mutual Misunderstanding between the Americans and the English

Basil Hall

It is generally taken for granted, that while travellers in other foreign countries are apt to misconstrue much that they hear, and often, also, to express what they do not mean to say, merely from their ignorance of the language, these embarrassments, in the case of an Englishman, will be entirely overcome in America, in consequence of English being spoken by both parties. But I have little doubt, after the experiences of this journey, that no inconsiderable portion of the mutual misunderstandings between the Americans and their guests, arises from an imperfect acquaintance with this very English language, supposed to be common to both.

It must be recollected, that the meaning of words does not depend upon their etymology, or upon the definitions of Johnson, or any other lexicographer, but entirely upon the usage of the society in which they are current. We see this strongly marked even in England itself, where many ex- **page 43/** pressions are used by one rank of persons, with perfect propriety, which, if whispered in another, would either be considered the grossest ill-breeding, or would be entirely misconceived, from carrying with them a sense totally dissimilar. Now, what holds good with regard to the different classes of society in one and the same country, may fairly be supposed still more striking in the case of different countries.

60

In America, it so happens — I don't at present enquire wherefore — that the English language is somewhat modified. I speak not alone of the meaning of individual words, in many of which also the change is abundantly perceptible; but chiefly of the general acceptation of language, as connected with a set of feelings, and a state of circumstances, materially different from those which exist in England. It would certainly be astonishing, if some difference were not to be produced in these two nations, both in the ideas, and in those forms of speech by which they receive expression, in consequence of the continued presence and operation of physical, moral, and political phenomena so essentially dissimilar, and in spite of the common origin, and the common language, of the two countries.

That part of the population in America who are acquainted with their own country, but who know   **page 44/**   little of any other, and who, of course, form an immense majority of the whole, naturally give the tone to thought, as well as to language, — that is to say, their authority, as to the value of all current expressions, will predominate. And it must inevitably happen, that if these persons, forming the great mass, have acquired the habit, whether wisely or not, of seeing every thing in a favourable light which respects America, and of depreciating every thing English; and if at the same time they have fallen into the uncontrolled practice of using, amongst themselves, a correspondent warmth of language to express these thoughts and feelings, they may well be supposed to acquire habits of self-admiration, and self-praise, beyond what they themselves are aware of. Their feelings and their language, therefore, may be strictly in keeping with each other, according to the current American acceptation of the words used, and they may often be speaking with perfect sincerity, with no want of a mutual and perfect understanding amongst themselves, when to a stranger the very reverse of all this may appear.

If it be the custom in England to apply different words, or a different form of words, from those used in America, to describe similar feelings and circumstances, an English traveller in that country, bringing with him his English ideas as to the   **page 45/**   acceptation of words, and the judgment of things, will naturally be struck with what he supposes a want of agreement between the facts he witnesses, and the verbal expression in which they are represented to him by the inhabitants of America.

Now, if this theory be true, both parties will often be as much dissatisfied, or perhaps more dissatisfied, and wider of the intended mark, than if their respective languages — as happens between our neighbours the French and us — were entirely different, not merely in their local usage or occasional idiom, but in their whole structure. According to this view, an American, accustomed to use a certain form of expression to explain an ordinary sentiment, will be disappointed to find that he does not carry the stranger along with him — whereas it is very possible that he and his guest may all the while be thinking pretty much alike; but still the native may fail to make himself understood, from using terms which the stranger has been taught to appropriate to things of a different character. And in the same way, the stranger may describe what he feels in terms which, if understood in the sense he means them, would give his audience pleasure instead of offence.

I do not say that all the misunderstandings, as they are well called, which separate the Americans   page 46/   from us, arise from this source, but I know by painful experience that many of them do; and I seriously believe, that things would now be better, in this respect at least, between the countries, if, when the Americans adopted a form of government so radically different from ours, they could likewise have reformed the dialect as thoroughly. It is curious enough, by the way, to see the discomfort that some scrupulous Americans show to the mere name of our common tongue; I have actually heard a grave proposal made to relinquish the practice of calling it the English language!

I remember reading in some old author, that when the Jesuits went to China, they found the religious ceremonies so like those of the Roman Catholic Church, that in their labours of conversion, they were more perplexed than assisted by this remarkable similarity, being often sorely bothered how to make the difference between the religions sufficiently manifest in the outward manners. They declared, accordingly, in writing to their countrymen at home, "that in all their travels amongst the Heathen, they had never before found the arch enemy concealed under so insidious a garb, and that it was far easier to convert a Gentoo to Christianity — though he worshipped a stick or a stone, and would rather kill one of his parents than   page 47/   leap over a cow — than it was to bring about a Chinese who cared neither for God nor Devil."

I don't go quite so far. But I will say this, that in all my travels, both amongst Heathens and amongst Christians, I have never encountered any people by whom I found it nearly so difficult to make myself understood as by the Americans. page 48/

from *Democracy in America*, Vol. II
by Alexis De Tocqueville
(Translated by Henry Reeves)
London and New York: The Colonial Press, 1900

The Effect of Democracy on Language

Alexis De Tocqueville

. . . American authors may truly be said to live more in England than in their own country; since they constantly study the English writers, and take them every day for their models. But such is not the case with the bulk of the population, which is more immediately subjected to the peculiar causes acting upon the United States. It is not then to the written, but to the spoken language that attention must be paid, if we would detect the modifications which the idiom of an aristocratic people may undergo when it becomes the language of a democracy.

Englishmen of education, and more competent judges than I can be myself of the nicer shades of expression, have frequently assured me that the language of the educated classes in the United States is notably different from that of the educated classes in Great Britain. They complain not only that the Americans have brought into use a number of new words — the difference and the distance between the two countries might suffice to explain that much — but that these new words are more especially taken from the jargon of parties, the mechanical arts, or the language of trade. They assert, in addition to this, that old English words are often used by the Americans in new acceptations; and lastly, that the inhabitants of the United States frequently intermingle their phraseology in the strangest manner, and sometimes place words together which are always kept apart in the language of the mother-country. These remarks, which were made to me at various times by persons who page 68/ appear to be worthy of credit, led me to reflect upon the subject; and my reflections brought me, by theoretical reasoning, to the same point at which my informants had arrived by practical observation.

In aristocracies, language must naturally partake of that state of repose in which everything remains. Few new words are coined, because few new things are made; and even if new things were made, they would be designated by known words, whose meaning has been determined by tradition. If it happens that the human mind bestirs itself at length, or is roused by light breaking in from without, the novel expressions which are introduced are characterized by a degree of learning, intelligence, and philosophy, which shows that they do not originate in a democracy. . . .

Democratic nations love change for its own sake; and this is seen in their language as much as in their politics. Even when they do not need to change words, they sometimes feel a wish to transform them. The genius of a democratic people is not only shown by the great number of words they bring into use, but also by the nature of the ideas these new words represent. Amongst such a people the majority lays down the law in language as well as in everything else; its prevailing spirit is as manifest in that as in other respects. But the majority is more page 69/ engaged in business than in study — in political and commercial interests than in philosophical speculation or literary pursuits. Most of the words coined or adopted for its use will therefore bear the mark of these habits; they will mainly serve to express the wants of business, the passions of party, or the details of the public administration. In these departments the language will constantly spread, whilst on the other hand it will gradually lose ground in metaphysics and theology. . . .

In the absence of knowledge of the dead languages, democratic nations are apt to borrow words from living tongues; for their mutual intercourse becomes perpetual, and the inhabitants of different countries imitate each other the more readily as they grow more like each other every day.

But it is principally upon their own languages that democratic nations attempt to perpetrate innovations. From time to time they resume forgotten expressions in their vocabulary, which they restore to use; or they borrow from some particular class of the community a term peculiar to it, which they introduce with a figurative meaning into the language of daily life. Many expressions which originally belonged to the technical language of a profession or a party, are thus drawn into general circulation.

The most common expedient employed by democratic na- page 70/ tions to make an innovation in language consists in giving some unwonted meaning to an expression already in use. This method is very simple, prompt, and convenient; no learning is required to use it aright, and ignorance itself rather facilitates the practice; but that practice is most dangerous to the language. When a democratic people doubles the meaning of a word in this way, they sometimes render the signification which it retains as ambiguous as that which it acquires. An author begins by a slight deflection of a known expression from its primitive meaning, and he adapts it, thus modified, as well as he can to his subject. A second writer twists the sense of the expression in another way; a third takes possession of it for another purpose; and as there is no common appeal to the sentence of a permanent tribunal which may definitely settle the signification of the word, it remains in an ambiguous condition. The consequence is that writers hardly ever appear to dwell upon a single thought, but they always seem to point their aim at a knot of ideas, leaving the reader to judge which of them has been hit. This is a deplorable consequence of democracy. I had rather that the language should be made hideous with words imported from the Chinese, the Tartars, or the Hurons, than that the meaning of a word in our own language should become indeterminate. Harmony and uniformity are only secondary beauties in composition; many of these things are conventional, and, strictly speaking, it is possible to forego them; but without clear phraseology there is no good language.

The principle of equality necessarily introduces several other changes into language. In aristocratic ages, when each nation tends to stand aloof from all others and likes to have distinct characteristics of its own, it often happens that several peoples which have a common origin become nevertheless estranged from each other, so that, without ceasing to understand the same language, they no longer all speak it in the same manner. In these ages each nation is divided into a certain number of classes, which see but little of each other, and do not intermingle. Each of these classes contracts, and invariably retains, habits of mind peculiar to itself, and adopts by choice certain words and certain terms, which afterwards pass from generation to generation, like their estates. The same idiom then page 71/ comprises a language of the poor and a language of the rich — a language of the citizen and a language of the nobility — a learned language and a vulgar one. The deeper the divisions, and the more impassable the barriers of society become, the more must this be the case. I would lay a wager, that amongst the castes of India there are amazing variations of language, and that there is almost as much difference between the language of the pariah and that of the Brahmin as there is in their dress. When, on the contrary, men, being no longer restrained by ranks, meet on terms of constant intercourse — when castes are destroyed, and the classes of society are recruited and intermixed with each other, all the words of a language are mingled. Those which are unsuitable to the greater number perish; the remainder form a common store, whence everyone chooses pretty nearly at random. Almost all the different dialects which divided the idioms of European nations are manifestly declining; there is no *patois* in the New World, and it is disappearing every day from the old countries.

The influence of this revolution in social conditions is as much felt in style as it is in phraseology. Not only does everyone use the same words, but a habit springs up of using them without discrimination. The rules which style had set up are almost abolished: the line ceases to be drawn between expressions which seem by their very nature vulgar, and others which appear to be refined. Persons springing from different ranks of society carry the terms and expressions they are accustomed to use with them, into whatever circumstances they may pass; thus the origin of words is lost like the origin of individuals, and there is as much confusion in language as there is in society.

I am aware that in the classification of words there are rules which do not belong to one form of society any more than to another, but which are derived from the nature of things. Some expressions and phrases are vulgar, because the ideas they are meant to express are low in themselves; others are of a higher character, because the objects they are intended to designate are naturally elevated. No intermixture of ranks will ever efface these differences. But the principle of equality cannot fail to root out whatever is merely conventional and arbitrary in the forms of thought. Perhaps the necessary classification which I pointed out in the last sentence will always be less respected by page 72/ a democratic people than by any other, because amongst such a people there are no men who are permanently disposed by education, culture, and leisure to study the natural laws of language, and who cause those laws to be respected by their own observance of them.

. . . Democratic nations are passionately addicted to generic terms or abstract expressions, because these modes of speech enlarge thought, and assist the operations of the mind by enabling it to include several objects in a small compass. page 73/ . . . .

These abstract terms which abound in democratic languages, and which are used on every occasion without attaching them to any particular fact, enlarge and obscure the thoughts they are intended to convey; they render the mode of speech more succinct, and the idea contained in it less clear. But with regard to language, democratic nations prefer obscurity to labor. I know not indeed whether this loose style has not some secret charm for those who speak and write amongst these nations. . . .

Amongst all nations, generic and abstract terms form the basis of language. I do not, therefore, affect to expel these terms from democratic languages; I simply remark that men have an especial tendency, in the ages of democracy, to multiply words of this kind — to take them always by themselves in their most abstract acceptation, and to use them on all occasions, even when the nature of the discourse does not require them.   page 74/

from *Blackwood's Magazine*, Vol. CLXXXIII
January, 1908

The American Language

Charles Whibley

To the English traveller in America the language which he hears spoken about him is at once a puzzle and a surprise. It is his own, yet not his own. It seems to him a caricature of English, a phantom speech, ghostly yet familiar, such as he might hear in a land of dreams. He recognises its broad lineaments; its lesser details evade, or confuse, him. He acknowledges that the two tongues have a common basis. Their grammatical framework is identical. The small change of language — the adverbs and prepositions, — though sometimes strangely used in America, are not strange to an English ear. And there the precise resemblance ends. Accent, idiom, vocabulary give a new turn to the ancient speech. The traveller feels as though he were confronted with an old friend, tricked out in an odd suit of clothes, and master of a new pose and unaccustomed gesture.

The Americans are commonly reputed to speak through their nose. A more intimate acquaintance with their manner belies this reputation. It is rather a drawl that afflicts the ear than a nasal twang. You notice in every sentence a curious shifting of emphasis. America, with the true instinct of democracy, is determined to give all parts of speech an equal chance. The modest pronoun is not to be outdone by the blustering substantive or the self-asserting verb. And so it is that the native American hangs upon the small words: he does not clip and slur the unimportant vocables, and what his tongue loses in colour it gains in distinctness.

If the American continent had been colonised by Englishmen before the invention of printing, we might have watched the growth of another Anglo-Saxon tongue, separate and characteristic. American might have wandered as far from English as French or Spanish has wandered from Latin. It might have invented fresh inflections, and shaped its own syntax. But the black art of Gutenberg had hindered the free development of speech before John Smith set foot in Virginia, and the easy interchange of books, newspapers, and other merchandise ensured a certain uniformity. And so it was that the Americans, having accepted a ready-made system of grammar, were forced to express their fancy in an energetic and multi-coloured vocabulary. Nor do they attempt to belittle their debt. Rather they claim in English an exclusive privilege. Those whose pleasure it is to call America "God's own country" tell us with a bluff heartiness that they are the sole inheritors of the speech which page 118/ Chaucer and Shakespeare adorned. It is their favourite boast that they have preserved the old language from extinction. They expend a vast deal of ingenuity in the fruitless attempt to prove that even their dialect has its roots deep down in the soil of classical English. And when their proofs are demanded they are indeed a sorry few. A vast edifice of mistaken pride has been established upon the insecure basis of three words — fall, gotten, and bully. These once were familiar English, and they are English no more. The word "fall," "the fall of the leaf," which beautifully echoes the thought of spring, survives only in our provinces. It makes but a furtive and infrequent appearance in our literature. Chaucer and Shakespeare know it not. Johnson cites but one illustration of its use — from Dryden:

> "What crowds of patients the town-doctor kills,
> Or how last fall he raised the weekly bills."

On the other side of the Atlantic it is universally heard and written. There the word "autumn" is unknown; and though there is a dignity in the Latin word ennobled by our orators and poets, there is no one with a sense of style who will not applaud the choice of America.

But if she may take a lawful pride in "fall," America need not boast the use of "gotten." The termination, which suggests either wilful archaism or useless slang, adds nothing of sense or sound to the word. It is like a piece of dead wood in a tree, and is better lopped off. Nor does the use of "bully" prove a wholesome respect for the past. It is true that our Elizabethans used this adjective in the sense of great or noble. "Come," writes Ben Jonson in "The Poetaster," "I love bully Horace."[1] But in England the word was never of universal application, and was sternly reserved for poets, kings, and heroes. In modern America there is nothing that may not be "bully" if it meet with your approval. "A bully place," "a bully boat," "a bully blaze," — these show how far the word has departed from its origin. Nor, indeed, does it come down from English in an unbroken line. Overlooked for centuries, it was revived (or invented) in America some fifty years ago, and it is not to Dekker and Ben Jonson that we must look for palliation of its misuse.

Words have their fates. By a caprice of fortune one is taken, another is left. This is restricted to a narrow use; that wanders free over the plain of meaning. And thus we may explain many of the variations of English and of page 119/ American speech. A simple word crosses the ocean and takes new tasks upon

---

[1] Inumerable examples might be culled from the literature of the seventeenth century. One other will suffice here, taken from Dekker's "Shoemaker's Holiday": "Yet I'll shave it off, and stuff a tennis-ball with it, to please my bully king."

itself. The word "parlour," for instance, is dying in our midst, while "parlor" gains fresh vigour from an increasing and illegitimate employment. Originally a room in a religious house, a parlour (or parloir) became a place of reception or entertainment. Two centuries ago an air of elegance hung about it. It suggested spinnets and powdered wigs. And then, as fashion turned to commonness, the parlour grew stuffy with disuse, until it is to-day the room reserved for a vain display, consecrated to wax-flowers and framed photographs, hermetically sealed save when the voice of gentility bids its furtive door be opened. The American "parlor" resembles the "parlour" of the eighteenth century as little as the "parlour" of the Victorian age. It is busy, public, and multifarious. It means so many things that at last it carries no other meaning than that of a false elegance. It is in a dentist's parlor that the American's teeth are gilded; he is shaved in a tonsorial parlor; he travels in a parlor-car; and Miss Maudie's parlor proves how far an ancient and respected word may wander from its origin. One example, of many, will illustrate the accidents which beset the life of words. No examples will prove the plain absurdity which has flattered the vanity of some American critics that their language has faithfully adhered to the tradition of English speech.

The vocabulary of America, like the country itself, is a strange medley. All the languages of Europe, besides Yiddish, have been pilfered for its composition. Some words it has assimilated into itself; others it holds, as it were, by a temporary loan. And in its choice, or invention, it follows two divergent, even opposite, paths. On the one hand, it pursues and gathers to itself barbarous Latinisms; on the other, it is eager in its quest after a coarse and living slang. That a country which makes a constant boast of its practical intelligence should delight in long, flat, cumbrous collections of syllables, such as "locate," "operate," "antagonize," "transportation," "commutation," and "proposition," is an irony of civilisation. These words, if words they may be called, are hideous to the eye, offensive to the ear, and inexpressive to the mind. They are the base coins of language. They bear upon their face no decent superscription. They are put upon the street, fresh from some smasher's den, and not even the newspapers, contemptuous as they are of style, have reason to be proud of them. Nor is there any clear link between them and the meaning thrust upon them. Why should the poor holder of a season-ticket have the grim word "commutation" hung round his neck? Why should the simple business of going from one place to another be labelled **page 120/** "transportation"? And these words are apt and lucid compared with "proposition." Now "proposition" is America's maid-of-all-work. It means everything or nothing. It may be masculine, feminine, neuter — he, she, it. It is tough or firm, cold or warm, according to circumstances. But it has no more sense than an expletive, and its popularity is a clear proof of a starved imagination.

And while the American language is collecting those dried and shrivelled specimens of verbiage, it does not disdain the many-coloured flowers of lively speech. In other words, it gives as ready a welcome to the last experiment in Slang as to its false and pompous Latinisms. Nor is the welcome given in vain. Never before in the world's history has Slang flourished as it has flourished in America. And its triumph is not surprising. It is more than any artifice of speech the mark of a young and changing people. Youth has a natural love of metaphor and imagery; its pride delights in the mysteries of a technical vocabulary; it is happiest when it can fence itself about by the privilege of an exclusive and obscure tongue. And what is Slang but metaphor? There is no class, no cult, no trade, no sport which will not provide some strange words or images to the general stock of language, and America's variety has been as quick an encouragement to the growth of Slang as her youth. She levies contributions upon every batch of immigrants. The old world has thus come to the aid of the new. Spanish, Chinese, German, and Yiddish have all paid their toll. The aboriginal speech of the Indians, and its debased lingo, Chinook, have given freely of their wealth. And not only many tongues but many employments have enhanced the picturesqueness of American Slang. Now, America has not lost touch with her beginnings. The spirit of adventure is still strong within her. There is no country within whose borders so many lives are led. The pioneer still jostles the millionaire. The backwoods are not far distant from Wall Street. The farmers of Ohio, the cowboys of Texas, the miners of Nevada, owe allegiance to the same Government, and shape the same speech to their own purpose. Every State is a separate country, and cultivates a separate dialect. Then come baseball, poker, and the race-course, each with its own metaphors to swell the hoard. And the result is a language of the street and camp, brilliant in colour, multiform in character, which has not a rival in the history of speech.   **page 121/**   ....

... The written word and the spoken word differ even more widely in America than elsewhere. The spoken word threw off the trammels of an uneasy restraint at the very outset. The written word still obeys the law of gradual development, which has always controlled it. If you contrast the English literature of to-day with the American, you will find differences of accent and expression so slight that you may neglect them. You will find resemblances which prove that it is not in vain that our literatures have a common origin and have followed a common road. The arts, in truth, are more willingly obedient than life or politics to the established order; and America, free and democratic though she be, loyally acknowledges the sovereignty of humane letters. American is heard at the street corner. It is still English that is written in the study.   **page 126/**

6

WHAT IS AN AMERICANISM?

from *The Works of the Rev. John Witherspoon*, Vol. IV
by The Rev. John Rodgers
Philadelphia: William W. Woodward, 1802

The Druid: Number V

John Witherspoon

... The English language is spoken through all the United States. We are at a great distance from the island of Great-Britain, in which the standard of the language is as yet supposed to be found. Every state is equal to and in- page 458/ dependent of every other; and, I believe, none of them will agree, at least immediately, to receive laws from another, in discourse, any more than in action. Time and accident must determine what turn affairs will take in this respect in future, whether we shall continue to consider the language of Great-Britain as the pattern upon which we are to form ours, or whether, in this new empire, some centre of learning and politeness will not be found, which shall obtain influence and prescribe the rules of speech and writing to every other part.

While this point is yet unsettled, it has occurred to me to make some observations upon the present state of the English language in America, and to attempt a collection of some of the chief improprieties which prevail, and might be easily corrected. I will premise one or two general remarks. The vulgar in America speak much better than the vulgar in Great-Britain, for a very obvious reason, viz. that being much more unsettled, and moving frequently from place to place, they are not so liable to local peculiarities, either in accent or phraseology. There is a greater difference in dialect between one county and another in Britain, than there is between one state and another in America. I shall also admit, though with some hesitation, that gentlemen and scholars in Great-Britain speak as much with the vulgar in common chit chat, as persons of the same class do in America: but there is a remarkable difference in their public and solemn discourses. I have heard in this country, in the senate, at the bar, and from the pulpit, and see daily in dissertations from the press, errors in grammar, improprieties and vulgarisms, which hardly any person of the same class, in point of rank and literature, would have fallen into in Great-Britain. Curiosity led me to make a collection of these, which, as soon as it became large, convinced me that they were of very different kinds, and therefore must be reduced to a considerable number of classes, in order to their being treated with critical justice. These I now present to the public under the following heads, to each of which I will subjoin a short explication, and a page 459/ number of examples, with remarks where they seem necessary.

1. Americanisms, or ways of speaking peculiar to this country.
2. Vulgarisms in England and America.
3. Vulgarisms in America only.
4. Local phrases or terms.
5. Common blunders arising from ignorance.
6. Cant phrases.
7. Personal blunders.
8. Technical terms introduced into the language.

It will be proper to put the reader in mind, that he ought not to expect that the enumeration under each of these heads can be complete. This would have required a very long course of observation; and indeed is not necessary to my purpose, which is by specimens to enable every attentive and judicious person to make observations for himself.

1. The first class I call American, by which I understand an use of phrases or terms, or a construction of sentences, even among persons of rank and education, different from the use of the same terms or phrases, or the construction of similar sentences, in Great-Britain. It does not follow, from a man's using these, that he is ignorant, or his discourse upon the whole inelegant; nay, it does not follow in every case, that the terms or phrases used are worse in themselves, but merely that they are of American and not of English growth. The word Americanism, which I have coined for the purpose, is exactly similar in its formation and signification to the word Scotticism. By the word Scotticism is understood any term or phrase, and indeed any thing either in construction, pronunciation, or accentuation, that is peculiar to North-Britain. There are many instances in which the Scotch way is as good, and some in which every person who has the least taste as to the propriety or purity of language in general, must confess that it is better, than that of England, yet speakers and writers must conform to custom. page 460/ . . . .

The examples follow.

1. "The United States, or *either* of them." This is so far from being a mark of ignorance, that it is used by many of the most able and accurate speakers and writers, yet it is not English. The United States are thirteen in number, but in English either does not signify one of many, but *one or the other* of two. I

imagine *either* has become an adjective pronoun, by being a sort of abbreviation of a sentence where it is used adverbially, *either the one or the other.* It is exactly the same with *ekateros* in Greek, and *alterutur* in Latin.

2. This is to *notify* the public; or the people had not been *notified.* By this is meant *inform* and *informed.* In English we do not notify the person of the thing, but notify the thing to the person. In this instance there is certainly an impropriety, *for to notify* is just saying by a word of Latin derivation, *to make known.* Now if you cannot   page 461/   say this is to make the public known, neither ought you to say this is to notify the public.

3. *Fellow countrymen.* This is a word of very frequent use in America. It has been heard in public orations from men of the first character, and may be daily seen in newspaper publications. It is an evident tautology, for the last word expresses fully the meaning of both. If you open any dictionary, you will find the word countryman signifies one born in the same country. You may say fellow citizens, fellow soldiers, fellow subjects, fellow christians, but not *fellow countrymen.*

4. These things were ordered delivered to the army. The words *to be* are omitted. I am not certain whether this is a local expression or general in America.

5. I wish we could contrive it to Philadelphia. The words *to carry it, to have it carried,* or some such, are wanting. It is a defective construction, of which there are but too many that have already obtained in practice, in spite of all the remonstrances of men of letters.

6. We may *hope* the assistance of God. The word *for* or *to receive* is wanting. In this instance hope, which is a neuter verb, is turned into the active verb, and not very properly as to the objective term assistance. It must be admitted, however, that in some old English poets, hope is sometimes used as an active verb, but it is contrary to modern practice.

7. I do not consider myself equal to this task. The word *as* is wanting. I am not certain whether this may not be an English vulgarism, for it is frequently used by the renowned author of Common Sense, who is an Englishman born; but he has so happy a talent of adopting the blunders of others, that nothing decisive can be inferred from his practice. It is, however, undoubtedly an Americanism, for it is used by authors greatly superior to him in every respect.

8. Neither to day *or* to morrow. The proper construction is, either the one or the other, neither the one *nor* the other.

9. A *certain* Thomas Benson. The word certain, as used in English, is an indefinite, the name fixes it precise-   page 462/   ly so that there is a kind of contradiction in the expression. In England they would say, a certain person called or supposed to be Thomas Benson.

10. Such bodies are *incident* to these evils. The evil is incident or ready to fall upon the person, the person liable or subject to the evil.

11. He is a very *clever* man. She is quite a *clever* woman. How often are these phrases to be heard in conversation? Their meaning, however, would certainly be mistaken when heard for the first time by one born in Britain. In these cases, Americans generally mean by *clever,* only goodness of disposition, worthiness, integrity, without the least regard to capacity; nay, if I am not mistaken, it is frequently applied, where there is an acknowledged simplicity, or mediocrity

of capacity. But in Britain, clever always means capacity, and may be joined either to a good or bad disposition. We say of a man, he is a clever man, a clever tradesman, a clever fellow, without any reflection upon his moral character, yet at the same time it carries no approbation of it. It is exceeding good English, and very common to say, He is a clever fellow, but I am sorry to say it, he is also a great rogue. When cleverness is applied primarily to conduct, and not to the person, it generally carries in it the idea of art or chicanery, not very honorable; for example — Such a plan I confess was very clever, i.e., sly, artful, well contrived, but not very fair.

12. I was quite mad at him, he made me quite mad. This is perhaps an English vulgarism, but it is not found in any accurate writer, nor used by any good speaker, unless when poets or orators use it as a strong figure, and to heighten the expression say, he was mad with rage.

These shall suffice for the first class.   **page 463/**

Number VI.

. . . The third class consists of vulgarisms in America only. This must be understood, so far as I have been able to observe, and perhaps some of them are local. It will not be necessary either to make the examples on this head numerous, or to say much upon them, because the introduction of vulgarisms into writing or public discourses is the same, whether they are of one country or another.

1. I have not done it yet, but am just going to. This is an imperfect construction; it wants the words *do it.* Imperfect constructions are the blemish of the English language in general, and rather more frequent in this country than in England. **page 466/**

2. It is *partly all* gone, it is *mostly all* gone. This is an absurdity or barbarism, as well as a vulgarism.

3. This is the weapon with which he defends himself when he is *attacted,* for attacked; or according to the abbreviation, attack'd.

4. As I told Mr. _____, for as I told you. I hope Mr. _____ is well this morning. What is Mr. _____'s opinion upon this subject? This way of speaking to one who is present in the third person, and as if he were absent, is used in this country by way of respect. No such thing is done in Britain, except that to persons of very high rank, they say your majesty, your grace, your lordship; yet even there the continuance of the discourse in the third person is not customary.

5. I have been *to* Philadelphia, for *at* or *in* Philadelphia; I have been *to* dinner, for I have dined.

6. Walk *in* the house, for *into* the house.

7. You *have no right* to pay it, where right is used for what logicians would call the correlative term obligation.

8. A *spell* of sickness, a long *spell,* a bad *spell.* Perhaps this word is borrowed from the sea dialect.

9. *Every* of these states; *every* of them; *every* of us; for *every one.* I believe the word every is used in this manner in some old English writers, and also in some old laws, but not in modern practice. The thing is also improper, because it should be every one to make it strictly a partitive, and subject to the same construction,

as some of them, part of them, many of them, &c. yet it must be acknowledged, that there is no greater impropriety, if so great, in the vulgar construction of *every*, than in another expression very common in both countries, viz. *all of them.*

Having finished these two classes, I shall make a remark or two upon vulgarisms in general. Probably many will think and say, that it would be a piece of stiffness or affectation to avoid them wholly, in conversation or common discourse. As to some of those which have been described above, perhaps this may be admitted; but as to the greatest part, it is certainly best to avoid them wholly, lest we should fall into them inadvertently where   page 467/   they would be highly improper. If a gentleman will not imitate a peasant, male or female, in saying *if so be,* and *forsooth,* and many other such phrases, because he knows they are vulgarisms, why should he imitate them in saying *equally as good,* or *I see him yesterday,* but because he does not know, or does not attend to the impropriety?

The reader is also desired to observe, that we are not by far so much in danger of the charge of affectation for what we omit saying, as for what we do say. When a man is fond of introducing hard words, or studies a nice or pompous diction, he brings himself immediately into contempt; but he may easily attain a cautious habit of avoiding low phrases or vulgar terms, without being at all liable to the imputation either of vanity or constraint.

I conclude with observing, that as bombast and empty swelling is the danger to which those are exposed who aim at sublimity, so low sentiments and vulgar terms are what those are most in danger of who aim at simplicity. Now, as it is my intention, in the course of these papers, to set a mark of reprobation upon every affected and fantastic mode of expression, and to recommend a pure, and, as it may be called, classic simplicity, it is the more necessary to guard the reader against that low and grovelling manner which is sometimes mistaken for it. page 468/

from *Harper's Magazine*, Vol. CXXVII
July, 1913

Differences in English and American Usage

Thomas R. Lounsbury

It has been intimated in a previous article that in the strictest and, it may be added, in the only really proper sense of the term, an Americanism is a word or phrase naturally used by an educated American which under similar conditions would not be used by an educated Englishman. The emphasis, it will be seen, lies on the word "educated." To set off the speech of the illiterate American against the speech of the cultivated Englishman is as unscientific as it would be to set off the speech of the London cockney against that of the cultivated American. Comparison of the usage of two different countries can properly be made only between members of the same social class.

Furthermore, this definition of Americanism needs another limitation, so far as these particular articles are concerned. They are in general given up to the consideration of the words and phrases found in the written tongue and not in the one spoken. In every country the colloquial speech of the most cultivated embraces a far wider range and variety of words and phrases than the same men would permit themselves to use in the printed page. Even he who is the most reckless in writing would never think of assuming to himself there a liberty of expression, not to call it license, which he indulges in unhesitatingly in conversation. The two general principles which have just been laid down are subject to certain modifications. Here, however, it is only important to say that the discussion of the subject is restricted to the written speech of educated men on both sides of the Atlantic. As a result, slang, vulgarisms, colloquialisms, and the grammatical blunders of the illiterate — which last are apt to be the same in all countries — do not come under consideration. This is not because all the terms excluded are in themselves unimportant. The language of low life is often picturesque and forcible. It is from that quarter that the literary language not infrequently recruits its own exhausted energies. But until such expressions have become embodied in the classical speech they have to be disregarded by him who limits his attention to that.

Restrictions such as these narrow largely the field to be covered. It is far, indeed, from being extensive. The truth is, the moment we give up the consideration of terms necessary to depict American scenery and American life, manners, and customs — for which no equivalents exist — we have, comparatively speaking, but a beggarly account of words to bring out sharply the differences of educated speech as found on the two sides of the Atlantic. Furthermore, these differences tend to become fewer with the increase of intercommunication. Still they exist. One cause for divergence of speech was inevitable in the nature of things. The American continues to retain words and meanings of words which were in frequent, if not in general use, both literary and colloquial, when his ancestors left their native land. It is to be kept in mind that a language transported from one country to another is fairly certain to undergo what is technically called an arrest of development. This is especially sure to be the case at periods when not only are distances vast but intercommunication infrequent. In the country emigrated from, words once familiar drop gradually out of use. New words are introduced to replace them. Others again change their meaning. Of two words once existing side by side and denoting essentially the same thing, one is taken and the other left. In this page 274/ movement of speech the transferred language has little or no part. Not only are the words which have been brought over retained; they are retained in their original sense. Hence in time the language of the colony as contrasted with that of the mother-country tends to seem, if not to be, archaic to the dwellers in the latter.

Such a result has been distinctly manifest in the language of this country. Many of our so-called Americanisms represent the English usage of the former half of the seventeenth century, when the original settlements were made here. Most of this class of transported words were heard then everywhere in cultivated speech. On the other hand, some had their native home in the English dialects. They have never been used in English literature, at least on any scale worth considering. But brought over to America, they became here part of the common tongue. Take one notable illustration. *Cracker*, as the designation of a thin, hard biscuit, is widely used with us by all classes. Now this term is not entirely unknown in English literature, but it cannot be said to have in it any recognized position. In the dialects of northern England and in parts of Scotland it is, however, not infrequent. From these quarters it was in all probability brought to America. Here it has come into general if not into universal use.

Very few, indeed, are the instances in which either the transported word or the meaning of it has died out in England itself. It is used at times; but still it is heard there so little, and so frequently heard here, that on both sides of the Atlantic it comes to be considered as a distinctive mark of American speech. No reader of Shakespeare needs to be told that he often uses *mad* in the sense of "angry." When Hotspur tells Henry IV. that the popinjay lord who had been sent to demand his prisoners made him mad, he makes use of an expression likely to be heard at any moment from the mouth of an American. Very noticeable, too, upon the speech of this country has been the influence of the Bible, the main reading of the early New England colonists. For instance, the authorized version uses the adjective *ill* half a score of times, but it never uses it of any bodily ailment. There is also in it no mention of *illness*. In both cases it is *sick* and *sickness* that are invariably found; and they are found very often. The same usage is generally characteristic of Shakespeare also. *Ill*, referring to physical indisposition, is employed by him about a dozen times, while *sick*, in the same general sense, can be found over a hundred. This practice remains with us. Though *ill* is used, it is not used so frequently as the word it has largely supplanted in the mother-country; for English speech, at least English colloquial speech, has largely abandoned the once general employment of *sick*. It practically limits it to sickness of the stomach. Or take again a common use of the adjective *homely*, as applied to personal appearance. The Bible has not the word at all in any sense. In this particular sense Shakespeare has it but three times. But when we reach a little later period it is a natural inference that such meaning must have been very prevalent. Otherwise Milton could hardly have represented Comus as saying:

> "It is for homely features to keep home,
> They had their name thence."

This now regular usage in America has never died out in England. It can be found in various later authors. But though surviving there, it has little of the vigorous life this meaning of the word retains here. Accordingly, so employed it may be called an Americanism.

It is almost needless to observe that the limitation of the differences between English and American usage, not merely to the speech of the educated, but to their written speech, restricts the consideration of the subject to a comparatively small number of words. Yet few as these are, they are too many to be treated in the pages of a magazine. Accordingly it is only for the sake of illustating and enforcing principles that examples are adduced. Some idea can be got of their character, however, by the examination of two words, one a noun and the other an adjective. Where an Englishman says *autumn*, the American generally says *fall*. Both terms have, indeed, been more or less in use in the two countries; but the frequency of the employment of   page 275/   the latter on this side of the ocean and its infrequency on the other entitle it to the right of being designated as an Americanism. The variation of usage extends even to the meaning. In popular speech *autumn* comprises in England the months of August, September, and October; in America it comprises September, October, and November. This difference of signification is very possibly due for its continuance, if not for its origin, to difference of climatic conditions. But when we come to the employment of the words themselves there is no reason in the nature of things for this particular divergence. *Autumn*, indeed, is common enough with us; but though somewhat frequent in literature, it is not often heard in colloquial speech. The exact reverse is true of England, save that there *fall* is altogether less used than *autumn* is here. . . .

The other word referred to is the adjective *rare*, as designating meat partially cooked. The corresponding English term is *underdone*. This history of the former is essentially the same as that just given of *fall*. Both *rare* and *underdone* are used in the two countries; in each, one is heard regularly, the other infrequently. Very many absurd derivations have been concocted for the word now generally regarded as an Americanism. It is hardly necessary to say that it is quite as distinct in its origin as in its meaning from the more common term derived from the Latin *rarus*. Thus our adjective is genuinely Anglo-Saxon. It is to be noted here that a number of words now beginning with the liquids *l*, *n*, and *r* once possessed an initial *h*. Thus *loaf* was originally *hláf*, *nut* was *hnut*, *roof* was *hróf*. When the aspirate ceased to be pronounced, our ruthless ancestors, not having the reverential attitude of their descendants toward unnecessary and misleading letters, began their work of ruining the language by incontinently dropping the initial *h* as having outlived its usefulness. To words of this class belonged our *rare*. Its original form was *hrér*. In Anglo-Saxon dictionaries it is defined as "raw, un-   page 276/   cooked." Like the rest of its class it also proceeded to treat contumeliously the initial *h*. In the spellings *rere*, *rear*, later *rare*, it had and continues to have a vigorous existence in certain of the English dialects. To some extent this remains true also of the cultivated speech. In the latter, however, it was for a long time mainly used to designate eggs boiled soft. Later it came to the front in a more general sense. Yet in spite of its occasional appearance in literature, it seems to have dropped out of the speech of educated men in England. The contrary is true of America. Apparently it was from the dialects that the word made its way into ordinary use in this country. Yet though *rare* is now exceedingly common and has been so for a long time, it is a singular fact that it does not appear in Pickering's early dictionary of Americanisms nor in the much fuller one of Bartlett, though the last edition of the latter's work came out as late as 1870.

These two examples serve to make clear the nature of the real distinction which exists between the speech of educated men in the two countries. . . .
277/

from *Americanisms Old and New: A Dictionary of Words, Phrases, and Colloquialisms Peculiar to the United States, British America, The West Indies, &c.*
by John S. Farmer
London: Thomas Poulter & Sons, 1889

What Is an Americanism?

John S. Farmer

Strictly speaking, an "Americanism" may be defined as a word or phrase, old or new, employed by general and respectable usage in America in a way not sanctioned by the best standards of the English language. As a matter of fact, however, the term has come to possess a wider meaning; and it is now applied not only to words and phrases which can be so described, but also to the new and legitimately born words adapted to the general needs and usages, to the survivals of an older form of English than that now current in the Mother Country, and to the racy, pungent vernacular of Western life. Hitherto, this divergence in speech has been of little moment, except to the curiously inclined in matters philosophical. Latterly, however, for good or ill, we have been brought face to face with what has been grandiloquently called "The Great American Language" oftentimes in its baldest form, and on its most repulsive side. The works, also, of the popular exponents of "American humor" itself an article as distinct in type as is the American character, have made the English people familiar with transatlantic words, phrases, turns of expression, and constructions, most of which, strange of sound and quaint in form, are altogether incomprehensible. Their influence is daily gaining ground — books in shoals, journals by the score, and allusions without stint, are multiplying on every hand. American newspapers, too, humorous and otherwise, circulate in England by hundreds of thousands weekly — all this and a good deal else is doing its work in popularising American peculiarities of speech and diction to an extent which, a few years since, would have been deemed incredible. Even our own newspapers, hitherto regarded as models of correct literary style, are many of them following in their wake; and, both in matter and phraseology, are lending countenance to what at first sight appears a monstrously crude and almost imbecile jargon; while   **page vii/**   others, fearful of a direct plunge, modestly introduce the uncouth bantlings with a saving clause. . . .

Such is the beginning; who can tell what the end will be; or how far American influences will modify the noble English language? . . .   **page viii/**

7

REGIONAL VARIETIES OF AMERICAN ENGLISH

from *The Century Magazine*, Vol. XLVIII
October, 1894

Folk-Speech in America

Edward Eggleston

. . . English travelers very early mention the differences between colonial speech and that of the mother country. This arose partly from the great number of new objects and processes that must have names, and partly from English provincial words adopted into general speech in America. . . .

There are indigenous words in our folk-speech, but our local rustic dialects are composed almost entirely of words in their older forms or older senses, of English words now quite obsolete, and of words from provincial page 867/ English dialects. When first I heard farmers in the Lake George region call a "cowslip" a "cowslop," I smiled to think how modern the corruption was, and how easy to imagine that the name had something to do with the feeding of a cow. But rash guesses in etymology are ever unsafe; "cusloppe" is given as a form of the Anglo-Saxon word nine centuries ago. The etymologists miss the history of this word, and of the word "slop," by not knowing that, both as noun and verb, "slop" refers to any liquid or semi-liquid food for cattle, and this over so wide a region of America as to make its antiquity certain.

Take another expression that seems strictly American. "She is in a perfect *gale*," one says of a little girl or a young woman in a state of effervescent mirth. It is easy and natural to suppose this to be modern, and to derive it from a sea-farer's figure of speech. But the "Danes" who settled in England spoke a tongue very much like the Icelandic, and there is in this speech the word *gáll*, — with a long vowel, — meaning "a fit of gaiety," so that Anglo-Danish ladies in the court of Knut probably "got into a perfect gale" as our American women and girls do now. In New England they have the verb to "train" for to romp. For this I can find no remote ancestry; it may have come from the New England "trainin'," with its rum, cider, and ginger-bread, but I do not think it so recent as that. . . .

Now an American feels something vulgar in the word "nigger." A "half-cut" American, though he might use it in speech, would hardly print it. It repels us even in Thackeray. The black man has taken to calling himself *negro* nowadays, and he puts no little race assertion into the word; but he is mortally averse to "nigger," which on this side of the sea has the tang of overseer's lingo. "Don't you call me niggah; de debbil is a niggah," is the way a South Carolina black woman uttered her objection a while ago. But there is nothing diabolical — indeed, there is nothing essentially vulgar — in the pedigree of the offensive word. The first blacks brought to Jamestown are not called in Captain Smith's history "negro," the Spanish word for "black," but "negar," from the French word for a black man. They were similarly called in Boston — in the records it is spelled "neger," but a will of 1653 made it "negar." This pronunciation "negar," or "neegur," was the commonest one on the Ohio River in my childhood, and is an older word in English than negro.

In the first anti-slavery tract printed in New England, in the year 1700, Judge Sewall writes not only "negro," but in one place "niger," which I take to be "nigger" in sound. Perhaps the sound of the old French word is most nearly kept in the Irishman's "naygur." **page 868/** . . . .

A good example of the attraction of one word for another is to be found in our American word "riffle," which gets the go-by from all the dictionaries and vocabularies, so far as I know, though it is present in the excellent proverbial phrase, "He cannot make the riffle," *i.e.*, he cannot achieve this purpose against opposing circumstances. The notion is that of a boatman or canoe-man struggling up-stream over a riffle, or ripple. The word "riffle" is common enough in this sense, and seems at first a corruption of "ripple." But this latter word is by the etymologists considered a modern form of "rimple," while riffle comes doubtless from "rift," which is the form given to the word in the letter-press to Evan's analysis of his famous "Map of the Middle British Colonies." Now "rift," as applied to a slight fall, or a "shoaly place," as the first English explorer of the Delaware has it, is but another form of "reef." Mr. Skeat cites from Hexham's "Dutch-English Dictionary" of 1658, "rif" or "riffe," defined by "a foard or shallow place," and of this the colonial "rift" was but another form. By attraction of "ripple," or mere effort to produce representative sound, we get "riffle." "Riff," "rift," and the more modern "riffle" are wholly omitted from the dictionaries, and the word "ripple," in the sense of *a slight fall in a stream,* is not known to lexicographers. I believe its use to be all but universal in the United States. I very much doubt the derivation of "ripple" from "rimple." **page 869/**

. . . Fashions may change, but the countryman is slow to give up the ways and words of his forefathers. If the world's changes knock the sense out of a word he will put another meaning into it with as little alteration as possible. **page 873/** . . . .

from *The Frontier in Perspective*
by Walker D. Wyman and Clifton B. Kroeber
Madison: The University of Wisconsin Press, 1957

Language on the American Frontier

Frederic G. Cassidy

It is currently fashionable, and has been for some years, to refer to the language we speak in the United States as "the American language." This phrase may, of course, be produced in several tones of voice — a patriotic tone, a tone vibrating with manifest   page 185/   destiny, a naïve tone, or a chauvinistic one. Our most recently published dictionary has rushed forth with the clamorous title of the *New World Dictionary of the American Language* — betraying clearly the tone of voice of its business office, which is out to make Americanism pay.

The student of language, however, uses this phrase in the tone of voice indicating quotation marks. By no acceptable linguistic definition can our language be called "the American language"; it is not a separate speech unintelligible to speakers in the British Isles, Australia, or Canada; it is merely one variant form of the language which already has an established name: the English language. Not even the sturdiest isolationist can deny the historic connections.

The term "the American Language" was given currency, as we all know, by the great popular success of H. L. Mencken's book, first published in 1919, of which it was the title. Mencken was nothing if not bold; he had an ax to grind; he enjoyed telling the English where to get off *at*. Evidently this struck a note of welcome to many American ears, for his book became surprisingly a best seller. Scholars, therefore, even while rejecting the linguistic validity of the phrase, owe Mencken a considerable debt of gratitude for at last making the public intelligently aware — as many a better scholar before him had failed to do — that among the most interesting achievements of our new nation has been a characteristically different idiom. The colony which grew away from the homeland politically and has since come of age has also developed its own ways of speech. It is fair to say that if the English language had only one pole or center a hundred years ago, today it has two. And this bipolarity is the direct result of what happened on the American frontier.

To begin with, of course, America itself was the frontier: so are all colonies with respect to their parent lands. The most striking characteristic of a frontier society is its fluidity. True enough, there is considerable carry-over of habits, customs, institutions, ideals from the homeland, insofar as these are desirable and possible under the new conditions. But the important thing is that the fixity, the settled and confining structure of society in the old country, is shaken loose. Thus the new country gives a new chance. It demands fresh ways — and it makes fresh ways possible. page 186/

The migrations of humanity that take place from time to time, seen through the long eye of history, are like the flowing of a stream of volcanic lava. Driven by an outburst from a center of pressure, this stream pours out, running wherever it may, over the unresisting flats, around the rockier protuberances, picking up and incorporating many things in its path, ever cooling and hardening as it goes, but always with that glowing, fluid edge. This edge is the frontier.

So in the past three centuries the pressures of Europe flung out the crowd of adventurers and refugees, the rebellious and the ambitious, the disinherited and the farsighted. To America they flowed, thinly at first, spreading along the coast, trickling inland in the lower places, slowed by the mountains and resistance of Indians, but always with the hot edge rising and creeping on. At last, after a century and a half the lava stream broke into the plains and rolled westward ineluctably. In some places it eddied to a stop, cooled and became sluggish; but there was always the hot edge, the frontier, flowing on and on, taking many new shapes, swallowing many things that it came upon, some of its own currents mingling with others or overflowing them wholly — molten, hungry, seething with bubbles of humanity.

What of language in all this? It would be impossible to imagine such a movement of peoples as taking place without the use of language. Language is at once the exclusive and the most characteristic property of human beings; in the movement to the world frontiers, language went along. The first comers, of course, spoke some variety of their European tongue as it existed at the time. Limiting ourselves to English, we may say that on the ships of the explorers probably every sort of local or dialectal speech could have been heard. Settlements, when those were made, were sometimes less miscellaneous linguistically, but they were never "pure." Mixture, a characteristic of the frontier, was present too in the settlers' speech.

In a valuable study of New England pronunciation published in 1927, Professor Anders Orbeck looked into the places of origin of some 680 early English-speaking settlers of the towns of Plymouth, Watertown, and Dedham, Massachusetts.[1] He discovered that page 187/ among the number there was one settler each from Scotland, Wales, and the Isle of Man; less than ten each from nineteen shires of England; and that the greatest number clearly came from Norfolk, Suffolk, Essex, and London. Stated in terms of the major language areas of England, this is to say that 7 per cent came from the North, 4 per cent from the West Midlands, 9 per cent from the Southwest, 5 per cent from the Southeast, and 75 per cent from the East Midlands. If this may be generally taken as representing the early settlement of New England, it means that the pronunciation and usage which furnished the basis of standard British English clearly predominated also on the New England frontier.

[1] *Early New England Pronunciation as Reflected in Some Seventeenth Century Town Records* (Ann Arbor, Mich., 1927), 119ff.

Evidence for the Virginia colony is not as satisfactory, but the language of the East Midlands seems also to have predominated there. Nevertheless, there was the other 25 per cent not from the East Midlands — an admixture which left its effect — and the compromise speech of the colonies was thus begun with elements deriving from the homeland even before elements newly acquired by the settlers could make themselves felt.

As this first flow of settlement in eastern New England began to cool, there came another of a somewhat different sort, deriving more from the North and West of England than from the East Midlands. Since lands along the coast were by now taken up, the new settlers moved inland, and eventually their speech became dominant in New England west of the Connecticut River, in the upper Hudson River Valley, and in eastern Pennsylvania. Then this current spread out farther to the south and west, and so the speech differences of these later comers took their place on the new frontier and rolled across the plains and mountains to the Pacific.   page 188/ ....

from *American Speech*, Vol. VII
December, 1931

Some Americanisms of a Hundred Years Ago

John Howard Birss

During December, 1829, an extensive list of Americanisms based largely on Pickering's early compilation appeared in *The Virginia Literary Museum* (Vol. I, No. 27, pp. 417ff.), a journal devoted to belles-lettres and the arts, published by the University of Virginia. The list included several terms not to be found in Pickering or other collections, and a few, when recorded elsewhere, with dissimilar definitions. Since these words are of considerable interest, and some are not to be found in the works of Bartlett, De Vere, Farmer and Henley, and Thornton, I believe they are worth reprinting. In all cases definitions have been transcribed verbatim, my own notes following in brackets. At the conclusion of the list may be found the full titles of volumes from which the several citations in the notes have been drawn. An incomplete file of *The Virginia Literary Museum*, 1829–31, may be consulted at the Harvard Library.

Cohogle, v. To bamboozle. Kentucky. [Related perhaps to *cog*, "to lie or cheat" and *coggerie*, "falsehood; cheating" cited by Halliwell, 262. Cf. also *The Slang Dictionary*, 124, "Anyone who has been hocussed or cheated is sometimes said to have been cogged."]

Delodgment, n. Exit. Kentucky.

Flunkt, p. part. Overcome, outdone. Kentucky. [The N.E.D. gives 1823 as the earliest use in *The Crayon*, a Yale periodical. Barrère and Leland, I, 375, suggest "Possibly a New York or New Jersey (Princeton) word from the Dutch *flonk, flonker, flonken*, to twinkle or sparkle like a star, bright at one instant and then invisible."]

Givy, adj. Muggy. The weather is said to be givy, when there is much moisture in the air. [Farmer, 266, cites *givy* as "pliable; easy to work; i.e., ready to 'give.'" Bartlett (4 ed.), 247: "A term applied to tobacco leaves, in a certain condition of their preparation for market. Yielding, pliable."]

Gostering, pr. part. Imperious, boasting. Variant-Gaustering. West. [This term has not been restricted to the United States. Halliwell, 393, under *gauster* gives "to laugh loudly; to be noisy; to swagger." Cf. also in Halliwell, 408, *goister*. The N.E.D. notes: "Dial. survival of ME 'galstre.'"]

Honeyfuggle, v. To quiz, to cozen. Kentucky. [Bartlett (4 ed.), 292, "to humbug, swindle, cheat. West and South." *Coney-fogle*, "to lay plots," a Lancashire word, noticed by Halliwell, 267, may be the origin of it.]

Hoppergrass, This is often used in the South for grasshopper. A vulgarism. ["Hopper" is listed by Farmer, 305, as a contracted form.]   page 96/

Hornswoggle, v. To embarrass irretrievably. Kentucky. [This is a curious definition of a term that is sometimes heard today with a changed but relative meaning. Farmer, 305, notes: "A Western creation signifying nonsense, follery or chaffing deception. Variants are skulduggery and shenanigan." It has evidently made its way to England for *The Slang Dictionary*, 195, gives "nonsense, humbug. Believed to be of American origin."]

Join the church, v. phr. To become a member of the church. [Included as evidence of an expression at one time in bad repute, but now acceptable in current usage.]

Means, n. Medicine. South.

Mollagausauger, n. A stout fellow. Kentucky.

Motivity, n. The quality of being influenced by motives, also the power of producing motion.

Nitre, n. This word is very improperly used in many parts, for "the sweet spirit of nitre," instead of "salt-petre."

Quiddle, v. To busy one's self about trifles. This word is also used as a substantive. New England. [Origin uncertain; cf. quibble, twiddle. Most probably related to *quiddity*, for early use of which, see *Hamlet*, V. i. 103, "Why might not that be a lawyer? Where be his quiddities now?" But nearer home, Emerson, in *Conduct of Life* (1861), "Neither will be driven into a quiddling abstemiousness. 'T is a superstition to insist on a special diet." Cf. Farmer, 466, *quiddling*, "uncertain, unsteady." Bartlett (4 ed.), 509, for the same word gives "mincing, as quiddling gait." Cf. the note under *quip* in Farmer and Henley, 364.]

Retiracy, n. Solitude. Western States. [Farmer, 458, under this word cites: "Retirement; a competency." Cf. Bartlett (2 ed.), 363, "It is said in New England of a person who left off business with a fortune to retire that he has a retiracy; i.e., a sufficient fortune to retire upon." Bartlett (4 ed.), 525, "This absurd word is often applied to the condition of politicians who have retired, willingly or unwillingly, to private life."]

Sniptious, adj. Smart, spruce. Variant, ripsniptious. South and West. [Barrère and Leland, II, 269: "Snippeny, snippy, sniptious, snippish (American), used in several ways, vain, conceited. 'Snippeny folks are not popular, and E. P. Roe says that almost anything will be forgiven sooner than thinking one's self better than other people' — Detroit Free Press. Also given to petty criticism, mincing and pert observation."]

Vine, n. Any creeping plant. In England it is restricted to the plant that bears the grape. [But Halliwell, 910, states: "Any trailing plant bearing fruit."]

REFERENCES

Barrère, A., and Leland, C. G. *A Dictionary of Slang, Jargon, and Cant.* Ballantyne Press, London, 1889.

Bartlett, John R. *Dictionary of Americanisms.* Little, Brown, and Co., Boston, 1859 (2 ed.); 1884 (4 ed.) **page 97/**

Farmer, John S. *Americanisms, Old and New.* Privately printed by T. Poulter and Sons, London, 1889.

Farmer, J. S., and Henley, W. E. *Dictionary of Slang and Colloquial English.* G. Routledge and Sons, Ltd., London, n.d. (5 ed.).

Halliwell, James O. *A Dictionary of Archaic and Provincial Words.* G. Routledge and Sons, Ltd., London, 1924 (7 ed.).

The Slang Dictionary. Chatto and Windus. London, 1922. **page 98/**

from *Americanisms; The English of the New World*
by M. Schele De Vere
New York: Charles Scribner & Company, 1872

The Great West

Schele De Vere

. . . The New England States have a dialect of their own, by far the most fully developed and the most characteristic of all the varieties of English spoken in America. It represents alike the effect which climate has upon the organs of speech in their favorite sounds — the nasal twang and the violent curtailment of words, — and the direction given to the choice of terms and the arrangement of sentences, by their favorite occupations and their leading lines of thought. But the Great West has impressed the stamp of its own life even more forcibly upon the speech of its sons. Everything is on such a gigantic scale there that the vast proportions with which the mind becomes familiar, beget unconsciously a love of hyperbole, which in its turn invites irresistibly to humor. Life is an unceasing fury of activity there, and hence speech also is racy with life and vigor; all is new there to those who come from older countries or crowded cities, and hence new words are continually coined, and old ones receive new meanings; nature is fresh and young there, and hence the poetic feeling is excited, and speech assumes unconsciously the rhythm and the elevation of poetry.

The language of Western men has been called high-flown, overwrought, grandiloquent — it may be so, but it is so only as a fair representation of the Western world, which God created on a large scale, and which in its turn grows faster, works harder, achieves more than any other land on earth has ever done. Nor must it be forgotten that the West has no severe critic to correct abuses, no court and no polite society to taboo equivocal words, no classic writers to impart good taste and train the ear to a love   **page 161/**   of gentle words and flowing verse. Speech, there, is free as the air of heaven, and moves with the impulsive energy of independent youth, conscious of matchless strength, and acknowledging no master in word or deed. It is an intensified, strangely impulsive language, just as the life's blood of the whole West throbs with faster pulse, and courses with fuller vigor through all its veins. There is no greater difference between the stately style of Milton and the dashing, reckless lines of Swinburne, than between the formal, almost pedantic echo of Johnsonian rhythm in Hawthorne's work, and the free and easy verses of Brett Harte. Hence, New England has wit, and what can be more caustic than Lowell's deservedly famous political squibs? But the West has humor, golden humor, full of poetry, dramatizing dry facts into flesh and blood, but abounding in charity and good-will to all men.

So it is with their sounds, that come full and hearty from broad chests, breathing freely the pure air that sweeps down from Rocky Mountains unhampered, across broad prairies, over a whole continent. Words are as abundant as food, and expressions grow in force and extent alike, till they sound extravagant to the more economical son of the East. Speech is bold, rejecting laws and rules, making one and the same word answer many purposes, and utterly scouting the euphemistic shifts of a sickly delicacy. It becomes vulgar — and it will become so, as the sweetest milk turns sour when the thunder rolls on high — the vulgarism is still what J. R. Lowell so happily calls "poetry in the egg." Its slang, also, is as luxurious as the weeds among the rich grasses, but at least it is home-made, and smells of the breath of the prairie or the blood of the Indian, and is not imported from abroad or made in the bar-room and betting-ring.

Hence the student of English finds in the West a rich harvest of new words, of old words made to answer new purposes, often in the most surprising way, and of phrases full of poetical feeling, such as could only arise amid scenes of great beauty, matchless energy, and sublime danger.   page 162/ . . . .

The almost boundless liberty with which Americans use the words of their language, was recently shown with painful impressiveness. In a fearful catastrophe which happened in February, 1871, on the Hudson River railway, all the horrors of the disaster and all the grief for the numerous victims could not efface the deep impression made by the useless but noble heroism of the engine-driver, who refused to escape, stood by his engine, and plunged with it into the abyss. It appeared afterward that in discussing with railroadmen the expediency of jumping from an engine in time of danger, Doc. Simmons had once said, "I would *squat!*" He meant he would *squat* down behind the boiler and trust to going through with whatever might obstruct the road, after having pulled the brakes, reversed the engine, and opened the throttle.   page 170/ . . . .

A very peculiar term, full of instruction in showing the origin of many similar words, is the name of *Maverick,* used in Texas to designate an unmarked yearling. It is derived from the Hon. Samuel Maverick, of San Antonio, who removed to Western Texas thirty years ago, driving with him some three thousand head of cattle, then the largest herd in all the country. He established a *ranche,* and placed an old negro there in charge of the cattle, to mark, brand, and see after them. Unfortunately this man was more given to the bottle than his business, and, as a natural consequence, many a calf and colt went unmarked. The neighbors, having much smaller herds, were very careful to mark and brand every one of their calves during the early spring and summer. The spring after the arrival of Mr. Maverick's large herd these *rancheros* noticed a number of unmarked yearlings, and, well acquainted with the habits of his steward, naturally concluded that they were the new-comer's property, and hence called them *mavericks,* so that the very absence of a mark and brand was taken as evidence of his ownership. . . .   page 211/

The tendency of all Americans to use high-sounding words of extensive meaning for comparatively small matters, is nowhere more fully developed than in the West. Here even small objects are not brought, but *crowded*, and thus the Rev. Mr. Cartwright even says quaintly: "God Almighty *crowded* me into the world bareheaded, and I think no more harm to enter Massachusetts bareheaded, than for the Lord to bring me into the world without a hat." (*Autobiography*, p. 473.) What elsewhere is great appears to him nothing less than *cruel*, although here also he only follows the example set him by his early ancestors, since Hakluyt already thus used the word. Mr. Bartlett tells the pleasant story of a man who, having been quite seriously ill, was asked by the physician who had calmed the paroxysm, how he felt, and replied: "Oh, doctor, I am powerful weak, but *cruel easy*." (*Dictionary*, p. 170.) On the other hand, the Western man takes the much debated word *cuss*, and employs it where he wishes to express anything but a curse, often even affection. There is a touching incident mentioned in F. B. Harte's *Luck of Roaring Camp,* page 213/ where a rough, wicked miner, Kentuck Joe, goes to see a new-born baby, and finding his finger clutched by the little creature, breaks forth ecstatically in the words: "The d—d little *cuss;* he *rastled* with my finger!" holding that finger a little apart from its fellows and examining it curiously. The question is, whether the term comes really from a vulgar pronunciation of *curse,* as most authorities state, or is an abbreviation of *customer,* with the primary idea of what is frequently called a *bad* or an *ugly customer.* The latter theory might be supported by the fact that a *cuss* is, as has already been stated, by no means always a *curse,* and that a low, miserly person is very apt to be called a mean *cuss,* which may be nothing more than a *mean customer.* This would apply even to a case like the following, taken from the New Orleans *Picayune:* "I had oft heard tell of Yankees, but never knew what *mean cusses* they were, until I met a few of them at Washington." . . . page 214/

from *Forty Years of American Life*
by Thomas Low Nichols
New York: The Telegraph Press, 1937

Peculiarities and Eccentricities

Thomas Low Nichols

Englishmen know the Yankee chiefly as he appears in literature and on the stage. He is well drawn in the novels of John Neal, Cooper, Paulding, and Mrs. Stowe, and in the writings of the author of *Sam Slick* and James Russell Lowell. Hackett, Hill, Jefferson, and other American actors and artists, have given us pretty good Yankees on the stage. We imagine that literary and dramatic portraitures are overdone. I do not think so. I have never seen a stage Irishman, Cockney, Yankee, or negro that came fully up to the genuine article. The trouble is not in overdoing, but in doing falsely. Many English writers confuse the American idioms and peculiarities of the East, West, and South. It is as if one should mix up Scotchmen, Irishmen, and Cockneys.

It is possible to travel through America without meeting many specimens of the thorough Yankee, the broad Western man, or the distinctive Southerner of the strongest type; but they all exist abundantly. There are districts in New England, in the rough mountain regions, where the Yankee flourishes as grotesque in the attire and speech as was ever described in story or seen upon the stage. Western and Southern peculiarities are still more common.

I know of no physiological reason why a Yankee should talk through his nose, unless he got the habit of shutting his mouth to keep out the cold fogs and drizzling north-easters of Massachusetts Bay. It is certain that men open their mouths and broaden their speech as they go West, until on the Mississippi they tell   page 65/   you "thar are heaps of bar (bears) over thar, whar I was raised." Southern speech is clipped, softened, and broadened by the negro admixture. The child learns its language from its negro nurse, servants, and playmates, and this not unpleasant patois is never quite eradicated. Southerners drawl: the Northern people accent sharply and are very emphatic.

Besides peculiarities of articulation and enunciation, there are forms of expression peculiar to and characteristic of each section of the American States. An old fashioned Yankee is shy of swearing; he says, "I vum," "I swon," "I swow," "I vow," "darn it," "gaul darn your picter," "by golly," "golly crimus"; and uses other ingenious and cowardly substitutes for profanity. The Western man rips out remorseless oaths, swearing a blue streak with a remarkable breadth of expression. Whereas a Hoosier describes himself as "catawampously chawed up," the Yankee is merely a "gone sucker." Inquire about his health, and he tells you he is "so as to be crawlin'!" He talks of "spunkin' up to an all-fired, tarnation slick gall, clean grit, I tell yeou neow"; and, naturally, he has "a kinder sneakin notion arter her." If she were to tell him to "hold his yawp," he would admit that he felt "kinder streaked, by golly!" He describes a man as being "handsome as a picter, but so darnation ugly"; or as "a thunderin' fool, but a clever critter as ever lived" — ugly being Yankee for wicked, and clever for good-natured. A plain girl is "as homely as a hedge-fence." A Yankee brags that he is "a hull team and a hoss to let." You can't "tucker him eout." It "beats all natur heow he can go it when he gets his dander up." He has "got his eyeteeth cut, true as preachin'." He gets "hoppin' mad," and "makes all gee agin." He is "dreadful glad to see you," and is "powerful sorry you enjoy such poor health"; but read Lowell's Zeke Bigelow or Mrs. Stowe's Sam Lawson.

I am inclined to think the Western vocabulary more copious than that of the Yankee proper. The language, like the country, has a certain breadth and magnitude about it. A Western man "sleeps so sound, it would take an earthquake to wake him." He is in danger "pretty considerable much," because "somebody was down on him, like the whole Missouri on a sand-bar." He is a "gone 'coon." He is down on all "cussed varmints," gets into an "everlasting fix," and holds that "the longest pole knocks down the persimmons." A story "smells rather tall." "Stranger," page 66/ he says, "in bar hunts I am numerous." He says a pathetic story sunk into his feelings "like a snagged boat into the Mississippi." He tells of a person "as cross as a bar with two cubs and a sore tail." He "laughs like a hyena over a dead nigger." He "walks through a fence like a falling tree through a cobweb." He "goes the whole hog." He raises "right smart of corn" and lives where there is "a smart chance of bars." "Bust me wide open," he says, "if I didn't bulge into the creek in the twinkling of a bedpost, I was so thunderin' savagerous."

In the south-west is found the combination of Western and Southern character and speech. The south-western man was "born in old Kaintuck, raised in Mississippi, is death on a bar, and smartly on a painter fight." He "walks the water, out hollers the thunder, drinks the Mississippi," "calculates" that he is "the genuwine article," and that those he don't like "ain't worth shucks." He tells of "a fellow so poor and thin he had to lean up agin a saplin' to cuss." He gets "as savage as a meat axe." He "splurges about," and "blows up like a steamboat."

The Southerner is "mighty glad to see you." He is apt to be "powerful lazy," and "powerful slow"; but if you visit him where he has located himself, he'll "go for you to the hilt agin creation." When people salute each other at meeting, he says they are "howdyin' and civilizin' each other." He has "powerful nice corn." The extreme of facility is not as easy as lying, but "as easy as shootin'." A man who has undressed has "shucked himself." To make a bet with a man is to "size his pile." Yankees guess everything, past, present and future; Southerners reckon and calculate. All these peculiarities of speech would fill a small volume. Most of the Yankeeisms can be found in the districts of England from which the country was first settled. The colloquialisms of the South and West are more original. Miners, gamblers, and all sorts of adventurers attracted by gold to California and the Rocky Mountains, have invented new forms of expression which will be found in the poems and prose writings of Colonel Hay, Bret Harte, and others.

American humour consists largely of exaggeration, and of strange and quaint expressions. Much that seems droll to English readers is very seriously intended. The man who described himself as "squandering about permiscuous" had no idea that his expression was funny. When he boasted of his sister — "She slings page 67/ the nastiest ankle in old Kentuck," he only intended to say that she was a good dancer. To escape rapidly, west of the Mississippi, might be "to vamose quicker'n greased lightnin' down a peeled hickory." "Vamose," and "vamose the ranch," were brought from Mexico by the Santa Fé traders. "Cut stick," and "absquatulate," are indigenous. A man cuts a stick when about to travel. Absquatulate comes from *a* or *ab* privative, and squat, western for settle. When a squatter removes, he absquatulates. As for the greased lightning and peeled hickory, Americans have a passion for making improvements on everything. The Mississippi boatmen improved the name of *Bois Brulé* into something they could understand, when they called it Rob Ruly's Woods. The story of land so rich that a squash vine, in its rapid growth, overtook and smothered a drove of pigs, was

a western exaggeration. The evidence of a witness in a life insurance case, when
the death was caused by the blowing-up of a steamboat on the Ohio, is droll,
just because it is characteristic. The witness knew the missing man. He saw him
on the deck of the steamboat just before the explosion. "When," asked the lawyer,
"was the last time you saw him?" "The very last time I ever set eyes on him," said
the careful witness, "was when the biler burst, and I was going up, *and I met him
and the smoke pipe coming down!*" . . .   page 68/

from *The New York Times Magazine*
January 10, 1932

Exploring in America's Vocal Jungle

Otis Skinner

It is highly improbable that a native American speech flowing from a pure
racial origin like that of the Latins and Teutons will ever become a reality. In our
conglomerate nation too much lingual wash from Europe, Asia, Africa and
Polynesia has polluted the stream of our English pure and undefiled to allow us a
verbal harmony. We do not agree on a method of saying things.

A charming Virginia acquaintance of mine on a visit to a New England town
was in a quandary about a certain address. The name she sought seemed unfamiliar to everyone. Finally she said: "I don't know how you-all call it, but I
want to find some one named C-a-r-t-e-r." It was this delightful lady who corrected the pronunciation of my infant daughter when she wanted to play a game
of cards. "Cornelia," she said, "you can't have them unless you ask for kyards."

At this same tender age my child was the guest in the home of a Philadelphia
friend. At the breakfast table she said she'd like some porridge. "My darling,"
said her hostess in reproof, "you must speak correctly — pourridge!"

My daughter still thought she would like some porridge. "Pourridge!" insisted
the lady. "Now, how do you say it?"

"Oatmeal!" replied Cornelia defiantly.

The name of Tremont is well known in Boston. There is a great diversity of
usage in its appellation. Trée-mont, Tremónt and Tremmunt. There used to be a
hotel of that name and I once directed a cabman to drive me to it. He did not
understand at first. Finally it dawned on him. "Oh!" he said, "you mean Tremmunt."

There is a Goethe Street in Chicago. Formerly the Clark Street car con-
ductors announced it as "Gooth Street." Now they rhyme it with "dirty."

What is the standard of American speech? Is it New England, Middle Atlantic, Pennsylvanian, Southern, midcontinental or Pacific? Each of these sections has its own tradition of verbal and tonal inflection, and when an inhabitant of one of them is overheard ordering his cocktail in the bar of Paris Ritz, his gloves at Jouvin's on the Avenue de l'Opera, or inquiring the rate of American exchange at the Guaranty Trust Company's office in Pall Mall, it is not too difficult to detect whether he comes from Nashua, New Hampshire; New York City; Lancaster, Pennsylvania; Richmond, Louisville, Mobile, Detroit, Topeka, or San Francisco. The task is much less difficult with the female than the male speaker, the voice of the former being far deadlier than that of the male, far more aggressive in its local pride and satisfaction.

Nothing is more expressive of the independence of our mother tongue than the letter R. It is the battle cry of our native land, the glory that is Umurrica. It pipes through New England nostrils, surges from the larynx of Pennsylvania, assaults us in Michigan and Indiana, and roams at large on our boundless prairies. So proud are we of this birthright of ours that we accord it the honor of an extra syllable whenever possible, as in de-ur, cle-ur, fi-ur, sh-ur. "Law" becomes "lor" and "saw" is changed to "sor."

It is hurtled at infant ears from the teacher's platform of our public schools, crawls into our homes through the radio, greets us from behind the counter of the department store, presides over shrilled debates in women's clubs, subdues us from the pulpit, echoes in court rooms and legislative halls, and prevents our going comfortably to sleep at bad plays in the theatre where actors transpose Hamlet's meaning and speak the speech rippingly on the tongue.

There is a native vitality and determination about it not to be withstood. It resembles that knuckle clutch of the fork displayed at the dining tables of the Waldorf-Astoria by pilgrims from mid-Western towns — a manoeuvre that always fascinates me, especially when by a difficult turn of the wrist food is deftly deposited on expectant tongues.

Are we as a nation tone deaf or have our eardrums become ossified by the vocal miasma rising from the American melting pot? The origin of much of our polyphone inflection is readily found. The Pilgrim Fathers who started the New England collection of cradles, spinning wheels and highboys also brought from non-conformist English pulpits the heritage of Puritan nasality, intensified as time went on by the rigors of the New England climate.

The followers of William Penn, together with certain Swedish and Welsh citizenry, bequeathed to the Philadelphians of today a flatness of tone still observable in Quaker families. As one proceeds southwesterly from Philadelphia he finds himself in the country of the so-called Pennsylvania Dutch, where the early immigrant, who was really not Dutch but German, has left a lasting burr on the speech of his adopted country.

In the coal districts the spoken word is infected by Bohemian and Polish accents, while in Pittsburgh there is a peculiar lilt, a possible mountaineer influence, as expressed in the familiar "Alle-ghé-ny."

Maryland has passed more unscathed through the years since her foundation by Lord Baltimore than some of her sister States. It is the dividing line between

North and South, the barrier against which have broken the rude surges of Puritan and Pennsylvania harshness and the lazy softness of the cotton fields.

What manner of speech was possessed by the company of Captain John Smith and the later Virginia Colonists it is difficult to determine. It is evident, however, that Virginian accent, like that of all the States below the Mason and Dixon line, has been under negroid influence for more than two centuries. It was inevitable that the Negro mammy should flavor the speech of the white children she brought up and the house slave that of his young master. More and more did each generation take on the Negro lilt that sang in their ears from every quarter. A pleasant voice, that of Virginia; utterly wrong in diction, its limpid caress stops our ears to its sins of mispronunciation.

Just why the Virginia voice should be gentle, while that of Kentucky and Tennessee is raucous and grating, I do not know. Something poisoned it at its source. I never hear its feminine shrillness without a rasp of my nerves and an "edge" to my teeth.

The further South we travel the more loose and sloppy becomes the spoken word, until finally it merges into the uncertain creole of New Orleans. The atmosphere of Texas would seem to have a beneficial influence on vocal effort. I have known many examples of fine voices and unaffected speech from the Lone Star State. It renews its vigor as it crosses tornado-swept Kansas, its unshackled R's reverberating in the great open spaces, and again subsides, into the J-less Scandinavian of Wisconsin.

Our American speech softens vastly as it nears the Pacific Ocean. Whatever the cause — the gentle rains of Oregon, or the fogs that roll through the Golden Gate of San Francisco, or contact with the sensuous language of Spain, or that the early pioneers cast aside from their prairie schooners into the alkali desert something of the rasping vocalization of the East — there is a perceptible absence of provincialism beyond the Sierra Nevada range.

But woe is me! What can one say of our New Yorkese, that incredible mélange born of every accent under the sun? There the tonal idiosyncrasies of Scandinavian and Australian, the Czech, the Slovak, the Pole, the Greek and the Filipino, the sons of Erin, of Spain and of Italy and Africa, the Russian and the Japanese, the Jew of Germany and the Balkans have compounded the mixture that is the Manhattan equivalent of Cockayne.

Not long ago the American Academy of Arts and Letters gave a medal to Mr. Holbrook of one of the broadcasting studios, in recognition of the excellent quality of his diction. In presenting the medal, Hamlin Garland took occasion to launch a few well-directed shots at the workaday speech of our country. In rebuttal, however, of his own arraignment he attacked the polyglot utterance of England, laying special stress on the almost unintelligible language of the Cockney.

Those of us who have wandered about Covent Garden Market amid the shouting of hucksters in the busy morning hour, who have attempted to follow the words of British curates reverberating through "long-drawn aisles and fretted vaults" at cathedral services and who have been mystified by the throated emanations of Oxford and Cambridge dons can appreciate Mr. Garland's point of view.

It is not the purpose of these reflections to assault the orthoepic sins of Great Britain. She has burdens enough to bear without that. It proves nothing to say that her little island enshrines some sixty or seventy different dialects. O'Farrell informs you that only in Dublin is English spoken in its purity, while MacPherson says that you hear the verra best English in the whole wurrld in Edinboro.

Who, then, shall decide when doctors disagree? What boots it for the pot to call the kettle black? The truth is that our mother tongue at its best is neither insular nor provincial; English is English, whether uttered in Liverpool or Chicago.

But have we no cultural speech in these United States? Are we a race of savages who should be forced out of our tepees and taught to speak like schoolmasters? Far be it from me to say so. To become a nation of precise prigs would not help our cause at all. It is Main Street against which my resentment is roused, and the fact that Main Street leads to Park Avenue. The proletariat of today become the plutocrats of tomorrow and carry   page 4/   to their new environment the lingual sins of their origin. . . . .   page 16/

from   *Scientific   American,*   Vol. **CLXXXII**
January, 1950

The American Languages

Hans Kurath

We are not accustomed to think of the U. S. language as a Babel of tongues, but if one were to make the experiment of assembling individuals from a number of different localities and listening carefully to their speech, he might note some rather curious results. For example, a Rhode Islander might speak of a "dandle," a Marylander of a "cocky-horse," a coastal North Carolinian of a "hicky-horse," a western North Carolinian of a "ridy-horse," a Block Islander of a "tippity-bounce," a Cape Codder of a "tilt," a native of the lower Connecticut Valley of a "tinter," a Hudson Valley native of a "teeter-totter" and a Bostonian of a "teeter-board." All of these expressions mean the same thing — a seesaw — yet it is entirely possible that some of the nine persons would not know what the others were talking about.

American English has a surprising wealth of such localisms. The casual foreign visitor is inclined to lump them all together as "Americanisms," and to suppose, erroneously, that they are generally current throughout the U. S. More sophisti-

cated observers are aware that New England, the South and the West show
certain differences in speech, but usually they have only the vaguest notions of
the actual location of these regionalisms. As a matter of fact, the expressions
commonly identified as "New Englandisms" are apt to be current only east of the
Connecticut River; "Southernisms" more often than not are confined to Virginia
or to certain sections making up the old plantation country of the South; "Westernisms" may be common only in the Spanish Southwest or the cattle country.
On the other hand there are regions with equally distinctive speech patterns
that have largely escaped notice; a notable example is the broad Midland area
embracing Pennsylvania and the Ohio Valley, where the vocabulary and pronunciation are as different from those of New England and the South as the latter are
from each other.

Since 1931 the writer and a group of associates have been making a study,
under the auspices of the American Council of Learned Societies, of local and
regional speech differences in the eastern United States. We now have the data
for a "Linguistic Atlas" providing a systematic record of the currency of selected
words and expressions in the coastal states from Maine to Georgia and in Pennsylvania, West Virginia and eastern Ohio. As in all scientific studies, the immediate
purpose was simply the collection of facts, without which a historical interpretation of American linguistic usage is impossible. In this case the results shed considerable light on U. S. migrations, settlement areas, trade areas, culture areas and
other aspects of human geography and population history.

In making the survey we used the sampling method. Trained linguists went to
nearly every county in these states and in each interviewed two persons — one
old-fashioned and unschooled, the other a member of the middle class who had
had the benefit of a grade-school or high-school education. They also interviewed
one or more cultured persons in each of the larger cities. The interviewers spent
from 10 to 15 hours with each individual to record his habitual usage on well over
a thousand points. Most of this field work was done by Bernard Bloch, Raven I.
McDavid and the late Guy S. Lowman, Jr.

All together more than 1,200 persons were interviewed, and full information
was obtained, among other things, on the diffusion of some 400 local or regional
expressions. A map was plotted for each expression. The boundary enclosing the
area in which a given expression is current is known as an isogloss. Wherever a
large number of isoglosses enclose a common area, i.e., wherever the people
share many folk expressions that are not current elsewhere, obviously they de-
limit a major speech boundary.

These studies showed that the eastern section of our country is divided into
three speech areas of first importance — the North, the Midland and the South.
These major areas are distinguished by certain region-wide expressions. They
are split, however, into a number of sub-areas, each with its own local folk words
and peculiarities of diction. . . . The Northern region in general includes the New
England settlement area, reaching west to the Great Lakes, and the Dutch
settlement in the Hudson Valley. Within it are no fewer than six distinct sub-
divisions; the people of northeastern, southeastern and southwestern New England, metropolitan New York, the Hudson Valley and western New York have
inherited from their forebears or developed certain definite speech differences.

Similarly the Midland, corresponding in general to the Pennsylvania settlement area, is segmented into several speech areas, of which one of the most distinctive is the section west and north of Philadelphia settled by the Pennsylvania Dutch. Natural geographical barriers have a great influence on population movements, and hence on language, as is demonstrated by the fact that the crest of the Alleghenies in Pennsylvania divides the eastern and western parts of the state into distinct speech areas. In the South one can find **page 48/** differing varieties of Southern speech in the Chesapeake Bay area, the Virginia Piedmont and the eastern sections of the Carolinas. The speech boundaries in the South tend to be sharper than in other regions, because its populations have clung more closely to the soil.

Now there are certain key expressions that characterize each major region. You can identify a person as a Northerner if he says pail for bucket, swill for garbage, whiffletree or whippletree for the bar to which a horse is harnessed, comforter or comfortable for a heavy quilt, brook for stream. A Midlander can generally be identified by his use of the word blinds for window shades, skillet for frying pan, spouting for roof gutters. A Southerner characteristically says light-bread for wheat bread, clabber for curdled sour milk, hay stock for haycock, corn shucks for cornhusks, lightwood for kindling, rock fence for stone fence, and of course "you-all." In some cases the three regions have three distinct expressions for the same thing. Thus salt pork is commonly called salt pork in the North, side meat in much of the Midland and middlin meat in much of the South. A Northerner generally calls a dragonfly a darning needle; a Midlander is likely to call it a snake feeder or snake doctor; a Southerner, a snake doctor or mosquito hawk. Corn bread is known as johnnycake in the North and corn pone in the Midland and South. To call a cow in the pasture, a Northern farmer cries "Come boss!" or "Co-boss!"; a Midlander calls "Sook!"; a Southerner calls "Co-ee!" or "Co-wench!" In New England farmers call a bull a critter, sire, toro or top cow; in the Midland they most often call it an ox, male cow or sire, in the South, a steer, male cow, beast or brute.

It is usually possible, however, to place a person much more precisely, to connect him with a particular area in his region. The areas that have been settled longest have the most distinctive speechways. Use of the word fritter for griddlecake and funnel for stovepipe spots a New Englander as a "Down-Easter." (In most of New England a funnel for pouring liquids is called a "tunnel.") The expression cleavestone peach for freestone peach, apple grunt for apple dumpling and porch for the kitchen ell place a man on Cape Cod. Dandle for seesaw and eace worm for earthworm put him on Narragansett Bay. If he calls a thunder shower a tempest and a pet lamb a cade, he is from Cape Cod or Narragansett Bay. If a New Englander says ivy for mountain laurel and angledog for earthworm, he lives in the lower Connecticut Valley. If he calls a coal hod a coal scuttle, a haystack a hay barrack and cottage cheese pot cheese, his home is in the valley of the Hudson or the Housatonic. In Maine children coast belly-bumper, **page 49/** in the upper Connecticut Valley belly-bunt, around Massachusetts and Narragansett Bays belly-bump, on the lower Connecticut belly-gutter and in the Hudson Valley belly-wopper.

In the South one finds even sharper local differences in speech. Around

Chesapeake Bay alone there are several distinct speech areas. Thus a cowpen is called a cowpen on the Maryland Western Shore, a pound on the Eastern Shore, a cuppin in the Virginia Piedmont and a brake in the Norfolk area on the south side of the Bay. A freestone peach is named an open peach on the Eastern Shore, an openstone peach on the Western Shore, a soft peach in the Virginia Piedmont and a clearseed peach in the Norfolk area. The Carolina Shore has at least five different speech areas. In various localities of the Carolinas a store-room is known as a lumber room, a plunder room or a trumpery room; a vest is called a wesket or a jacket; bacon is known as breakfast bacon, breakfast strips or breakfast meat; a screech owl is a scrich owl, a scrooch owl, a squinch owl or a shivering owl, the pig call is "Chook!", "Wookie!", "Vootsie!", "Goop!" or "Woopie!"

How can we account for the existence, and particularly the persistence, of so many regional and local expressions? We must first understand clearly that there are social "isoglosses" as well as geographical ones. Three levels of speech can be distinguished in the U. S.: 1) cultivated speech, which is most widespread in urban areas; 2) common speech, the language of the large middle class; 3) folk speech, which is found in rural areas. Cultivated speech tends to be national or regional in character. The homely expressions that we have been considering come mostly from the second and third levels. They are the speechways of relatively unschooled people who read little, travel little, and acquire their language largely by ear from the older generation in their immediate vicinity.

Our studies indicate that the different places of origin of the colonial settlers, geographical barriers, colonial isolation, expanding frontiers and transportation facilities, trade, social stratification, educational facilities, religious activities and political activities have all played their parts in localizing or disseminating linguistic usages. The colonists who settled the Eastern seaboard were a heterogeneous group to start with. Even among those from the British Isles a great variety of dialects, peasant and urban, were spoken; there were Yorkshiremen, Lancashiremen, Kentishmen, Hampshiremen, Ulstermen, and a small minority who spoke the dialect of the upper classes of London.

In the course of several generations in the New World each colony developed its own unique blend of provincial dialects, adding to the old-country speech a few expressions taken from the Indians and others invented as names for unfamiliar plants and animals found in their new environment. As the settlements expanded westward, the frontiersmen developed new blends of speech, dropping many of the more local expressions but retaining the more widely used regional expressions. Thus west of the Alleghenies and the Appalachians speech is less diversified than in the East and speech boundaries are less clearly defined. It is this lack of clear boundaries in the central states that is largely responsible for the fiction that a "general American" type of English exists. Actually three regional types of English are spoken in the Middle West — the Northern type in the Great Lakes Basin and upper Mississippi Valley, the Southern type in the Gulf States, and the Midland type in the valleys of the Ohio and its tributaries and along the middle course of the Mississippi.

Speech areas are not stable; they expand or shrink. The nucleus of an expanding area's growth is usually a large metropolitan center or a dominant social class whose speech is regarded as superior. In the East the cities of Boston, New York and Philadelphia have been important centers of expanding areas in speech. Boston, which has dominated eastern New England since the days of the Massachusetts Bay Colony, reached the heyday of its linguistic influence in the middle of the 19th century, when the literary and intellectual accomplishments of its writers and scholars gave it a hearing not only in New England but throughout the country. Metropolitan New York has had a striking effect upon the speechways, particularly in pronunciation, of the surrounding areas; its unique speech has supplanted New Englandisms and other local expressions on Long Island, in southwestern Connecticut, in eastern New Jersey and in the lower Hudson Valley. The linguistic influence of Philadelphia has spread westward almost to Baltimore and southeastward into Delaware and the Maryland Eastern Shore.

The shrinking speech areas in general are those that lack a prominent population center and fall under the influence of one or more adjoining areas of expansion. Examples of such areas are Narragansett Bay, central New England and the Virginia Tidewater, which is coming under the domination of the expanding Piedmont area. To students of language the speechways of a shrinking area provide important clues to usages of the past; those of an expanding area, to developments of the future.   **page 50/**   . . . .

8

REFLECTIONS OF AMERICAN CULTURE

 from *Chronicles of The Pilgrim Fathers of The Colony of Plymouth, from 1602–1625*
by Alexander Young
Boston: Charles C. Little and James Brown, 1841

A Letter Sent from New England

Edward Winslow

Loving and Old Friend,

Although I received no letter from you by this ship, yet forasmuch as I know you expect the performance of my promise, which was, to write unto you truly and faithfully of all things, I have therefore at this time sent unto you accordingly, referring you for further satisfaction to our more large Relations.

You shall understand that in this little time that a few of us have been here, we have built seven dwelling-houses and four for the use of the plantation, and have made preparation for divers others. We set the last spring some twenty acres of Indian corn, and   **page 230/**   sowed some six acres of barley and pease; and according to the manner of the Indians, we manured our ground with herrings, or rather shads, which we have in great abundance, and take with great ease at our doors. Our corn did prove well; and, God be praised, we had a good increase of Indian corn, and our barley indifferent good, but our pease not worth the gathering, for we feared they were too late sown. They came up very well, and blossomed; but the sun parched them in the blossom.

Our harvest being gotten in, our governor sent four men on fowling, that so we might, after a special manner, rejoice together after we had gathered the fruit of our labors. They four in one day killed as much fowl as, with a little help beside, served the company almost a week. At which time, amongst other recreations, we exercised our arms, many of the Indians coming amongst us, and among the rest their greatest king, Massasoyt, with some ninety men, whom for three days we entertained and feasted; and they went out and killed five deer, which they brought to the plantation, and bestowed on our governor, and upon the captain and others. And although it be not always so plentiful as it was at this time with us, yet by the goodness   page 231/   of God we are so far from want, that we often wish you partakers of our plenty.

We have found the Indians very faithful in their covenant of peace with us, very loving, and ready to pleasure us. We often go to them, and they come to us. Some of us have been fifty miles by land in the country with them, the occasions and relations whereof you shall understand by our general and more full declaration of such things as are worth the noting. Yea, it hath pleased God so to possess the Indians with a fear of us and love unto us, that not only the greatest king amongst them, called Massasoyt, but also all the princes and peoples round about us, have either made suit unto us, or been glad of any occasion to make peace with us; so that seven of them at once have sent their messengers to us to that end. Yea, an isle at sea, which we never saw, hath also, together with the former, yielded willingly to be under the protection and subject to our sovereign lord King James. So that there is now great peace amongst the Indians   page 232/   themselves, which was not formerly, neither would have been but for us; and we, for our parts, walk as peaceably and safely in the wood as in the highways in England. We entertain them familiarly in our houses, and they as friendly bestowing their venison on us. They are a people without any religion or knowledge of any God, yet very trusty, quick of apprehension, ripe-witted, just. The men and women go naked, only a skin about their middles.

For the temper of the air here, it agreeth well with that in England; and if there be any difference at all, this is somewhat hotter in summer. Some think it to be colder in winter; but I cannot out of experience so say. The air is very clear, and not foggy, as hath been reported. I never in my life remember a more seasonable year than we have here enjoyed; and if we have once but kine, horses, and sheep, I make no question but men might live as contented here as in any part of the world. For fish and fowl, we have great abundance. Fresh cod in the summer is but coarse meat with us. Our bay is full of lobsters all the summer, and affordeth variety of other fish. In September we can take a hogshead of eels in a night, with small labor, and can dig them out of their beds all the winter. We have muscles and clams at our doors. Oysters we have none   page 233/   near, but we can have them brought by the Indians when we will. All the spring-time the earth sendeth forth naturally very good sallet herbs. Here are grapes, white and red, and very sweet and strong also; strawberries, gooseberries, raspas, &c.; plums of three sorts, white, black, and red, being almost as good as a damson; abundance of roses, white, red and damask; single, but very sweet indeed. The country wanteth only industrious men to employ; for it would grieve your hearts if, as I, you had seen so many miles together by goodly rivers uninhabited; and withal, to consider those parts of the world wherein you live to be even greatly burthened with abundance of people. These things I thought good to let you understand, being the truth of things as near as I could experimentally take knowledge of, and that you might on our behalf give God thanks, who hath dealt so favorably with us.

Our supply of men from you came the 9th of November, 1621, putting in at Cape Cod, some eight or ten leagues from us. The Indians that dwell there- **page 234/** about were they who were owners of the corn which we found in caves, for which we have given them full content, and are in great league with them. They sent us word there was a ship near unto them, but thought it to be a Frenchman; and indeed for ourselves we expected not a friend so soon. But when we perceived that she made for our bay, the governor commanded a piece to be shot off, to call home such as were abroad at work. Whereupon every man, yea boy, that could handle a gun, were ready, with full resolution that, if she were an enemy, we would stand in our just defence, not fearing them. But God provided better for us than we supposed. These came all in health, not any being sick by the way, otherwise than by sea-sickness, and so continue at this time, by the blessing of God. The good-wife Ford was deliv- **page 235/** ered of a son the first night she landed, and both of them are very well.

When it pleaseth God we are settled and fitted for the fishing business and other trading, I doubt not but by the blessing of God the gain will give content to have a very good bread-room to put your biscuits in. Let your cask for beer and though it be not much, yet it will witness for us that we have not been idle, considering the smallness of our number all this summer. We hope the merchants will accept of it, and be encouraged to furnish us with things needful for further employment, which will also encourage us to put forth ourselves to the uttermost.

Now because I expect your coming unto us, with other friends, whose company we much desire, I thought good to advertise you a few things needful. Be careful to have a very good bread-room to put your biscuits in. Let your cask for beer and water be iron-bound, for the first tier, if not more. Let not your **page 236/** meat be dry-salted; none can better do it than the sailors. Let your meal be so hard trod in your cask that you shall need an adz or hatchet to work it out with. Trust not too much on us for corn at this time, for by reason of this last company that came, depending wholly upon us, we shall have little enough till harvest. Be careful to come by some of your meal to spend by the way; it will much refresh you. Build your cabins as open as you can, and bring good store of clothes and bedding with you. Bring every man a musket or fowling-piece. Let your piece be long in the barrel, and fear not the weight of it, for most of our shooting is from stands. Bring juice of lemons, and take it fasting; it is of good use. For hot waters, aniseed water is the best; but use it sparingly. If you bring any thing for comfort in the country, butter or sallet oil, or both, is very good. Our Indian corn, even the coarsest, maketh as pleasant meat as rice; therefore spare that, unless to spend by the way. Bring paper and linseed oil for your windows, with **page 237/** cotton yarn for your lamps. Let your shot be most for big fowls, and bring store of powder and shot. I forbear further to write for the present, hoping to see you by the next return. So I take my leave, commending you to the Lord for a safe conduct unto us, resting in him,

Your loving friend,
E. W.

Plymouth, in New England, this 11th of December, 1621. **page 238/**

from *Domestic Manners of the Americans*, Vol. I
by Mrs. Frances M. Trollope
New York: Dodd, Mead & Company, 1901

Yankees

Frances Trollope

The Quakers have been celebrated for the pertinacity with which they avoid giving a direct answer, but what Quaker could ever vie with a Yankee in this sort of fencing? Nothing, in fact, can equal their skill in evading a question, **page 242/** excepting that with which they set about asking one. I am afraid that in repeating a conversation which I overheard on board the Erie canal boat, I shall spoil it, by forgetting some of the little delicate doublings which delighted me — yet I wrote it down immediately. Both parties were Yankees, but strangers to each other: one of them having by gentle degrees, made himself pretty well acquainted with the point from which every one on board had started, and that for which he was bound, at last attacked his brother Reynard thus:—

"Well, now, which way may you be travelling?"

"I expect this canal runs pretty nearly west."

"Are you going far with it?"

"Well, now, I don't rightly know how many miles it may be."

"I expect you'll be from New York?"

"Sure enough I have been at New York, often and often."

"I calculate, then, 'tis not there as you stop?"

"Business must be minded, in stopping and in stirring." **page 243/**

"You may say that. Well, I look then you'll be making for the Springs?"

"Folks say as all the world is making for the Springs, and I expect a good sight of them is."

"Do you calculate upon stopping long when you get to your journeys end?"

" 'Tis my business must settle that, I expect."

"I guess that's true, too; but you'll be for making pleasure a business for once, I calculate?"

"My business don't often lie in that line."

"Then, may be, it is not the Springs as takes you this line?"

"The Springs is a right elegant place, I reckon."

"It is your health, I calculate, as makes you break your good rules?"

"My health don't trouble me much, I guess."

"No? Why that's well. How is the markets, sir? Are bread stuffs up?"

"I a'nt just capable to say."

"A deal of money's made by just looking after the article at the fountain's head."

"You may say that." **page 244/**

"Do you look to be making great dealings in produce up the country?"

"Why that, I expect, is difficult to know."

"I calculate you'll find the markets changeable these times?"

"No markets ben't very often without changing."

"Why, that's right down true. What may be your biggest article of produce?"

"I calculate, generally, that's the biggest as I makes most by."

"You may say that. But what do you chiefly call your most particular branch?"

"Why, that's what I can't justly say."

And so they went on, without advancing or giving an inch, 'till I was weary of listening; but I left them still at it when I stepped out to resume my station on a trunk at the bow of the boat, where I scribbled in my note-book this specimen of Yankee conversation. **page 245/**

from *The New Purchase; or, Early Years in the Far West*
by Robert Carlton, Esq. (B. R. Hall)
New Albany, Indiana: Jno. R. Nunemacher, 1855

Backwoods Dialogue

B. R. Hall

"Well, I'm powerful rite down glad you kin eat sich like food! what mought your name be — if it's no offence?"

"Carlton, ma'am; I live in Woodville —"

"Well — that's what I suspish'nd. Ned Stanley was out here last winter a huntin, and I heerd him tell on you — as how you was a powerful clever feller — albeit a *leetle* of a big-bug. But *I'll* take your part arter this — and *King* shill too."

"Oh! Mrs. King, if we were all better acquainted with one another, we'd all think better of our friends and neighbours. But I must be off — what's the damage?"

"Bless me! Mr. Carltin, I don't take nothin for sich a meal! Put up that puss, if you want to be friends — I'm powerful sorry King's away — call here next time, sir, and I allow you'll git somethin good enough for a white man."

"Thank you! Mrs. King, thank you. Well — please give me directions — I'm not much of a woodsman."

"Well, you're comin on. Howsever you've kim the wust ind of the trace, and won't find no diffikilty till about fifteen miles on at the next settlement, Ike Chuff's — whare you mought foller a cow path — and so you'd better stop thar and axe."

In due time, and after a hard ride of thirty miles from the burnt cabin, we came in sight of Ike Chuff's clearing. As the trace ran plain and broad round the fence and across a small ravine, I was unwilling to waste time with needless inquiries, and, therefore, followed the line of path with undiminished confidence.

The trace, indeed, narrowed — once or twice vanished — all that was no novelty; but at last we seemed to reach the vanishing point, for now, after the last vanish, the path never reappeared! In place of the one however, were seen four! and those running in as many different directions and evidently, like Gay's road — to no places at all! And so, for the neglect of inquiring, Kate and I had been judiciously following a cow path! **page 443/**

"Why not steer by the sun?"

That is easy enough, my friend, in a country where there is a sun. I had, indeed, seen little of that "Great Shine" all day; and for the last two hours nothing, a rain having then commenced which lasted till our reaching Woodville.

"What *did* you do then?"

Trusted to Kate to find the way back to Chuff's; — as we had hardly gone two miles astray — and that she did in fifteen minutes.

"What then?"

You shall hear for yourself — "Hilloo! the house!"

"Well — hilloo! what's wantin?"

"The trace to Woodville — I missed it just now."

"Sorter allowed so, when I seed you take the cow path to the licks —"

"Well, my friend, why didn't you hollow to me?"

" 'Cos I allowed you mought a axed if you ain't a woodsman, and if you be, you know'd the way to the licks as well as me."

"Thank you, sir; will you show me now?"

"Take the path tother ind of the fence."

Neighbour Chuff's settlement differs, you see, in suavity from King's. Still, the Hoosier's direction was right; and with nothing more romantic than our *feed* in the morning, we arrived pretty much used up to a late dinner in the evening at Woodville — having done more than forty *wilderness* miles in about twelve hours! For the whole, however, I was rewarded, when Dr. Sylvan that night called at our house and said with an approving smile:

"Pretty *well* done! pretty well *done!* After this I think we may dubb you a backwoodsman." **page 444/**

from *The Knickerbocker*, Vol. XLVI
August, 1855 (speech made by General
Buncombe, in the House of Representa-
tives, in the days of 'Fifty-Four Forty or
Fight')

Specimen of Eloquence from an Authentic Speech

'Mr. Speaker: When I take my eyes and throw them over the vast expanse of this expansive country: when I see how the yeast of freedom has caused it to rise in the scale of civilization and extension on every side; when I see it growing, swelling, roaring, like a spring-freshet — when I see all *this*, I cannot resist the idea, Sir, that the day will come when this great nation, like a young school-boy, will burst its straps, and become entirely too big for its boots!

'Sir, we want *elbow-room!* — the continent — the *whole* continent — and nothing *but* the continent! And we will *have* it! Then shall Uncle Sam, placing his hat upon the Canadas, rest his right arm on the Oregon and California coast, his left on the eastern sea-board, and whittle away the British power, while repos-ing his leg, like a freeman, upon Cape-Horn! Sir, the day *will* — the day *must* come!'   page 212/

from *Roughing It*, Vol. II
by Mark Twain
New York and London: Harper &
Brothers, 1899

Buck Fanshaw's Funeral

Mark Twain

"Are you the duck that runs the gospel-mill next door?"
"Am I the — pardon me, I believe I do not understand?"
With another sigh and a half-sob, Scotty rejoined:

"Why you see we are in a bit of trouble, and the boys thought maybe you would give us a lift, if we'd tackle you — that is, if I've got the rights of it and you are the head clerk of the doxology works next door."

"I am the shepherd in charge of the flock whose fold is next door."   **page 62/**

"The which?"

"The spiritual adviser of the little company of believers whose sanctuary adjoins these premises."

Scotty scratched his head, reflected a moment, and then said:

"You ruther hold over me, pard. I reckon I can't call that hand. Ante and pass the buck."

"How? I beg pardon. What did I understand you to say?"

"Well, you've ruther got the bulge on me. Or maybe we've both got the bulge, somehow. You don't smoke me and I don't smoke you. You see, one of the boys has passed in his checks, and we want to give him a good send-off, and so the thing I'm on now is to roust out somebody to jerk a little chin-music for us and waltz him through handsome."

"My friend, I seem to grow more and more bewildered. Your observations are wholly incomprehensible to me. Cannot you simplify them in some way? At first I thought perhaps I understood you, but I grope now. Would it not expedite matters if you restricted yourself to categorical statements of fact unemcumbered with obstructing accumulations of metaphor and allegory?"

Another pause, and more reflection. Then, said Scotty:

"I'll have to pass, I judge."

"How?"

"You've raised me out, pard."   **page 63/**

"I still fail to catch your meaning."

"Why, that last lead of yourn is too many for me — that's the idea. I can't neither trump nor follow suit."

The clergyman sank back in his chair perplexed. Scotty leaned his head on his hand and gave himself up to thought. Presently his face came up, sorrowful but confident.

"I've got it now, so's you can savvy," he said. "What we want is a gospel-sharp. See?"

"A what?"

"Gospel-sharp. Parson."

"Oh! Why did you not say so before? I am a clergyman — a parson."

"Now you talk! You see my blind and straddle it like a man. Put it there!" — extending a brawny paw, which closed over the minister's small hand and gave it a shake indicative of fraternal sympathy and fervent gratification.

"Now we're all right, pard. Let's start fresh. Don't you mind my snuffling a little — becuz we're in a power of trouble. You see, one of the boys has gone up the flume —"

"Gone where?"

"Up the flume — throwed up the sponge, you understand."

"Thrown up the sponge?"

"Yes — kicked the bucket —"

"Ah — has departed to that mysterious country from whose bourne no traveller returns." page 64/

"Return! I reckon not. Why, pard, he's *dead!*"

"Yes, I understand."

"Oh, you do? Well I thought maybe you might be getting tangled some more. Yes, you see he's dead again —"

"*Again!* Why, has he ever been dead before?"

"Dead before? No! Do you reckon a man has got as many lives as a cat? But you bet you he's awful dead now, poor old boy, and I wish I'd never seen this day. I don't want no better friend than Buck Fanshaw. I knowed him by the back; and when I know a man and like him, I freeze to him — you hear *me*. Take him all round, pard, there never was a bullier man in the mines. No man ever knowed Buck Fanshaw to go back on a friend. But it's all up, you know, it's all up. It ain't no use. They've scooped him.

"Scooped him?"

"Yes — death has. Well, well, well, we've got to give him up. Yes, indeed. It's a kind of a hard world, after all, *ain't* it? But pard, he was a rustler! You ought to seen him get started once. He was a bully boy with a glass eye! Just spit in his face and give him room according to his strength, and it was just beautiful to see him peel and go in. He was the worst son of a thief that ever drawed breath. Pard, he was *on* it! He was on it bigger than an Injun!"

"On it? On what? page 65/

"On the shoot. On the shoulder. On the fight, you understand. *He* didn't give a continental for *any*body. *Beg* your pardon, friend, for coming so near saying a cuss-word — but you see I'm on an awful strain, in this palaver, on account of having to cramp down and draw everything so mild. But we've got to give him up. There ain't any getting around that, I don't reckon. Now if we can get you to help plant him —"

"Preach the funeral discourse? Assist at the obsequies?"

"Obs'quies is good. Yes. That's it — that's our little game. We are going to get the thing up regardless, you know. He was always nifty himself, and so you bet you his funeral ain't going to be no slouch — solid silver door-plate on his coffin, six plumes on the hearse, and a nigger on the box in a biled shirt and a plug hat — how's that for high? And we'll take care of *you*, pard. We'll fix you all right. There'll be a kerridge for you; and whatever you want, you just 'scape out and we'll 'tend to it. We've got a shebang fixed up for you to stand behind, in No. 1's house, and don't you be afraid. Just go in and toot your horn, if you don't sell a clam. Put Buck through as bully as you can, pard, for anybody that knowed him will tell you that he was one of the whitest men that was ever in the mines. You can't draw it too strong. He never could stand it to see things going wrong. He's done more to make this town quiet and   page 66/   peaceable than any man in it. I've seen him lick four Greasers in eleven minutes, myself. If a thing wanted regulating, *he* warn't a man to go browsing around after somebody to do it, but he would prance in and regulate it himself. He warn't a Catholic. Scasely. He was down on 'em. His word was, 'No Irish need apply!' But it didn't make no difference about that when it came down to what a man's rights was — and so, when some roughs jumped the Catholic boneyard and started in to stake out town-lots in it he *went* for 'em! And he *cleaned* 'em, too! I was there, pard, and I seen it myself."

"That was very well indeed — at least the impulse was — whether the act was strictly defensible or not. Had deceased any religious convictions? That is to say, did he feel a dependence upon, or acknowledge allegiance to a higher power?"

More reflection.

"I reckon you've stumped me again, pard. Could you say it over once more, and say it slow?"

"Well, to simplify it somewhat, was he, or rather had he ever been connected with any organization sequestered from secular concerns and devoted to self-sacrifice in the interests of morality?"

"All down but nine — set 'em up on the other alley, pard."

"What did I understand you to say?"

"Why, you're most too many for me, you know. When you get in with your left I hunt grass every   page 67/   time. Every time you draw, you fill; but I don't seem to have any luck. Let's have a new deal."

"How? Begin again?"

"That's it."

"Very well. Was he a good man, and —"

"There — I see that; don't put up another chip till I look at my hand. A good man, says you? Pard, it ain't no name for it. He was the best man that ever — pard, you would have doted on that man. He could lam any galoot of his inches in America. It was him that put down the riot last election before it got a start; and everybody said he was the only man that could have done it. He waltzed in with a spanner in one hand and a trumpet in the other, and sent fourteen men home on a shutter in less than three minutes. He had that riot all broke up and prevented nice before anybody ever got a chance to strike a blow. He was always for peace, and he would *have* peace — he could not stand disturbances. Pard, he was a great loss to this town. It would please the boys if you could chip in something like that and do him justice. Here once when the Micks got to throwing stones through the Methodis' Sunday-school windows, Buck Fanshaw, all of his own notion, shut up his saloon and took a couple of six-shooters and mounted guard over the Sunday-school. Says he, 'No Irish need apply!' And they didn't. He was the bulliest man in the mountains, pard! He could run faster, jump higher, hit harder, and hold   page 68/   more tanglefoot whisky without spilling it than any man in seventeen counties. Put that in, pard — it'll please the boys more than anything you could say. And you can say, pard, that he never shook his mother."

"Never shook his mother?"

"That's it — any of the boys will tell you so."

"Well, but why *should* he shake her?"

"That's what *I* say — but some people does."

"Not people of any repute?"

"Well, some that averages pretty so-so."

"In my opinion the man that would offer personal violence to his own mother, ought to —"

"Cheese it, pard; you've banked your ball clean outside the string. What I was a drivin' at, was, that he never *throwed off* on his mother — don't you see? No indeedy. He give her a house to live in, and town lots, and plenty of money; and he looked after her and took care of her all the time; and when she was down with the smallpox I'm d—d if he didn't set up nights and nuss her himself! *Beg* your pardon for saying it, but it hopped out too quick for yours truly. You've treated me like a gentleman, pard, and I ain't the man to hurt your feelings intentional. I think you're white. I think you're a square man, pard. I like you, and I'll lick any man that don't: I'll lick him till he can't tell himself from a last year's corpse! Put it *there!"* [Another fraternal hand-shake — and exit.]   page 69/ . . . .

from *Balaam and His Master and Other Sketches and Stories* by Joel Chandler Harris
Boston and New York: Houghton, Mifflin and Company, 1891

The Trial of Ananias

Joel Chandler Harris

The cross-examination of the witness by Ananias's counsel was severe. The fact was gradually developed that Mr. Jones caught the negro stealing potatoes at night; that the night was dark and cloudy; that he did not actually catch the negro, but saw him; that he did not really see the negro clearly, but knew "in reason" that it must be Ananias.

The fact was also developed that Mr.   page 142/   Jones was not alone when he saw Ananias, but was accompanied by Mr. Miles Cottingham, a small farmer in the neighborhood, who was well known all over the county as a man of un-doubted veracity and of the strictest integrity.

At this point Lawyer Terrell, who had been facing Mr. Jones with severity painted on his countenance, seemed suddenly to recover his temper. He turned to the listening crowd, and said, in his blandest tones, "Is Mr. Miles Cottingham in the room?"

There was a pause, and then a small boy perched in one of the windows, through which the sun was streaming, cried out, "He's a-standin' out yander by the horse-rack."

Whereupon a subpoena was promptly made out by the clerk of the court, and the deputy sheriff, putting his head out of a window, cried:

"Miles G. Cottingham! Miles G. Cottingham! Miles G. Cottingham! Come into court."

Mr. Cottingham was fat, rosy, and cheerful. He came into court with such a dubious smile on his face that his friends in the room were disposed to laugh, but they   page 143/   remembered that Lawyer Terrell was somewhat intolerant of these manifestations of good-humor. As for Mr. Cottingham himself, he was greatly puzzled. When the voice of the court crier reached his ears he was in the act of taking a dram, and, as he said afterward, he "come mighty nigh drappin' the tumbeler." But he was not subjected to any such mortification. He tossed off his dram in fine style, and went to the court-house, where, as soon as he had pushed his way to the front, he was met by Lawyer Terrell, who shook him heartily by the hand, and told him his testimony was needed in order that justice might be done.

Then Mr. Cottingham was put on the stand as a witness for the defense.

"How old are you, Mr. Cottingham?" said Lawyer Terrell.

"Ef I make no mistakes, I'm a-gwine on sixty-nine," replied the witness.

"Are your eyes good?"

"Well, sir, they er about ez good ez the common run; not so good ez they mought be, en yit good enough fer me."

"Did you ever see that negro before?" The lawyer pointed to Ananias.

"Which nigger? That un over there?   page 144/   Why, that's thish yer God-forsakin' Ananias. Ef it had a-bin any yuther nigger but Ananias I wouldn't 'a' bin so certain and shore; bekaze sence the war they er all so mighty nigh alike I can't tell one from t'other sca'cely. All eckceppin' of Ananias; I'd know Ananias ef I met 'im in kingdom come wi' his hair all swinjed off."

The jury betrayed symptoms of enjoying this testimony; seeing which, the State's attorney rose to his feet to protest.

"May it please the court" —

"One moment, your honor!" exclaimed Lawyer Terrell. Then, turning to the witness: "Mr. Cottingham, were you with Mr. Jones when he was watching to catch a thief who had been stealing from him?"

"Well, sir," replied Mr. Cottingham, "I sot up wi' him one night, but I disremember in pertickler what night it wuz."

"Did you see the thief?"

"Well, sir," said Mr. Cottingham, in his deliberate way, looking around over the court-room with a more judicial air than the judge on the bench, "ef you push me close I'll tell you. Ther wuz a consid'able flutterment in the neighborhoods er whar we sot, an' me an' Wash done some mighty sly slip-   page 145/   pin' up en surrounderin'; but ez ter seein' anybody, we didn't see 'im. We heerd 'm a-scufflin' an' a-runnin', but we didn't ketch a glimpse un 'im, nuther har ner hide."

"Did Mr. Jones see him?"

"No more'n I did. I wuz right at Wash's elbow. We heerd the villyun a-runnin', but we never seed 'im. Atterwards, when we got back ter the house, Wash he 'lowed it must 'a bin that nigger Ananias thar, an' I 'lowed it jess mought ez well be Ananias ez any yuther nigger, bekaze you know yourself —"

"That will do, Mr. Cottingham," said Mr. Lawyer Terrell, blandly. The State's attorney undertook to cross-examine Mr. Cottingham; but he was a blundering man, and the result of his cross-examination was simply a stronger and more impressive repetition of Mr. Cottingham's testimony.

After this, the solicitor was willing to submit the case to the jury without argument, but Mr. Terrell said that if it pleased the court he had a few words to say to the jury in behalf of his client. The speech made by the State's attorney was flat and stale, for he was not interested in the case; but Lawyer Terrell's appeal to the jury is still   page 146/   remembered in Rockville. It was not only powerful, but inimitable; it was humorous, pathetic, and eloquent. When he concluded, the jury, which was composed mostly of middle-aged men, was in tears. The feelings of the spectators were also wrought up to a very high pitch, and when the jury found a verdict of "not guilty," without retiring, the people in the court-room made the old house ring again with applause.   page 147/   . . . .

9

THE AMERICAN SLANGUAGE

from *November Boughs*
by Walt Whitman
Philadelphia: David McKay, 1888

Slang in America

Walt Whitman

View'd freely, the English language is the accretion and growth of every dialect, race, and range of time, and its both the free and compacted composition of all. From this point of view, it stands for Language in the largest sense, and is really the greatest of studies. It involves so much; is indeed a sort of universal absorber, combiner, and conqueror. The scope of its etymologies is the scope not only of man and civilization, but the history of Nature in all departments, and of the organic Universe, brought up to date; for all are comprehended in words, and their backgrounds. This is when words become vitaliz'd, and stand for things, as they unerringly and soon come to do, in the mind that enters on their study with fitting spirit, grasp, and appreciation.

Slang, profoundly consider'd, is the lawless germinal element, below all words and sentences, and behind all poetry, and proves a certain perennial rankness and protestantism in speech. As the United States inherit by far their most precious possession — the language they talk and write — from the Old World, under and out of its feudal institutes, I will allow myself to borrow a simile even of those forms farthest removed from American democracy. Considering Language then as some mighty potentate, into the majestic audience-hall of the monarch ever enters a personage like one of Shakspere's clowns, and takes position there, and plays a part even in the stateliest ceremonies. Such is Slang, or indirection, an attempt of common humanity to escape from bald literalism, and express itself

113

illimitably, which in highest walks produces poets and poems, and doubtless in pre-historic times gave the start to, and perfected, the whole immense tangle of the old mythologies. For, curious as it may appear, it is strictly the same impulse-source, the same thing. Slang, too, is the wholesome fermentation or eructation of those processes eternally active in language, by which froth and specks are thrown up, mostly to pass away; though occasionally to settle and permanently chrystallize.

To make it plainer, it is certain that many of the oldest and solidest words we use, were originally generated from the daring and license of slang. In the processes of word-formation, myriads die, but here and there the attempt attracts superior meanings,   **page 68/**   becomes valuable and indispensable, and lives forever. Thus the term *right* means literally only straight. *Wrong* primarily meant twisted, distorted. *Integrity* meant oneness. *Spirit* meant breath, or flame. A *supercilious* person was one who rais'd his eyebrows. To *insult* was to leap against. If you *influenc'd* a man, you but flow'd into him. The Hebrew word which is translated *prophesy* meant to bubble up and pour forth as a fountain. The enthusiast bubbles up with the Spirit of God within him, and it pours forth from him like a fountain. The word prophecy is misunderstood. Many suppose that it is limited to mere prediction; that is but the lesser portion of prophecy. The greater work is to reveal God. Every true religious enthusiast is a prophet.

Language, be it remember'd, is not on abstract construction of the learn'd, or of dictionary-makers, but is something arising out of the work, needs, ties, joys, affections, tastes, of long generations of humanity, and has its bases broad and low, close to the ground. Its final decisions are made by the masses, people nearest the concrete, having most to do with actual land and sea. It impermeates all, the Past as well as the Present, and is the grandest triumph of the human intellect. "Those mighty works of art," says Addington Symonds, "which we call languages, in the construction of which whole peoples unconsciously co-operated, the forms of which were determin'd not by individual genius, but by the instincts of successive generations, acting to one end, inherent in the nature of the race — Those poems of pure thought and fancy, cadenced not in words, but in living imagery, fountainheads of inspiration, mirrors of the mind of nascent nations, which we call Mythologies — these surely are more marvellous in their infantine spontaneity than any more mature production of the races which evolv'd them. Yet we are utterly ignorant of their embryology; the true science of Origins is yet in its cradle."

Daring as it is to say so, in the growth of Language it is certain that the retrospect of slang from the start would be the recalling from their nebulous conditions of all that is poetical in the stores of human utterance. Moreover, the honest delving, as of late years, by the German and British workers in comparative philology, has pierc'd and dispers'd many of the falsest bubbles of centuries; and will disperse many more. It was long recorded that in Scandinavian mythology the heroes in the Norse Paradise drank out of the skulls of their slain enemies. Later investigation proves the word taken for skulls to mean *horns* of beasts slain in the hunt. And what reader had not been exercis'd over the traces of that feudal custom, by which *seigneurs* warm'd   **page 69/**   their feet in the bowels of serfs, the abdomen being open'd for the purpose? It now is made to appear that the serf was only required to submit his unharm'd abdomen as a foot cushion while his lord supp'd, and was required to chafe the legs of the seigneur with his hands.

It is curiously in embryons and childhood, and among the illiterate, we always find the groundwork and start, of this great science, and its noblest products. What a relief most people have in speaking of a man not by his true and formal name, with a "Mister" to it, but by some odd or homely appellative. The propensity to approach a meaning not directly and squarely, but by circuitous styles of expression, seems indeed a born quality of the common people everywhere, evidenced by nick-names, and the inveterate determination of the masses to bestow sub-titles, sometimes ridiculous, sometimes very apt. Always among the soldiers during the Secession War, one heard of "Little Mac" (General McClellan), or of "Uncle Billy" (Gen. Sherman.) "The old man" was, of course, very common. Among the rank and file, both armies, it was very general to speak of the different States they came from by their slang names. Those from Maine were call'd Foxes; New Hampshire, Granite Boys; Massachusetts, Bay Staters; Vermont, Green Mountain Boys; Rhode Island, Gun Flints; Connecticut, Wooden Nutmegs; New York, Knickerbockers; New Jersey, Clam Catchers; Pennsylvania, Logher Heads; Delaware, Muskrats; Maryland, Claw Thumpers; Virginia, Beagles; North Carolina, Tar Boilers; South Carolina, Weasels; Georgia, Buzzards; Louisiana, Creoles; Alabama, Lizzards; Kentucky, Corn Crackers; Ohio, Buckeyes; Michigan, Wolverines; Indiana, Hoosiers; Illinois, Suckers; Missouri, Pukes; Mississippi, Tad Poles; Florida, Fly up the Creeks; Wisconsin, Badgers; Iowa, Hawkeyes; Oregon, Hard Cases. Indeed I am not sure but slang names have more than once made Presidents. "Old Hickory," (Gen. Jackson) is one case in point. "Tippecanoe, and Tyler too," another. **page 70/** . . . .

Certainly philologists have not given enough attention to this element and its results, which, I repeat, can probably be found working every where to-day, amid modern conditions, with as much life and activity as in far-back Greece or India, under pre-historic ones. Then the wit — the rich flashes of humor and genius and poetry — darting out often from a gang of laborers, railroad-men, miners, drivers or boatmen! How often have I hover'd at the edge of a crowd of them, to hear their repartees and impromtus! You get more real fun from half an hour with them than from the books of all "the American humorists."

The science of language has large and close analogies in geological science, with its ceaseless evolution, its fossils, and its numberless submerged layers and hidden strata, the infinite go-before of the present. Or, perhaps Language is more like some vast living body, or perennial body of bodies. And slang not only brings the first feeders of it, but is afterward the start of fancy, imagination and humor, breathing into its nostrils the breath of life. **page 72/**

from *The Autocrat of the Breakfast Table*
by Oliver Wendell Holmes
Boston: Houghton Mifflin Company, 1858, 1882, 1886, 1891

Dish-Water from the Washings of English Dandyism

Oliver Wendell Holmes

— I think there is one habit, — I said to our company a day or two afterwards, — worse than that of punning. It is the gradual substitution of cant or slang terms for words which truly characterize their objects. I have known several very genteel idiots whose whole vocabulary had deliquesced into some half dozen expressions. All things fell into one of two great categories, — *fast* or *slow*. Man's chief end was to be a *brick*. When the great calamities of life overtook their friends, these last were spoken of as being *a good deal cut up*. Nine tenths of human existence were summed up in the single word, *bore*. These expressions come to be the algebraic symbols of minds which have grown too weak or indolent to discriminate. They are the blank checks of intellectual bankruptcy; — you may fill them up with what idea you like; it makes no difference, for there are no funds in the treasury upon which they are drawn. Colleges and good-for-nothing smoking-clubs are the places where these conversational fungi spring up most luxuriantly. Don't think I undervalue the proper use and application of a cant word or phrase. It adds piquancy to conversation, as a mushroom does to a sauce. But it is no better than a toadstool, odious to the sense and poisonous to the intellect, when it spawns itself all over the talk of men and youths **page 256/**   capable of talking, as it sometimes does. As we hear slang phraseology, it is commonly the dish-water from the washings of English dandyism, schoolboy or full-grown, wrung out of a three-volume novel which had sopped it up, or decanted from the pictured urn of Mr. Verdant Green, and diluted to suit the provincial climate.

— The young fellow called John spoke up sharply and said, it was "rum" to hear me "pitchin' into fellers" for "goin' it in the slang line," when I used all the flash words myself just when I pleased.

— I replied with my usual forbearance. — Certainly, to give up the algebraic symbol because *a* or *b* is often a cover for ideal nihility, would be unwise. I have heard a child laboring to express a certain condition, involving a hitherto undescribed sensation (as it supposed), all of which could have been sufficiently explained by the participle — *bored.* I have seen a country-clergyman, with a one-story intellect and one-horse vocabulary, who has consumed his valuable time (and mine) freely, in developing an opinion of a brother-minister's discourse which would have been abundantly characterized by a peach-down-lipped sopho-more in the one word — *slow.* Let us discriminate, and be shy of absolute pro-scription. I am omniverbivorous by nature and training. Passing by such words as are poisonous, I can swallow most others, and chew such as I cannot swallow. page 257/ . . . .

from *The New York Times*
December 14, 1932

Nation's Best Textbook of Slang Formed by Congressional Record

Chicago, Dec 13 (AP). — The nation's best textbook of slang is the Congres-sional Record and the White House is a fount of the American vernacular, ac-cording to Sir William S. Craigie, University of Chicago lexicographer and co-editor of the Oxford English dictionary.

In his search for characteristic expressions with which Americans have colored the English language since the Pilgrims landed, Professor Craigie said his best sources had been, not the jargon of street corners or the dialect of the under-world, but the volumes wherein are recorded the speeches of national legislators and the missives of the Presidents.

The Congressional Record before the middle of the last century was almost free from slang, Professor Craigie said.

"Before then legislators were very formal," he continued. "They were con-servative in their speech, purists. The old school of oratory flourished. Men spoke as men wrote. Again, some sort of unofficial censorship may have existed. Speeches, in being transferred to the page may have been edited to conform to grammatical rules."

Lawmakers are not especially careless in their choice of words, Professor Craigie pointed out. Representing the demands of different parts of the country, they also represent their peculiarities. At Washington, colloquialisms are cen-tralized and made public for the rest of the country to grasp. Soon they become national and find their way into the language of the people. . . . **page 16/**

from *The Forum*, Vol. XC
December, 1933

They Don't Speak Our Language

H. T. Webster

"They don't speak our language" — and we don't speak theirs.

If you have a tendency to be smug about your large vocabulary and just a shade snooty about that of the so-called Booboisie — lay off your lofty lid, laddie, and let your hair dry. The chances are that the "saps" savvy conversation you wouldn't even suspect.

Take on a cargo of this:

Two shopgirls in the seat ahead of me on a street car. Judged by their looks Binet wouldn't even let them *enter* an intelligence test. Call them Jennie and Dollie for convenience.

JENNIE. Why not buzz Eddie for the brawl?

DOLLIE. That flat hoop! He wouldn't rate a blind date with a cold biscuit.

JENNIE. Wassa mat? He outdoor you? I thought he was the principal rave and the real McCoy in your y.l.

DOLLIE. That's torn. And I turned on the fan myself. I glimmed him with a snuggle-puppy in a can and I told him he couldn't double-clock me with that kind of a number. Anyhow, he's no bargain, and does he spread the frosting thin!

At this point I reeled off the car ten blocks from my stop. What is laughingly known as the brain, bean, nut, etc. of this performer now at the mike was — to coin a phrase — all haywire. I had gathered that a young man named Eddie was under discussion, but Dollie and Jennie had kept the rest from me as effectively as though they chattered Chaldean.

But most of the words sank into my subconscious, and I was able to repeat them to a sapient — no relation to sap — youth who honors this ancient with his tolerant companionship at times.

"Where have you bean?" he jeered. "Those janes weren't spilling anything but plain U.S.

"One of them wanted to phone this bird Eddie for a party, but the other frail said he was a wet smack — a social dud to you — who wasn't fit to be selected as an escort for a girl he didn't know, even a dame who lacked sex appeal and otherwise wouldn't do. Then the first baby wanted to know what was the big idea, had Eddie given her the air, put her under the oxygen tent, gated her — in other words thrown her over? Hadn't he been her chief enthusiasm and the genuine goods in her young life?

"The other one simply said that was all washed up, fini. That if anybody did any airing she'd done it herself because she saw Eddie taking one of these eager neckers out in an automobile, and she had told him he couldn't page 367/ two-time her — double-cross her, to speak dictionary stuff — with that kind of a doll. Besides, she said he wasn't so hot and that he was no spendthrift."

Well, that's how it all began, my dears, that's how it all began. Jennie and Dollie started those "They Don't Speak Our Language" cartoons. Or at least they were the direct inspiration, though the idea might readily have germinated from the day in '96 when Bill Lambert came back to my home town of Tomahawk, Wis. (pop. 2,500) after a visit to Chicago.

Bill hailed me from afar and paralyzed me with:

"How's your couverosity sagaciating this morning?"

In those ante-syndicate, ante-radio, ante-talkie days, argot spread less swiftly than now, but Bill and I knocked all of Tomahawk for a loop with *that* one inside twenty-four hours.

It was not until lately that I found "sagaciate" in the dictionary, there defined as "to do or be in any way; think, talk or act, as indicating a state of mind or body: as, how do you sagaciate this morning? (Slang, U.S.)" But the Rosetta stone, the key for interpreting the motive if not the meaning of all slang, was contained in the given example of its usage. This was taken from Joel Chandler Harris' Uncle Remus stories:

"'How duz yo' sym'tums seem ter sagashuate?' sez Brer Rabbit, sezee."

Caste Marks of Speech

I have a notion all of us are Uncle Remusing when we adopt an esoteric system of speech — chemists, cartoonists, doctors, lawyers, merchants, thieves. It is the caste mark, or if you insist upon being old-fashioned, the snake's hips! Everybody seems to indulge in it. And do I go for it in a big way! For me it amounts to very nearly the equivalent of one day off a week. This is about as often as I dare to base a panel of drawings on a cartoon idea which is captioned, "They Don't Speak Our Language."

I had relocated "sagaciate" in a dictionary of the approximate dimensions of a doghouse, but anybody who tries to issue a one-volume lexicon of American slang will have something the size of a cow barn.

Slanguage, argot, jargon, lingo — where does it all come from? The Big Towns are still largely the clearing houses of slang, but not so much of it originates on the Main Stems as when I was a boy. Ade, once a daily geyser of fresh whimsies, spouts now only once in a while. Hughey, McKeogh, Tad, H. C. Witwer, and Ring Lardner, creators of lines and phrases still current, are trading wise wheezes with Rabelais and Mark Twain in Valhalla. Bugs Baer, Bill McGeehan, Bud Fisher, Damon Runyon, Walter Winchell, Rube Goldberg, and Milt Gross initiate and chronicle much vivid and picturesque street speech, but the bulk of it flows into the reservoir of language from shops, mills, factories, laboratories, jails, speakeasies, colleges, the sea, sports, and the stage.

Not all of these languages of ours which "they" do or don't speak, are slang. Many of them are pure technology, codes to which only the initiated have the

key. But technology, argot, or slang — these various examples of dialect and
patois drive conscientious philologists gaga.

As there are not so many philologists, the real burden is borne by hosts and
hostesses, of whom there are a great many. The Websters of Shippan Point,
Connecticut, for instance, decide to entertain a group of friends, with the
notion of making everyone feel neighborly. Enter Mr. and Mrs. Bushmiller. He
is in the banana business, and they promptly spot Mr. and Mrs. Gross, likewise
in the banana business. At once they rush together as if they were particles of
quicksilver.

"Nice cargo of Santa Marta eights and nines that came in yesterday," says
Mr. Bushmiller.

"Yeah," says Mr. Gross. "Guatemala is running heavier average this year. They
only cut full three quarters."

"Hummp," continues Mr. Bushmiller, "I'm sticking to count bunches for the
city trade, and there's good dough in reds and lady fingers for the fancy fruit
stores."

"But," says Mr. Gross, "try to pull out the color on a bunch of bananas not up to
grade. Y'gotta sweat 'em and gas 'em."

Meantime the Williamses and the Gordons are in an insurance huddle, discussing skips, lapses, coverage, fiduciaries, and groups — while Doctor Frink and
Doctor Hogan are   page 368/   adding to the general chumminess of the occasion with light and airy badinage about accommodative asthenopia, emmetropia,
binocular fusion, achromatic orthogons, visual axes, and diopters of esophoria.
As a further flux for these divergent elements of the party we have Professor and
Mrs. Leech, who will talk on helminthology with anybody and on anthropology
with nobody — and whom I suspect of making up all the words they use over
six syllables. There just ain't no such words.

And when Mrs. Webster and I introduce a broad general topic of conversation
such as the relative merits of Lenz, Culbertson, Official, or One-Over-One and
use such simple terms as demands, overcalls, sikes, slams, open hands, fourteen
counts, yarboroughs, and double ruffs, we find we've unfortunately gathered
together a bunch of impossible dubs who Don't Speak Our Language. And the
party does a dive.

The Greeks Had a Word for It

It's tough on the host and hostess, but it takes all kinds to make a language as
well as a world. And language, like men, if it isn't fed, dies. It's the corruptions,
the vulgarisms, the slang that keep speech vital. The only pure language is a
dead one. And even the pellucid Greek of Aristotle and the limpid Latin of
Vergil were compounds of the lexicographers' dicta and the diction of Athenian
bars and Roman gladiatorial spectators. Take any modern slang, and I'm betting
eight to five the Greeks had a word for it. It's classic, now, but the pedants must
have crabbed when they first heard it.

I hazard the guess that if a Spartan dick (detective, if you haven't never heard
nuthin') were describing a case to a group of his fellows, his speech would have

just about the same relation to that in the grammars of his time as that of a New York plainclothesman, whom I overheard one day, bears to the book English of now. (A clumsy sentence — but I'm only a cartoonist.)

"This peterman," quoth he, "has a keister full of power.

"He cases the joint and skeletons in. He just gets the jug souped when the dark horse makes him. Well, this gun is a bangster, all snowed up, so he gives the dark horse the heat and lams. He gets away in a heap, but we nab his gander, and, besides, his calling cards are all over the crib. The gander squawks, and the mobster gets rapped for the hot squat. His lip couldn't spring him. He's lying in state in the dance hall now."

I'll give you the glossary and you can roll your own story. Peterman — safe-blower; keister — suit case; power — explosive; cases the joint — looks over the place; skeletons in — uses skeleton keys; soup — another word for nitroglycerin; jug — safe; dark horse — night watchman; gun — crook; bangster — drug addict; snowed up — full of dope; gives the heat — shoots; lam — you know that one; heap — automobile; gander — lookout; calling cards — fingerprints; crib — safe; mobster — crook, again; rapped — sentenced; lip — lawyer; spring — free; lying in state — imprisoned; dance hall — death house; hot squat — electric chair.

Supposedly, criminal argot is a means by which crooks talk without revealing anything to non-crooks. Actually, I never knew a detective who hadn't a better vocabulary of that stuff than the average yegg.

Which will be enough about the underworld.

From more legitimate sources we get stuff **page 369/** almost equally esoteric. I read in *Billboard* the other day ads for a Hot Sax; Med. People; Tent Rep.; Bannerman; Fast Trumpet, modern go; Ballyhoos, Bingos, and Puritans; and Sousaphonist, single and SOBER. But I suppose a sousaphonist has something to do with an instrument named after the late great bandmaster and not after "souse."

Which reminds me. How many words do you know as synonyms for drunk? Soused, shined, shellacked, edged, jingled, pie-eyed, pickled, lit, petrified, para-lyzed — and plenty more. But look for most of them in the dictionary — with that popular meaning — and you'll find They Don't Speak Our Language. I don't think you'll find "hey-hey" or "making whoopee," either.

But back to the *Billboard*. I also ran into "flesh-shows," which doesn't mean burlesque, but merely flesh-and-blood shows in contrast to "grinds" — movies. I also found "neighb. house" and "deluxer" — small neighborhood cinema and big one infested with ushers.

Musicians have their code, of course. I learned recently that a grunt iron is a tuba, and among other things that when the bull-fiddler (viol player) plucks the strings of his instrument like a harp he is slapping the doghouse.

From the stage we have "wow," "frost," "riot," "ham," and "upstage" — to pick five from five thousand phrases. From the track "gee" is all I think of now — I never paddocked much. I'm inclined to think that "blah," "bunk," "blither," "poppycock," "hooey," and "bushwa" came from politics. "Banana oil," "apple-sauce," and "baloney" are the inspirations of individual comic-strip men — and darn good ones, too.

Circus Slanguage

But the slanguage that's nearest to my heart is circus and carnival argot. You see, when I was a appleknocker in the sticks, my ambition (what boy's isn't?) was to travel with a circus. Well, I rated it — about ten years ago.

A number of cartoonists, the late Clare Briggs and myself among them, had the luck to be invited to tour with the circus; and the hick kid from Tomahawk wouldn't have had more fun than I did.

It was no surprise to discover that on the lot zebras are convicts; that the big carnivora of the menagerie, lions, tigers, and leopards, are cats; or that musicians are windjammers. Made-up as a clown, it was my daily custom to cavort around the arena with the professional funnies, and I began to fancy myself a real trouper by such aids as the mental process of thinking of elephants, in my old-fashioned way, as bulls. There was a kick in that.

But I didn't begin to feel a real sophisticate in this circus life until I learned that when the bulls were used to push wagons out of the mud they were rubber mules; that blues were general admission tickets; that an ace was a dollar; that a connection was the tent corridor between menagerie and big tent; that a dolly was a movable crane; that to get with it was to join the outfit; that a gilly was a small show traveling in hired cars; a mender an adjuster of disputes and such with the town authorities; a jig a Negro; a mitt a palmist; and a sucker a monkey.

Other items in this circus curriculum were "pipe" for letter (or talk), "razor-backs" for roustabouts, "bloomer" for bad business, and "red" for a town where business was good. (Same color as "in the red" but opposite in meaning.) Then there was "grinder" for a ballyhoo man (but only for one who stayed out- page 370/ side), "advertise" for being noisy in public, "shack" for a train brakeman, and, of course, "Annie Oakleys" for passes.

Often in railroad coaches I puzzle over mysterious phrases spoken in conversation between American business men. They talk about rack losses, surface leakages, electrostatic capacities, lawning machines, and pug mills. As I move away out of earshot, I have a better understanding of what Professor Charles A. Beard means when he says civilization is getting too complicated for human minds to run it.

Some words take different color from varied trades. Hardly had I become aware that "job" was the current term among automobile men for any car, when Fred Kelly reported, from Peninsula, Ohio, another application of the word. A tombstone-maker had been showing Fred some of his samples in the local cemetery. On the drive back to town the monument man jerked his thumb at a passing woman. "That," he said, "is the widow of the Blue Granite job I showed you!"

Boat- and casket-makers use it, it's probably current among shovers of the queer for a phony note, and no doubt missionaries are now substituting it for "convert."

Hollywood Version

There is a constant need of new words and phrases to describe implements and situations that did not exist in the days when Addison and Steele were writing pure English. Both, I am sure, would make uncritical and grateful notations if they could follow a Hollywood cameraman and listen to his responses to his wife's questions on the day's work.

"What a day!" they would hear. "I cranked over five thousand feet of raw stock."

"Actually?"

"Yeah. All panchromatic and heavy emulsion. Sprocket holes bad, too."

"You'd better crash that kodak. When the last batch came out of the soup it wasn't fit to drum. Are you sure the grips got your gobos right?"

For the benefit of Addison and Steele and more recent laymen, who may possibly know that grips are stagehands, soup is developing fluid, and a drum is the reel on which film is wound, "gobos" should be more carefully explained. Why a black panel screen that shields a camera lens from bright lights should be called a gobo, I dunno, but gobo it is.

There's an old movie story of a director who hired a bunch of New York toughs and their molls as extras for a riot scene. After much drill he suddenly shouted: "Strip the sils off the broads."

The East Siders began to rip the clothes off the nearest girls. "Stop!" yelled the director. "Not you extras! I'm talking to the juicer."

What the extras had interpreted as a rough-house command was an order to the electrician to take the silk screens off the stage lights — "broads."

"Dubbin" is another word found only in movieland. It's the process by which films are prepared for export to countries speaking Another Language. The scheme is to synchronize the alien words with the lip movements of American stars — thus making it appear, for example, that Greta Garbo speaks Japanese as well as other languages, including the Scandinavian. It's an intricately technical piece of deception — and "dubbin" is its name, a corruption of "doubling."

The talkies require so many new devices that it's not strange they create a new language. The "boom," for instance, is a telescopic arm on a rubber-tired carriage which will carry a microphone to any part of the set. It's not a bit like a ship's boom now, but that's where the word came from originally. "Blimp" is the sound-proof box that muffles the noise of the camera. Originally it was a bag-like affair resembling a small dirigible. Hence blimp. It's a verb, too. The cameraman spends his day blimping.

Synchronization is the operation of timing the sound track to the action on the screen. It's much too long a word for daily use, so it becomes "sink." When the adjustment is being made in the laboratory, the picture is in sink.

And there are more subtle matters to be disposed of by the director. He might have his face slapped if he spoke frankly what is in his mind when he wants the star to leave off a brassiere or drape a leg over the arm of her chair or in some other manner to inject sex appeal. "Now sweetheart," he says impersonally and euphemistically, "right here, if you please, some of the old McGoo." Who is McGoo? I page 371/ don't know. I merely know the important thing: what McGoo is.

Just the other day I heard what was for me a new one that served to revive a boyish thrill. Long ago in Tomahawk, Willie Miller, who acted as janitor of the Opera House, in one of the dressing rooms found an abandoned set of false gray whiskers. On the basis of a library loan I gained temporary possession of them. There were incisions in the sides which enabled me to hang the beard from my ears in a swift adjustment. Unhappily everyone recognized me. When I mentioned it recently to Charles Coburn and described the incisions, he defined its purpose. When there is need in a play for a minor character to walk across the stage carrying a trunk or leading a dog, some member of the cast doubles in this part, and the disguise is a beard of the sort I borrowed. "It was," Mr. Coburn informed me, "a cross-over beard."

Remember Bill Frawley who played the tough sergeant in *Sons o' Guns?* Recently he walked into Marty Forkins' booking office and there encountered an old friend — a vaudevillian. This chap's act had died because his wife, who had played with him, spoiled most of his lines. The vaudeville man was about to go to Hollywood to make a short picture as a low comedian, with something better in prospect for the autumn.

"How're things?" said Bill.

"Colder than a well-digger's feet. The point killer took up my badge. I'm drifting west to put on big pants. I'm through with the mousetraps. Big time next season. My new partner's hotter than a pistol. She'll burn up the first five rows."

I asked Frawley to interpret "hotter than a pistol" for me. "The new partner in the act," he said, "is a red-haired girl."

Dumbing It Down

If there is one fact which is clear about the genesis of such words of slang as are worth repetition, it is that they are blown off as naturally as lava from lively minds cramped by a limited lexicon when under the pressure of a need for expression. Occasionally in times of stress, just as a stricken community gets help from the fire department or militia of adjoining regions, a word is borrowed. The theater has frequent need of a word for failure, and the cipher of the baseball scoreboards has served its people well. Consequently, when stock market prices dropped in 1929 as they had not dropped since 1873, the theater had a word for it, and *Variety* placed over the news story this headline: "Wall Street Lays an Egg."

It is the strictures of column rules in tabloid newspapers that gave us "love nest" and other crisp phrases with which to talk about what one of the colored help in the New York Newspaper Club was accustomed to speak of as "female trouble." The mass circulation of the tabloids is a forcing bed, guaranteeing a swift growth of their terse and often euphemistic phrases; but the boot-and-shoe trade, the morgue-keepers, the delicatessen men, each, I am sure, have a language as little understood by outsiders as if it were Choctaw. I don't mind that. But I do dislike the pretentious jargon of some professions.

Take some such simple matter as an old prize fighter walking on round heels. A couple of psychiatrists if appealed to for a diagnosis of the case will stumble around among a bewildering undergrowth of strange and invariably long words; but another prize fighter after one glance will say with authority: "Slug-nutty." This is one I like.

I can cheer, too, for the Hollywood gag men in conference on a comedy which has been revealed as too subtle, when they determine they must dumb it down. That phrase saves time and wearying gestures. And "switcheroo" has value in the state department as well as in the mouth of gag men.

"We can have him drunk and eating all the cherries out of the cocktails," proposes one gag man.

"No," objects another. "Lloyd did that."

"Oke," says the chief gag man. "We'll pull a switcheroo. We'll use olives instead."

Which may be why it is my private opinion that the quick passing of technocracy as an idea for conducting human affairs as well as a publicity device was due largely to its esoteric vocabulary. In other words, it laid an erg. And I doubt if we'll ever get far with currency stabilization or other international economic adjustments until economists begin abandoning the argot of celestial mathematicians.

The trouble with the Better Minds is that They Don't Speak Our Language.
page 372/

10

WORD-SPINNING AND PATTERNS
OF INNOVATION

from *The Independent*, Vol. LXV
October 1, 1908

The New Vocabulary

James Herbert Morse

Professor Lounsbury of Yale in a recent essay presses the question whether we may not reasonably let up a little on the rules of a too exact definition of adjectives. It is not a generation since Professor James Russell Lowell admitted that "no man, or body of men, can dam the stream of language." Where the masters of English in two great universities thus lift the boards, is it for the young generation to be too nice in the use of vocables?

We are just now in a wild hurly-burly of the vernacular. From every quarter freshly washed vocables are streaming in — some rolled down the sands of time, page 765/ some recently thrown up in the latest linguistic convulsion. The youth from the college classroom contributes what is to him a taking rendering of some Æschylean compound that has given life to a dull hour. The young clerk, home with sweet company from the comic opera, whistles the latest air just tiptoed over the stage, and the glad pair burst into song together. A bit of the technical jargon of the ball-field is caught up by the unfledged schoolboy and, generally incoherently connected with unrelated topics, is reproduced at the family table. It thus of course becomes slang; it may be innocent slang, soon to be relegated to a corner lot, in the comprehensive dictionary. "Bally," and "snide," and "hike," and "corking," will very naturally have but a brief day. The new words are often clean and wholesome, amusing, and altogether harmless.

There is much to recommend the argument of some easy-tempered old gentlemen, who say: "If the words do not require shutters, why should they not for a brief time swell the racy list of joy-giving vocables? They show what the weather is in youth — what the April winds are saying. There is the bubbling of springs about the rootlets of language. Occasionally a blossom will come of it — a new, fresh, aromatic Sophoclean word. The lexicon will be permanently enriched, and the nations be gladdened. Old men will smile, and maidens clap glad hands."

Addison, in his day, gently complained of those mild abbreviations — "mayn't," "can't," "sha'n't," "won't." We have very much untuned the language, he says. "To favor our natural taciturnity, when obliged to utter our thoughts, we give as quick a birth to our conceptions as possible." But how little he understood the necessities of an expanding civilization! In these hurly-burly days we draw the very poetry of language from the mills, the sporting field, the prize ring, the pool room, — most notably perhaps from the expressive vocabulary of Wall Street. On the ball-field, for instance, we "put up a gilt-edge game"; we "grab a lead"; "bunch a couple of hits." In emergencies, we "pop up to B," "gobble up a sizzler," "slam out a win," "come to the scratch at the show-down," "start the fireworks with a clean single," or "rap out a hot single," and then unhappily "stagnate on first base."

How eminently condensed all this is, and yet how joyfully Sophoclean! Fresh from college, the reporter evidently is, and yet how much he has lost of what a great metropolitan daily calls "the flashing note of femininity!" A first degree has been taken in the "manly arts." There were college "sports" fifty years ago who read approvingly in the public journals of the day how an eminent compatriot with his "bunch of fives" leveled on the "peepers" of an equally eminent gentle-man of foreign extraction, — how he "drew the claret" from his "mug," and touched his lips with an ungentle osculation. For the parlor these of course were vulgar expressions. But then they seldom got admission to the parlor. They belonged wholly to the stable, and it stands to reason that words wholly from the stable will not always have company manners. There will be words — "rotten," for instance — touching even the electric bell, that are "best recom-mended by frequent intervals of absence." They should only occasionally attach themselves to good company. Then there are dingy words, that barely escape stripes; explosive words, peculiarly adapted to the use of "our army in Flanders"; they should not be heard in Sunday-school, or seen in the Sunday papers. Sunday has its privileges; clean hands, clean dickeys, clean and wholesome words are among them. There are also ill-assorted words, like winter greenings in March, — the sound tumbled in with the "spect," so that the whole collocation leaves in the nostrils the sensation of decay. "Blooming" was once an excellent word; it went in good company; but of late it has taken to evil association, and it is at least suspi-cious. A blooming maid is still always welcome; but a "blooming cuss," a "bloom-ing shame," only at rare intervals. Frequent absences are desirable. Not that one may object to the word "cuss." Like the poor, it is always with us. Yet let it sometimes be a "knowing cuss," a "radiant cuss." Again, one is willing to see, at a distance, a "bum" fellow — even a long succession of him — always in one pattern of trousers — checked. But to have grace at table "bum," the meats "bum," and all

the guests "bum" we feel, with lit- page 766/ tle Marjorie Fleming, that we
would like to be "transported far beyond the wicked sons of men, where there is
nothing but strife and envying, pilfering and murder, where neither contentment
dwells, but there dwells drunkenness."

It is hardly ten years — contemporary, in fact, with the beginning of automo-
biliary record, that a modest and learned professor at Harvard was described, not
as lecturing to his class, but as "blowing off his mouth," "letting out hot air."
These are now archaic expressions. New times, new men, new vocables! The
college youth is now on the more public "oval." He wears a jauntier air; breathes
in his manners the fragrance of violets sometimes. He advises a distinguished
statesman who aspires to the Presidency to "go west and spread fragrance" in
Ohio. He has become a reporter, and is picturesque in his linguistic artistry.
From the "diamond," the racecourse — one hardly knows what — he fills his daily
column with Pindaric odes, singing how so-and-so "got in a whirlwind of a lick,"
with his bat, and then "rammed a homer"; how A., "like a human cornucopia,
poured out his gifts with lavish hand"; how B. "spread himself out to catch the
hurtling sphere"; how C. "wrapt his feet around his foe." These are all manly
heroes. Turning to the softer sex, he lets us for a moment admire the girlish
gaiety of a pair of mares that merrily "romped home from a second race" at the
jockey club meet. There was joy in Israel. Another day, haunting the athletic
field, he observes "a lull punctured with games." What an airy restfulness in that
"punctured lull!" If we did not know exactly "where we were at," it was restful
to be there. The words had on their "glad rags." They smacked of parlor associations. We feel the presence of ladies, and not, as in the case of those faint
adumbrations of far-off explosives, "bum" and "blooming," a suggestion of
Milton's nether notables —

"Princes, potentates,
And powers of heaven, once ours, now lost."

In this new stream that refuses to be dammed, there is everywhere the tumult
of contention. Human thought is on the "rush line"; it is determined to "get
there." Events mean to "arrive." Great powers are "pooling their interests." A
whole contingent is "lining up" for a game. On every side the "shouters," the
"heelers," the "backers," the "bummers," the "grafters," are "in evidence." Is it not
a time when we should be easy on the language — when the young journalists
should be allowed to "set the pace," and "leg it home" with the vocabulary?
page 767/

from *The New York Times Magazine*
September 8, 1957

About: New Words

Martin Tolchin

Lexicographers are perplexed daily by the problems that arise from our nation's unceasing efforts to increase its vocabulary. What is a word? At what point does it come into existence? And who is the authority for it?

Currently, dictionary men are wrestling with such terms as "exurbanite," "duopoly," "musicology," "medic," "litterbug," "hardtop," "elasticize," "desegregation," "egghead," "tranquilizer" and "paperback." Are these words? Not to mention the television meaning of "compatible" and "ghosts" and the "bop" meaning of "dig," "cool" and "crazy." Are these valid uses of established words? Finally, how might they achieve the dignity of a dictionary listing? . . .

While most laymen look to the dictionary to see if a particular "combination of sounds" is actually a word, lexicographers have come around to the opposite point of view. The authority for a word — in fact, the authority for a language — they now agree rests with the users of the language. Thus the process of adding new words to the dictionary begins with a systematic examination of almost everything printed in English, including best-selling novels, regional newspapers, mail order catalogues, menus, consumer magazines, trade journals, house organs — even the labels on canned goods.

Most new words are absorbed gradually into the language, but there are exceptions. An awesome example is the phrase "atomic bomb." When it crossed the desk of a Merriam-Webster editor back in 1917 (it had been clipped from a sentence in The Yale Review, which read, "When you can drop just one atomic bomb and wipe out Paris or Berlin, war will have become monstrous and impossible"), it drew the penciled comment: "Fanciful." During the Thirties, the phrases "atomic energy" and "atomic ray" warranted dictionary listings, but "atomic bomb" remained in the realm of the improbable. It was not until 1945 that it exploded into print, when the bomb was dropped on Hiroshima.

"Freeway" presents a more typical case. It first appeared in The New York Times, The Saturday Evening Post, Time and Harper's during 1948–49. In these first references the word was cradled in quotes. Later the quotes were dropped and the word was bolstered by parenthetical explanations. By 1952 it was listed with the addenda of the big dictionaries and today can be found in the regular listings of recently revised works.

Once a new word is sighted (and cited), it becomes a candidate for the dictionary, and is taken up and mulled over at periodic conferences. The decision to include a word is made on the basis of its frequency and range of use. But lexicographers do not simply tally up the number of citation slips. From the citations comes clues on definition, etymology, pronunciation, variant spellings and the like.

Sometimes the file on a new word is barren. This happens with words and phrases that gain speedy acceptance. To determine the etymology of the phrase "Iron Curtain," for example, lexicographers wrote to Sir Winston Churchill, who had coined it. Sir Winston, it turned out, had reference to the iron curtain (since replaced by one made of asbestos) that separated the stage from the orchestra in legitimate theatres.

Practical considerations play their part in the march of a word into the bold-face listings of a dictionary. Chief among these is the scope of the dictionary and the physical limitations imposed by the patching or resetting of large numbers of plates. Space for new entries is created mainly by rewriting definitions on the same page to eliminate runovers. To make space for "cybernetics," for example, the editors of the American College Dictionary took one line from the definition of "cyanine"; reduced the illustration of a "cycloid"; cut an example of the usage of the word "cut"; shortened the space separating the end of the "C" listings from the beginning of the "D" listings and cut five runovers.   page 68/ . . . .

from *The New York Times Magazine*
August 18, 1935

Our American English Marches Onward

Sir William Craigie

Whether we call it American English or American speech or the American language (a matter on which writers have long differed and even disputed) does not really matter a great deal, so long as the name carries with it a clear understanding of what it implies. The one misconception to be avoided at all costs is to suppose that any of these terms is equivalent to American slang. No one is likely to fall into this error with regard to English itself. There has been an abundance of English slang from at least the sixteenth century to the present time, but it has always been recognized as such, and has at no time been supposed to be anything but a minor part of the English language.

The fact that slang has had an exuberant development in the United States in recent years, and is one of the features that most readily attract attention, ought not to be allowed to blur the distinction between the language as a whole and this particular manifestation of its vitality. American English of the present day includes an extensive vocabulary of slang, but is so far independent of it that in the greater part of what is written and printed in the country it makes no appearance at all.

In any comparison between the English of the United States and that of Britain or other parts of the world, the slang element may be altogether ignored, and yet there will remain more points of difference than either the American or the Englishman will readily think of.

The interest in slang which creates this misconception is natural enough. Slang is forcible and novel, and obtains a vogue by these qualities, and by its convenience for use in familiar or informal talk. It has also the attraction of so frequently springing out of obscurity, giving little or no indication of its origin. Even within a week or two after a slang word or phrase has made its appearance it may be hopeless to trace it to its source.

The human mind, however, is an inquiring mind, and does not like to remain in ignorance; hence the constant endeavors to discover the origin of slang terms not only when they are new but sometimes many years after they have come into general use. The mystery of their origin adds to their interest, and gives them an undue prominence, which tends to obscure the fact that in the record of American English as a whole they play only a limited part, and that most of them appear only in the very latest period of its history.

A historical dictionary of American English is thus something very different from a dictionary of American slang; it also covers much more than a dictionary of Americanisms would do. It has to include, as far as possible, not only every word, usage or phrase which has originated on this side of the Atlantic from the days of the first Colonies but every one which has a clear connection with the development of the country and the culture of its inhabitants. The most ordinary English word may call for insertion on the latter ground, as having not only a real but often a vital connection with the life of the settlers and their descendants.

Log and *shingle* were words which the Colonists brought from home, but they have never had the same importance for everyday life in England that they have had here. *Corn* is a word as old as English itself, but in New England it not only acquired a new meaning but a fresh significance, giving it a different place in the American vocabulary from that which it holds in England. Such words are entitled to the same recognition and treatment in a historical dictionary as those of purely American origin.

It would be easy to illustrate this and other points by words taken at random throughout the alphabet, but that would give no idea of the number of such terms or of the labor involved in compiling their history. This can be much more clearly shown by taking a single section from one letter, and pointing out the special features of American English which it exhibits.

A survey, then, of the words beginning with BE, as already prepared for the historical dictionary now in progress, presents the following points of interest:

The ordinary word *beach* has to be entered because of its special meaning on the New Jersey coast, where it is applied to certain islands. It also gives rise to the compounds *beach-comber*, first recorded in 1840 and now in common use; *beach-grass* and *beach-plum* from the later years of the eighteenth century, and the more modern *beach-bird*, *beach-pea*, *beach-sand* and *beach-wagon*, a light open wagon with two or more seats, which dates from 1869. These compounds appear to be all of American origin. In English a *beach-bird* would more naturally be called a *shore-bird*.

Bead is entered for two reasons: because of its importance in early trading with the Indians, when "a fathom of beads" was a standard of value and for its application to the small knob on the sight of a gun. This appears as early as 1831, and gave rise to the expression "to draw a bead on" (from 1861 onward), which is rather a natural colloquialism than an example of true slang.

The common *bean* is not only employed in the colloquial or slang phrases "not to know beans" (from 1833) and "to amount to beans" (from 1876), but also enters into a number of distinctively American compounds, as *bean-blow, bean-patch, bean-hole, bean-shooter, bean-tree* (the catalpa) and *bean-vine*. So far, these have not been found earlier than the nineteenth century. . . .

It was inevitable that the *bear* should acquire a place in American life which it could not have in England, and consequently that from the seventeenth century onward an increasing number of new terms appear, *bear* being freely prefixed to such words as *bacon, chowder, dance* (among the Indians), *dog, fat, grass, hunt, hunter, hunting, meat, sign* (traces or tracks), *skin, steak, trap*, and *wallow*.

Such terms, if used by English writers, could only refer to other countries; in America they arose naturally out of the experiences of ordinary life. On the other hand the Stock Exchange in London was in operation earlier than that of New York, and the use of *bear* to designate a speculator for a fall in stocks, not recorded as current here before 1800, was merely carried over from England, where it is as old as 1744.

The noun *beat* developed several new senses in this country, of which the most natural is "the track of a wild animal." Others belong to the category of slang, as where one declares that he has never seen or heard "the beat of that"; when a reporter gets in with earlier news than a rival, or when the word denotes a broken-down loafer.

All of these are inventions of the nineteenth century, but the corresponding verb took on a special sense at the very beginning of the colonization, that of pounding corn into meal. That this was something of a task is shown by the records of Maryland, where in 1661 a prisoner was sentenced "to be kept in chaynes and beat his own bread."

Recent uses, like those of the noun, are mainly colloquial or slang, as in "to beat one's way," "to beat one to it," "to beat it" (make off), or "to beat up" (beat severely). A puzzling formation from this base is the colloquial or dialect adjective which from 1833 onward appears in the varying forms *beatemest, beatomest, beatermest, beatenest*, and *beatinest*, with the meaning of "superlative."

Like the bear, the *beaver* was an animal unknown to the ordinary inhabitant of Britain, but well known to the Colonist. Hence the word plays a great part in the early American vocabulary, frequently denoting not the animal itself but its most valuable part, the pelt or fur. Its industry gave rise to the familiar phrase "to work like a beaver," which is at least as old as 1741, while "busy as a beaver," "mad as a beaver," and others appear at later dates. Like the bear also, the beaver lent its name to the formation of many compounds, some very early as *beaver-dam, -meadow, -pond* and *beaver-coatskin,* to which at least a dozen more in common use were added in the course of time. Most of these were not wanted in England, although the *beaver-hat* had been known there from the time of Chaucer. . . .

Three special senses of the verb *to bed* are typical of successive developments in the new country. Forestry is represented by bedding a tree, that is, preparing a place for it to fall when cut down, evidenced in 1792. Agriculture gives rise to the sense of plowing ground in beds, as for cotton from at least 1830, and finally in the same century, to "*bed down cattle*" becomes one of the tasks of the cowboy, while the place where this is done becomes their "*bed-ground.*"

Even the noun *bed* has some significance in its compounds. *Bed-chamber* and *bed-cord* survived longer (the latter much longer) in common use than they did in England. *Bed-spread* is clearly of American origin (from about 1845), and so apparently are *bed-clothing* and *bed-quilt.* One of the most noticeable of the new formations is *bed-rock,* known in its original mining sense as early as 1850.

The *bee* was actually unknown in the country until introduced by the settlers; one writer records that the Indians had no name for it and called it "the Englishman's fly." Yet the word enters into compounds unknown in England, as *bee-gum, bee-hunt, -hunting, bee-martin, bee-range, bee-tree.* The acceptance of *bee-line* as a natural term for a straight line is an interesting example of American influence on English, which on the other hand has not accepted the equivalent *air-line.*

Although the *beech* is a tree well known in England, as in the United States, various attributive uses of it are significant of the different history of the two countries. The first settlers found that tracts of land were commonly characterized by different kinds of trees and, naturally, began to distinguish them by the names of these, as *cedar-swamp.*

In England there was less opportunity or need for similar designations, consequently the origin and currency of such terms as *beech-bottom, -flat, -ground, -land, -ridge, -swamp* are distinctively American. The geographical range of the tree may account for the fact that none of these appears to be earlier than 1770.

An everyday word like *beef* might be expected to have a parallel history in the two countries, but this is far from being the case. The old plural *beeves* for "oxen" may still be used in English, but the singular in this sense is obsolescent and the plural *beefs* unknown, while both are still common in American use. More remarkable, however, is the extent to which the word has been used to form attributive compounds unknown or unfamiliar in England. Thus, an animal reared for the purpose of providing beef becomes a *beef-animal, beef-cow, beef-creature, beef-ox,* or, collectively, *beef-cattle, beef-stock.*

In spite of possibilities, American English has been very little influenced by German; *beer-garden* (1870) and *beer-soup* (1789), however, are clearly from that source. On the other hand, *beer-fountain* and *beer-saloon* appear to be of native origin. . . .

The creation of new colloquial phrases is one of the points in which American English has excelled; many of them are so expressive and concise that, once introduced, their place in the language is assured. One of these happy inventions is the new use of *begin*, which thus makes its appearance in 1833, and was no doubt in use for some years before that. "The one in Bleecher Street cost ten thousand dollars, and that does not begin to be so expensive as that."

A less usual, though not uncommon, type of Americanism is the verb *belittle*, first used by Jefferson in 1782 (quoting an opinion of Buffon) in the literal sense of "to make smaller," and apparently not employed in its modern sense of "to depreciate," "minimize," until fifty years later. The number of literary Americanisms is really greater than is commonly known, and not a few have been accepted by English writers without any suspicion as to their place of origin.

Attributive uses of *bell* are frequent in English, but the American speaker has been able to increase the number by adding *bell-boy, bell-cord* (a bell-pull), *bell-crown* (of a hat), and *bell-crowned*, and the *bell-punch* of a conductor. A *bell-button* was popular as a jacket button for some time during the nineteenth century, but the writers who mention it fail to explain exactly what it was. The use of a bell hung on an animal which serves to guide others, familiar in English from the fifteenth century in *bell-wether*, has in the West given rise to the new compounds *bell-horse, bell-mare, bell-mule* and *bell-cow*.

To *belong* has in English always been normally accompanied by the preposition *to*; a book belongs *to* a person or a library. It was left to American speakers to extend the use to indicate place instead of possession, so that a book may belong *in* a library, when that is the natural or appropriate place for it. "I have never known whether he belonged above or below," Fenimore Cooper wrote in 1821, perhaps the earliest example of this usage. Even the *below* in this sentence, meaning lower down on a river, exhibits rather an American than an English sense of the word.

Words of Indian origin are not really numerous in American English, though a score or more are familiar to all. With these, however, it is legitimate to class a few English words which are used to render Indian equivalents, and have a currency entirely due to that circumstance. Thus in Southern documents of the eighteenth century we find from this source a special use of *beloved*, in the phrases *beloved man*, for a white man who was a favorite with the Indians, *beloved ground*, and *beloved day* for Sunday.

The use of *belt* to denote a stretch of country, narrow in proportion to its length, was perhaps not American in origin, but is certainly so in frequency of use, both in its simple form and with defining additions, as *belt of timber*, the *cotton-belt* or *corn-belt, the black-belt,* &c. . . .

The enumeration of so many words of a practical character from a small portion of the alphabet should be sufficient to show that American English has a serious side, of more real importance than the lighter vein which is too frequently regarded as its main claim to attention. As the words beginning with BE are barely the hundredth part of those which make up the language, their number gives some idea of the extent to which English has grown in its new surroundings.

The task of tracing all this fresh growth involves the reading and excerpting of literary works, documents and writings of all kinds during the entire period, and selecting from these such material as is likely to be of value for the purpose.

So many Americanisms have already been identified by previous investigators, from Witherspoon and Pickering down to Thornton, that there is no chance of overlooking these. No one at all acquainted with their work would fail to note an earlier or instructive example of "bogus" or "caucus" or "Yankee," or any other of the many words which have attracted general attention and whose origin has been the subject of much discussion. But only systematic and extensive collecting will yield the evidence necessary to present the history of such words as have been dealt with in this article, prove the genuinely American character of the new uses to which they have been put and show the date at which they have become a part of the language.

For a large part of this vocabulary there is no need to search for origins; these are given in any ordinary dictionary. Etymologizing becomes necessary only when the new word has come from some foreign tongue without first passing through English or when it has no obvious parentage.

The best that can be done in many cases is to exhibit the earliest evidence which can be found and be content with uncertainty until, or unless, more light can be obtained. This may come unexpectedly and put an end to a long-debated question, as in the recent discovery of Captain William Lynch of Pittsylvania in Virginia as the undoubted originator of Lynch law.

American English has been steadily developing for the last three centuries, and many of its special features have been recognized for more than a hundred years. The full presentation of its history will in many respects exhibit it in a new light and give evidence of its importance not only for the country of its origin but for the wider area in which English is the ordinary tongue.   page 16/

from *Americanisms; The English of the New World*
by M. Schele De Vere
New York: Charles Scribner & Company, 1872

Politics

Schele De Vere

Congress holds its *sessions* after the precedent of the British Parliament; but the same term is applied in some of the States to special courts of justice, engaged in regulating merely local affairs, like the granting of licenses or the building of bridges. The members, who, after English precedent, are styled *Honorable,* but, with American fondness for titles, retain the prefix for life, here have, or try to get, the *floor,* in order to deliver their speeches. page 258/ These are said to be not unfrequently delivered for *Buncombe,* an expression which has made its way with a large number of American political terms to England, and is almost naturalized there. The imported term denotes there false sentiments in speaking, as pretended enthusiasm or fictitious sympathy. The term originated thus: "A grave member of the Lower House of Congress, from the venerable State of North Carolina, representing a district, which included the County of *Buncombe,* in which he resided, whose style of speaking produced the very common effect of driving the members from the Hall, was one day addressing the House, when, as usual, coughing and sneering commenced, and the members began leaving. He paused a while, and assured the House that there need be no uneasiness on their part, and that for himself it mattered not how many left, for he was not speaking to the House, but to *Buncombe.*" (Richmond *Compiler,* August 17, 1841.) Henceforth *Buncombe* became the generic name for any constituency, and politicians, who speak not on what interests their audience, but what may influence those who have chosen them as their representatives, are said to be *talking Buncombe.*

The work done by Members of Congress is very largely influenced by agents from without, and by certain established usages of their own. The former is collectively called the *Lobby,* a term which, originating in the German *Laube,* a bower or small summer-house, meant for many centuries nothing more than a small hall or entering-room, preceding a larger room. In America, the rooms and passages surrounding the hall, in which legislative bodies hold their meetings, soon monopolized the term, and in a short time the men who assembled there to exercise whatever outside pressure they could bring to bear upon the legislators, were themselves called the *Lobby.* All who had petitions to be page 259/ granted, contracts to be given, or favors of any kind to be bestowed, either went themselves or sent well-qualified agents to Washington, to *lobby* their cause, as it was called. . . .

The members themselves are apt to have some favorite project which allows them to appear generous while they act from a selfish motive; in that case they are said to have *an axe to grind.* The incorporation of a trading company, the chartering of a new railway, the renewal of a valuable patent — all such schemes are *axes to grind.* The term is attributed to J. K. Paulding, but occurs before his time in a newspaper sketch in the style of Benjamin Franklin's "Too much for your whistle." It introduces a boy, who was induced by a clever fiction to turn the grindstone for another man to *grind his axe.* (Professor S. S. Haldeman.) "Special legislation in behalf of private interests is one of the curses of this country, otherwise so blessed by the smiles of Divine Providence. The number of *axes* which are taken to the various State Capitols, to be *ground* at the public expense, is perfectly enormous." (New York *Tribune,* March 23, 1871.)

As many members are apt to be in the same position, parliamentary usage has established a system of *log-rolling,* as it is called, by which they engage to help each other mutually. The term is taken from the habit of *loggers,* in the great lumber regions of the Northern States, to help each other in the hardest work they have to perform — the rolling of their immense logs from the place where the tree has been felled, to the water on which they are to be floated down. Each *logging-camp* thus assists the others in accomplishing a work which would be beyond page 260/ the power of any single one. In like manner, one member of the legislative body, unable to command sufficient votes for his own purpose, says to another member in the same position: Vote for my bill and I will vote for your bill; and this is called *log-rolling*. . . .

In more recent times *log-rolling* has lost much of its former prestige, as now-a-days all schemes of importance are taken up and pushed through by *rings*, combinations made outside the House, by whose activity and ample means everything is prepared beforehand, and all interests are secured, before the matter is reached by the House. Men who are not in the ring, either from conscientious scruples or because they command no influence on the floor, are called *outsiders,* and are *left out in the cold. Wire-pulling* is not an American custom exclusively, as the figure of speech is as old as the Marionettes of Italy and France, on whose miniature stage the actors were set in motion by wires, which the exhibitor pulled from above; but *wire-working*, as it is also called, has probably reached a higher degree of perfection here than abroad. . . . Great skill in this art is facetiously called *sculduggery* in the West. *Pipe-laying,* on the contrary, is an original term here, derived from a fictitious and treacherous correspondence, which pretended to give an account of the method by which voters from Philadelphia were brought to the polls in page 261/ New York, while the fraudulent scheme was concealed under the form of a contract for the laying of water-pipes from the Croton Aqueduct. The whole scheme was first denounced by the press, then examined in Court, and discovered to have been devised purely for the purpose of casting odium upon a political party. It made, however, so deep an impression upon the public, that the term *pipe-laying* was at once incorporated in the dictionary of political terms and is still used to designate the employment of persons as voters, who are not entitled to vote, by fraudulent means. . . . page 262/

from *Publications of the Modern Language Association*, Vol. LXXII
March, 1956

Contraction and Expansion

Louise Pound

V

. . . What are some of our leading devices for reducing verbal length to the simpler? Most obvious perhaps is our phenomenally increased liking for substituting initials for naming in full. This practice greatly increased after World War I and it is now at its height. Many have commented on it. Tonight I have consciously said MLA instead of Modern Language Association of America. The designation of our society by capital letters only (it may now be written without periods) would hardly have been tolerated in a formal address by our founding fathers. The initials were introduced into the Merriam Webster Unabridged of 1909 by P. W. Long, who worked for Webster's before coming to us as our Secretary. Other dictionaries followed, and MLA is now a standard abridgment **page 8/** alongside COD, DAR, YMCA and the alphabetical flood ("alphabet soup") that came with the New Deal. To MLA and PMLA we may now add FL. The initials sharply distinguish it from its parent organization and give unity to the body of scholars and teachers hitherto scattered in place and effort and suffering from *apartheid*. Such groupings of capital letters do save the utterance of many syllables. If they are pronounceable they often pass into words, as radar (radio detecting and ranging). The learned name for such coinages is acronyms; a popular designation, I think, might well be initialisms. AWOL and SHAPE are other examples. Later dictionaries recognize that AWOL need not always be capitalized but may be "awol." ACTH may go the same way. NATO and SNAFU may be pronounced as words. For GI only initials appear. One never hears "Ji." A. W. Read has shown us that the initials OK were floated in New York City in a presidential campaign of 1840. Often the written words "okay," or "okeh" are preferred. VIP exists as initials only, but UNESCO and UNRRA are spoken as words. Recall too the wartime WACS and WAVES and the English WRENS. One sympathizes with the now classic old lady who complained, "At that distance I could not see whether she was a WAC or a WAVE or a SPAM."

Another factor in the trend toward shrinkage for acceleration is no doubt the influence of the sound films. In these the quantity of words needs watching as much as in a ten-word telegram. Contributing too are the daily telegraphic headlines for the hurried reader. These must be fitted into available space and as a consequence short words, preferably striking ones, are favored. To this we owe the stock ascendancy of tot for child, cops for police, sleuth, graft, loot, and blast for inveigh against. Orb saves two letters over world. Many picturesque locutions such as sob sister, brain washing, trust buster save space effectively. Passing mention only may be made of our tendency to curtail longer words by suppressing initial, medial, or final syllables. No doubt this has always been with us but it gains rather than loses in popularity. To it we owe such abridgments as phone, auto, cab, wiz, gym, Yank. Jefferson may never have appeared in print as Tom but Ike and Winnie are overworked. I have been told that Chi-Coms and Chi-Nats for Chinese communists and nationalists are popular abbreviations in the Pentagon and elsewhere as time-saving.

An especially familiar method of lessening wordage, impossible to overlook, is our contemporary addiction to condensing expression by welding or agglutination. Words are merged, usually leaving their elements distinguishable. This is a stock device in the coining of trade-names. Amalgam trade-names are now thick as Vallombrosa leaves. New devices, gadgets, fabrics, whatnot appear in vast quantities and they have to be **page 9/** named. Sciences such as chemistry, medicine, sociology, psychology have long created new designations by joining elements involved. When I printed *Blends; Their Relation to English Word-Formation* as far back as 1914, such formations appeared only occasionally, mostly in the wake of Lewis Carroll's coinages such as "chortle," chuckle and snort, "galumphing," galloping and triumphing. Now the device is wildly overworked. The lid is off. A first impulse when a name is to be found for something new is to fall back on conflation. "Conoco" saves many syllables from Continental Oil Company. "Quink" makes a one-syllable name for quick-drying ink. "Vegemato" explains itself. In film and theatrical advertising have appeared such striking and none-too-admirable formations as "stupeficent (stupendous and magnificent), and "magnossal" (magnificent and colossal). "Chicagorilla" and terpsicorker" catch the attention readily. A certain highly paid columnist uses this device to the limit, hoping, I suppose, to both daze and faze.

Telescoped formations are coined on higher levels also. They do not always emerge from informal or casual usage or from attempts to arrest attention by departing from the accepted. Dignified circles do not ban them. We are familiar with Benelux, the coined name of an economic union of Belgium, the Netherlands, and Luxemburg. The formation is acceptable to most persons. It sounds impressive and its first syllable and its last give it something of the dignity of Latinity. Newspapers of the post-war period told of another economic union proposed on the model of Benelux but not carried out, that of France and Italy, to be termed Fritalux. Such a name might have been enough to kill it. Next the Scandinavian nations and England were said at one time to be pondering seriously an economic union to be named Uniscan. Sir Stafford Cripps, I think it was, said in a published item that the name should be Ukiscan (United Kingdom). Neither was accepted. The agglutinated Scandanglia, more intelligible, was suggested by the London *Times*, probably in a spirit of spoof. Before our two wars the proposal of such welded names would have been impossible.

Also not to be overlooked as contributing to verbal shrinkage is the tendency of our time for speech itself to give way to pictures. Picture writing was the primitive means of communication. We revive it as quicker in delivering its message than voice or print. We grow used to thin lines of type, mere trickles of explanation, below or about a photograph. Pictures of all types, dispensing with as much language as may be, face us on billboards and in magazines and are conspicuous features of advertisements. They are supposed to draw immediate attention to what is advertised and they probably do. Thus printed and auditory speech are economized on as though words were obstacles to communi- **page 10/** cation. To educationalists they are time savers, for many learn more quickly from them than from print or speech. The visual helps of maps and charts and photographs play an increasingly larger role. No doubt too the vogue of the pictorial has been helped by the growth by leaps and bounds of amateur photography, and has been helped yet more by the cinema.

I have heard it predicted that such verbal curtailments as the familiar and easily uttered "gotta," "hafta," "wanta" will ultimately find acceptance as standard much as "onto," "always," "already," have agglutinated in the past, with "alright" well on its way. To many this may seem hardly likely; yet their increasing use by cartoonists, radio speakers, and writers of the vernacular in fiction familiarize them more and more. Another tendency, namely the determined mauling of words, deserves passing attention. There have always been word-manipulations for humorous purposes, or amusing folk-etymological formations or dialectal perversions. We go far beyond these now. Our contemporary mutilations of standard words by professional columnists and humorists and by advertisers — this in order to arrest attention, or to give an effect of *grotesquerie,* or to startle through weird spellings — owes much to a New York City character Sime (Simon) Silverman, for a time the editor of the magazine *Variety.* Originally writing ordinary humdrum English, he moved on to a fresh eccentric type of word treatment. It was taken up by his assistants and by disciples such as Winchell. *Time* too and the *New Yorker* have sometimes manipulated standard expressions, compressing for space saving or for accelerated tempo but on a higher plane even when launching blends (cinemaniacs, intelligentsiacs, ballyhooligans). In general will not the weird spellings, eccentric syntax, whimsicalities, distortions, acrobatic flourishes of speech of our word-maulers and would-be humorists of today ultimately grow stale and fade? In any case they give most of us acidosis of the esprit. The exception is Ogden Nash. "It is strange," to quote from a Hollywood magnate, "what some authors auth."

The effects on our prose today of these devices for lessening wordage are not always admirable. The old repose is out of date, transformed into prose that speeds and jerks. Our rhythms are those of talk, fast, raucous, emphatic, fitting the pace of modern life.

What will become of our linguistic heritage if we continue indefinitely our addiction to departing from the established? Will it go the way of one phase of it, Poetry, which seems now to bypass the beautiful in pursuit of the arresting? Or of present-day Art, which also seems to have lost its sensitivity to the beautiful in quest of the striking or the grotesque? **page 11/**

VI

Alongside and in contrast with the trend toward trenchancy, condensation, compression, abridgment — the extreme reached in the substitution of pictures for language — there exists of course the opposite trend. This is the tendency toward elaboration and expansion, to enhance exactness, precision, perhaps sometimes merely to be impressive. This appears in the technical language of many fields, witness the jargons of science, nuclear phenomena, aviation, education, philology too. Since it comes oftenest into our horizon, the technical jargon of educationists attracts especial critical attention. Law, however, though it is said to have been somewhat simplified of late, is probably the worst offender as regards attenuated expression. From law, I think, derives the language of the Pentagon. As we know, official language tends toward impressive elaboration. A large envelope becomes a brief case, a brief case a portfolio, a portmanteau. In official jargon food becomes units of nutritional intake, the poor are the underprivileged or those in lower income brackets. To mend or revive is to recondition, rehabilitate, reactivate. To an educator of high status a baby sitter is the custodial supervisor of juvenile activities and recreation. All is not literature that litters but there is considerable litter about our official language as there is about professional jargons in general. We have cause to know that in an endeavor to be explicit or impressive, officialese is sometimes expanded to the point of being unintelligible. I have often heard Gertrude Stein accused of being unintelligible. I found her title "Tender Buttons" unintelligible. But on occasion she is brief and as lucid as sunshine compared to writers of officialese. Listen to her words on the money question. "The money is always there but the pockets change; it is not in the same pockets after a change, and that is all there is to say about money." **page 12/** . . . .

from *Variety: The Magazine of Show Business*

January 6, 1960

The 'Variety' of Language

Primer on the Workaday VARIETY Style in News Writing and Editing — Do-It-Yourself Lexicon for Beginners

Abel Green

Always a newspaperman's newspaper, *Variety* made no fuss, with rare exceptions, when big city and hinterland columnists and writers helped themselves. Credits have more than equalized in *Variety's* favor. It is because of this generous cross-fertilization of trade terms into the dailies that many a lay reader digs headlines in the dailies about "pix" that "click" and do 35G biz, and femme stars loaded with "s.a" who are "socko" at the "b.o." . . .

Writing what comes naturally to *Variety* staffers, an "ozoner" becomes a ready-made synonym for a drive-in, chiefly because of its variation in language, much as *Variety* some years back coined "whisperlow" as a substitute for speakeasy, and Mazda Lane as an alternative for Great White Way. Similarly, the term "hard-top" is useful to describe the conventional covered theatre (as against the drive-in). When Maria Callas creates a hub-bub at the Met Opera it becomes "Callasthenics." A story about income-tax devices in Hollywood reads LOOK, MA, I'M A CORPORATION.

Variety editors are congenital punsters. It's the fun part of the job that makes for punny reading. Here are some samples:

PEEL WILL RING AGAIN AT VEGAS' THUNDERBIRD refers to the strippers (peelers). The sparkling tv salute to the late Manie Sacks is captioned A MANIE-SPLENDORED THING. A kilted Scotch tenor who is boffo b.o. in his hoot-mon homeland is heralded ROBT. WILSON KILTS 'EM IN SCOTLAND. The NBC brass on the convention bandwagon are captioned NBC BAND-AIDES. When a certain diskery plots a bullmarket recording spree it is headlined DALE RECORDS IN AN UP-&-ETCH 'EM BEAT.

A film gross headline is completely clear to the initiates: ANCIENTS' HISTORY: ALMIGHTY TODD 37G, 53d; DEMILLE THOU SHALLS 32½G, 10th. (This was when Todd's "80 Days" and DeMille's "10 Commandments" were concurrent boxoffice champions). Anybody hip to pop music-makers needs no interpretation of TEA-GARDEN OF AUG. MOON (OR HOW SEXTET BROUGHT DIXIE TO ORIENT). Or the story datelined Frankfurt, REICH CATS & JAMMERS FETE SET FOR JUNE 7–10.

Film or legit gross stories lend themselves to plays on the slanguage. 'CAMILLE' COUGHED AWAY ONLY $7,000 OFF-BROADWAY is as clear as 'FLOWER' DRUMMING UP BIG LOOT SONG AT B.O.

PENNSY CENSORS TURN IN PENCILS means only one thing — the blue laws have been kayoed. In turn, influenced by other wordsters, a story about Gonzales-Gonzales and two competing Perez Prado brothers in the jazz field emerges captioned GERT STEIN WOULD HAVE HAD SOME PICNIC-PICNIC WITH THESE NAMES-NAMES. A story about a gambling license inspires GREENLIGHT FOR GREENFELT.

Sometimes a classic head is worth a retake. PITT CAUGHT WITH ITS PLANTS DOWN (when unseasonal heat caught the Pittsburgh exhibitors without their cooling systems) echoes a decade later as TV CAUGHT WITH PILOTS DOWN, this time referring to the shortage of vidpix pilot scripts. MOOLA FOLLOWS HULA AS 50TH STATE JUMPS means that, with Hawaii's statehood, tourism is up.

Proper names are automatic fodder to the head-writing punsters. GBC' boffo b.o. gives rise to SHAWMANSHIP. Actor Donald Crisp's hearty homecoming in his native Scotland is captioned TOASTING CRISP. When Ralph Bellamy shifts roles from Roosevelt to Thomas Jefferson, out comes SUNRISE AT MONTICELLO. Of course the two headlines of greatest quotation are now very old hat to staffers — to wit WALL STREET LAYS AN EGG and STICKS NIX HICK PIX.

Coinages

Variety has long been identified with telescoped coinages, and news events spark new ones. Its long-ago origination disk jockey became deejay, and when a femme platter-chatterer got on the air it was natural to caption her a "deejane." The formal master of ceremonies evolved into emcee; a distaff m.c. becomes femcee. Globallyhoo describes the recent trend for international publicity. A gent may be billed the veep in charge of public affairs but he's a "puffair" in *Variety*. Even when used for the first time, the readers usually get the message.

If hi-fi is what it is, then hi-si (for high society) and ci-fi (for science-fiction) is just as clear. J. Arthur Rank's attempt to click in the U.S. distribution market becomes RANK-YANK. Shows appealing to both juveniles and grownups are labeled "kidult" and a few questions get asked.

There are occasional and unconscious rebellions against the trite but true, and thus yesteryear's stripper becomes peeler.

Occasionally directives go forth for staffers and correspondents to lay-off some overly used term like "hypo" or "admish." Convenience coins many words.

Old films kept off tv are "vaulties." Thumbing old issues turns up "chowmein-ery" and "the oo-long circuit," alternately "the fried-rice belt." When Japanese jazz pianist Tohsiko Akiyosha played Boston, *Variety* captioned it HIP NIP IN HUB. (Of late, Jap and Nip are tabu, because of sensitivities expressed to the paper in vox pop form). Nearly all racial nicknames were long ago erased but geography expresses itself in Aussie or Anzac, hoot-mon or the auld-lang syne country; Volga belt or the steppes; fandango, carioca or cha-cha-cha locale, as the case may be, etc.

Then there are geographical juxtapositions which write their own heads, viz., YUGO B.O. SRO VIA WORD-OF-SATCHMOUTH. Or, another instance, MOSCOW EXPO-SOCKO B.O. King Hussein's kingsize bed at the White House comes out AND SO TO BEDOUIN.

Or when MGM Records is rushing out "Ben-Hur" albums, the same idea of punny caption tells it best: MGM'S IN-A-'HUR'-RY DISKS.

Modified simplified spelling is Style, viz., cigaret, brunet, soubret, but not thru, tho, nor even $15–Mil., or the Time-style $2 million; all the ciphers are preferred in $15,000,000 and $2,000,000, excepting where headwriting sometimes compels the contractions. Autobiog, prez, veepee are run-of-the-mine usages.

Actually *Variety* is quite circumspect, betimes almost prissy, when it comes to earthier language. No hells or damns. She may be a pushover, a B-girl, a prostie, a femme du pave, a joy-girl or round-heels, but nothing rougher. The breed may be a "shim," a limp-wrist, soprano-hipped set, and even AC–DC, but nothing stronger than that for the third sex. "Panze" and "pansy" are tabu.

In other orbits readers will recognize: out-fronters, hand-to-hand music (applause), hoofology, legmania, moujiks or peasants, silo circuit, barnyard Belascos, strawhats, citronella circuit, el foldo, plushery, posh spots, gimmick, Poverty Row, a Charles Addams (ghoulish), canary, Yanqui (for Latin-American parlance), Steinwaying, 88er (pianist), biopic, vidpic, telepic, oater, sage-brusher, mesquiter, they-went-that-awayer, torso-tosser (cooch-dancer), ofay (interracial).

Part of the Lexicon

Tin Pan Alley knows exactly what "the Brill Bldg. set" means as it does when terms like these are used: demo, biscuit, platter, payola, "cool," hip (nee hep), P.D. (public domain), thrush, belter, chirp, chantootsie bary, combo, group, dansapation, terper, "race" records (now obsolete), "the beat," waffle, r&b, r&r, billies, cornballs, cut-in, d.j., deejay, platter-chatter, "Lady Day," Der Bingle, j.d. (juvenile delinquency), BG, "Pops" (Whiteman), TD, "Uncle Nick," "Patty poem" the Groaner, sweater-levi set, record hops, pubbery, EP, ET, LP, 33–45–78rpm, "10 Downing St." (Lindy's).

The sudden public discovery in 1959 of "payola," a time dishonored Tin Pan Alley term, inspired the AP to get an "official" translation from *Variety*, and wonder about the "ola" part of it. Cuffola, torchola, boffola were explained. From that came frequently utilized *Variety* terms, such as foldo, el foldo, a fold-eroo.

More Varietyisms: Doing a Boone (scouting talent), borscht circuit, freeloader, juve, gabber, inside stuff, bellylaff, looker (for beauty), depresh, admish, fil-musical, exhib, distrib, org, burly (burlesk), grunter, rassler or grunt 'n' groaner (for wrestler), authored, jetted, Pan-Amed, TWA'd, Superchiefed, sickniks (for the new crop of neo-beatnik "sick" comedians). Although outlawed in current style sheet megger (for film director) keeps bobbing up even though the mega-phone technique of film direction went out of style, circa 1927, with the talkers.

"Nitery" once inspired the late drama critic John Anderson to observe that if *Variety* calls a night club a nitery what is a dairy?"

Chauvinistic guardian of its own intra-trade loyalties, *Variety* will, on occasion, let the world know that when Rita Hayworth married Aly Khan or when Grace Kelly married Prince Ranier III, femmes were "film stars"; their grooms simply "non-pros." **page 12/**

from *The Progressive*, Vol. XXIII
August, 1959

Madison Avenue's Ring-Tailed Roarers

C. Merton Babcock

Anyone with half an ear for linguistic nuances will detect in the commercial hyperbole emanating from Madison Avenue these days distinct echoes of frontier extravagance and backwoods vigorosity. For example, in a word like *fabuluscious*, which is an adman's recent coinage, one can note the same superlative quality, the same explosive outburst of roaring rowdyism apparent in such Westernisms as *scallywampus* or *expolagolluscious*. In both cases there is a lusty wolf-call of impetuous indecorum, a sort of wayward unrefinement and swaggering magniloquence.

The frontiersman, or backwoods screamer, bolstered his morale in the face of unknown terrors by splitting the firmament right down the middle and setting the Mississippi on fire with words like *spizarinctum*, *exflunctificate*, *absquatulate*, and *bolwoggoly*. Just so, the modern word-spinner knocks whole populations for a lula-kapoodler with slambangerisms like *fantabulastic*, *kebobanana*, and *jet-jamboree*.

The ideological meaning of these words is, of course, unimportant. The noise is the thing, the phoneto-semantic impact, the commotionality, the blood-pressure-raising potency. Words with strong acoustical reverberations are more purse-pick-acious than mere pantomimic locutions. *Aqua*, for example, is employed as though it were some magic ingredient like chlorophyll. Tone magic or sound witchery is clearly evident in *lickety-split*, *zippo*, *wisk*, *swirl*, and *plum-luscious*. Sonorous hues and tinkling aromas make strong multiple-sensory appeals: "a serenade in fragrance," "flying, reckless, madcap colors" — fizzy pinks, whirly blues, breezy yellows.

Razzle-dazzlement is another characteristic of tall talk, both varieties. Shockingly ribald effects are gained by upsetting established verbal patterns and by offending phonetic rules of decency. *Hogglebumgullop* is certainly a fugitive from linguistic justice. *Spandangalous* is a shotgun marriage of *spangle* and *dangle. Sockdologer* is outright blasphemy. *Deluscious, dish-appear, sale-a-bration, smileage,* and *slasharama* are the infamous results of premeditated linguicide.

The roaring commercial is in so many respects similar to its frontier counterpart that, given a locution out of context, one would be hard put to determine to which class it rightly belongs. *Scrumptious* appears in both vocabularies. *Glycohenphene,* which sounds for all the world like a miracle drug, is a legendary reptile with red legs, a yellow body, and blue scales along its backbone. *Neoquadrin,* on the other hand, is not a deep-sea monster, but a throat lozenge. *Hyclorothene* is a fabulous creature from the natural history of folk nonsense, along with the *gilly-galoo* (a bird that lays square eggs), and the *glyptodont* (a ferocious variety of kangaroo).

A hi-fi-lutin' superexpressivity is made possible by what H. L. Mencken called "cacophonous miscegenation": the incessant piling up of high-voltage intensifiers on an already overburdened linguistic circuit. Thus *monstrous* becomes *monstropolous; firm* becomes *firmacious; ferocious* becomes *helliferocious;* and *totally* becomes *teetotally* and *teetotatiously.* In Adspeak, *extravagance* is boosted to *extravaganza; elegant* is blown up to *swellelegant; fabulous* is inflated to *fantabulastic.*

Such words are mere pikers as compared to the recent coinage, *colossafabulgreat,* which promises almost too much for the money. Perhaps someone will eventually erect a tower of babble that will all but touch the sky: *supercolossomagigargantitanibrobdingnagian.* If a thing like that ever got out of control it could tear up the earth from here to Jackson Hole and actually topple the Tetons. There is a smidgin of hope though. Remember Skippoweth Branch of Salt River fame? He swore no living mortal could ever match his yell. And then one night he screamed himself to death to show his spirit.   **page 17/**

11

THE SCHOOLMA'AM VERSUS THE PEOPLE

from "Introduction to the Second Series of Biglow Papers," in *The Complete Poetical Works of James Russell Lowell*

Boston and New York: Houghton, Mifflin and Company, 1896

Truly Masculine English

James Russell Lowell

. . . In choosing the Yankee dialect, I did not act without forethought. It had long seemed to me that the great vice of American writing and speaking was a studied want of simplicity, that we were in danger of coming to look on our monther-tongue as a dead language, to be sought in the grammar and dictionary rather than in the heart, and that our only chance of escape was by seeking it at its living sources among those who were, as Scottowe says of Major-General Gibbons, "divinely illiterate." President Lincoln, the only really great public man whom these latter days have seen, was great also in this, that he was master — witness his speech at Gettyburg — of a truly masculine English, classic, because it was of no special period, and level at once to the highest and lowest of his countrymen. I learn from the highest authority that his favorite reading was in Shakespeare and Milton, to which, of course, the Bible should be added. But whoever should read the debates in Congress might fancy himself present at a meeting of the city council of some city of Southern Gaul in the decline of the Empire, where barbarians with a Latin varnish emulated each other in being more than Ciceronian. Whether it be want of culture, for the highest outcome of that is simplicity, or for whatever reason, it is certain that very few American writers or speakers wield their native language with the directness, precision, and force that are common as the day in the mother country. We use it like Scotsmen, not as if it belonged to us, but as if we wished to prove that we belong to it, by showing our intimacy with its written rather than its spoken dialect. And yet all the while our popular idiom is racy with life and vigor and originality, bucksome (as Milton used the word) to our new occasions, and proves itself no mere graft by sending up new suckers from the old root in spite of us. It is only from its roots in the living generations of men that a language can be reinforced with fresh vigor for its needs; what may be called a literate dialect grows ever more and more pedantic and foreign, till it becomes at last as unfitting a vehicle for living thought as monkish Latin. That we should all be made to talk like books is the danger with which we are threatened by the Universal Schoolmaster, who does his best to enslave the minds and memories of his victims to what he esteems the best models of English composition, that is to say, to the writers whose style is faultily correct and has no blood-warmth in it. No language after it has faded into *diction,* none that cannot suck up the feeding juices secreted for it in the rich mother-earth of common folk, can bring forth a sound and lusty book. True vigor and heartiness of phrase do not pass from page to page, but from man to man, where the brain is kindled and the lips supplied by downright living interests and by passion in its very throe. Language is the soil of thought, and our own especially is a rich leaf-mould, the slow deposit of ages, the shed foliage of feeling, fancy, and imagination, which has suffered an earth-change, that the vocal forest, as Howell called it, may clothe itself anew with living green. There is death in the dictionary; and, where language is too strictly limited by convention, the ground for expression to grow in is limited also; and we get a *potted* literature, Chinese dwarfs instead of healthy trees. . . . **page 443/**

from *Review of Reviews,* Vol. XCV
March, 1937

Stepchildren of the Mother Tongue

Walter Barnes

We need to define and develop in America a style of language which is more natural, idiomatic, and comfortable.

The schools, from the elementary grades clear through the college, have accepted and have done their best to teach the formal expository writing style as the usual, the regular mode of expression and communication. Conventional propriety has been played up as the highest virtue, breaking the "laws" of grammar looked upon as the lowest crime. Even when the schools have given a little grudging attention to oral language, they have regarded this dignified, straitlaced, ultra-correct writing dialect as the desirable manner in speech.

Texts in grammar and rhetoric, hand-books of usage, courses of study, all the traditions and the machinery of the schools have stressed the necessity of knowing the rules and sticking to them. Pedants and purists have fussed and fumed about so many small points and trivial distinctions, have passed so many linguistic blue laws that to most people English has seemed a maze of prescriptions, cautions, and negations. To watch your step has seemed more important than going places, to observe the table etiquette of language more important than having something to eat.

Other lovers of conformity have ganged up with the schools. Certain correspondence courses, two or three magazines on "correct language," a number of radio announcers, occasional editorials and letters to the editor add to the impression that language is a ritual of formal conventions, prim manners, and genteel observances.

Language is a mode of individual and social behavior, of personal and group conduct. People who are by temperament dignified, staid, and highhat, who go in for fine manners and correctness at any cost, will naturally prize conventionality in language: it's their kind of game, it's down their alley. But no one has appointed or anointed these gentry to be the custodians of our language, the judges of what is good, the arbiters of usage and taste. Hair-splitters, gerund-grinders, fuss-budgets are surely not the wisest teachers and safest leaders in language, or in any kind of human behavior.

The style of language most effective is that which is most appropriate on the specific occasion. Sometimes the occasion calls for formal, careful, meticulously proper language. But for most of the circumstances of life the desirable style is the informal, easy style of conversation, the pleasant, acceptable American vernacular. Particularly does this apply in this present generation, which in all its ways and manners, in dress, etiquette, and behavior is casual and easygoing.

Surely, we need to define and develop and to use a style of language which is more natural, idiomatic, and comfortable.

The conventionalists in language rely upon several lines of defense. Perhaps their strongest one is composed of "rules" of grammar. One must not say, for example, "It is *me*," because this violates the rule "the copulative verb is followed by the nominative form of the pronoun." But that so-called rule has no regulatory powers. Like all such statements, it has validity only insofar as it is a true generalization from all the facts.

The facts concerning the case of "It is *me*" are: 1. This expression is in accepted use in informal situations. 2. It is preferable to "It is *I*" whenever the speaker wishes to emphasize his own personal identity. It is so used and has been so used by dozens of reputable writers from Shakespeare to the present, including such men as Emerson, Meredith, and Stevenson. 3. So far as

page 60/

anyone knows, it has been in good colloquial use for three or four centuries, though for most of that time, the grammarians have been grumbling about it. 4. Many careful, sensitive speakers and writers employ both "It is *me*" and "It is *I*," depending on the desired shade of meaning.

Why, then, have the grammarians got so hot and bothered over "It is *me*"? Because, no doubt, they have "made up their minds" (a revealing phrase!) that this "rule" concerning the copulative verb and the nominative case does represent *nearly all* the facts; that it is a neat, handy, general statement; that since the language is nicer and tidier when usages are made to conform to such rules, therefore "It is *I*" is the right form. By such reasoning "It is *me*" seems to be a mistake, a lapse from a proper standard.

Many people, it would appear, assume that the language once had an ideal grammar-structure which has been debased by illiterates. Study of the language, from old English to the present, reveals nothing of the sort. It does show a peeling off of inflectional forms, but that change has given the language ease and springliness. And at every such simplification the contemporary grammarians groaned and warned. The history of the English language can be visualized as a continued though irregular war between the people, generally including the literary artists, in one army, and the grammarians in the other. And the grammarians, though victors in a few skirmishes, have never won a pitched battle.

page 61/ . . . .

from *Harper's Magazine*, Vol. CXXXV
June, 1917

Our Upstart Speech

Robert P. Utter

. . . If we grant slang its metaphor, and assume, as we safely may, its democracy, we have advanced by two axioms toward the problem of it; that there is a problem few who have to do with slang either as producers or consumers will be disposed to deny. If we put these axioms in relation with two propositions which seem mutually exclusive, there may be generated light that will enable us to see the problem steadily and see it whole. This hope we may have, too, with no fear of ever reaching the deadly finality of an answer. The two propositions are: first, slang is a principle of decay in language; second, slang is a principle of growth in language.

About the first, any schoolma'am can tell us. When Johnny in the "English" class declares that "Claudio gave Hero an awful bawling out in the church when they went to get married," she will, unless she knows more than most of her kind about Shakespeare's own use of slang, expatiate on the decay of the language (due to slang) since the poet fixed its standard of purity. She will show that slang indicates lack on the user's part of both vocabulary and ideas, and that if Johnny persists in using it he will have neither, and that if all the Johnnies use it, both will disappear from the face of the earth. Very likely she looks to some authority who says, "Slang is the great corrupting matter; it is perishable itself, and corrupts what is round it." She draws the obvious inference, and deals with such slang as comes under her jurisdiction as if any one using it or countenancing it were in a conspiracy against the bone and sinew of the language. But Johnny thinks he knows a bit about slang himself. "Oh, piffle!" he mutters under his breath; he would say it aloud if he could quote the words of the sage who says, "Slang may be called almost the only living language." Johnny is less articulate; he only "has a hunch" that slang is always to be encouraged because it is the language of the future, and that any one who tries to suppress it is "standing right in front of the band-wagon."

Most of us agree with both Johnny and the teacher and are not troubled by the paradox, for it lies at the very heart of our democracy, and we believe that that heart beats true. We look on with "keen untroubled face" (our own idiom phrases it less academically) while Mr. Kipling points out to his puzzled country-men the paradoxes of our democracy. We are "hedged with alien speech" he tells them, and "flout the law we make," never ceasing the while to "make the law we flout." Of our language we may fairly imagine Englishmen thinking, as one of them is said to have spoken, of the city of New York — "It will be wonderful when it is finished." We in our turn look to the other side of the Atlantic and think we notice that most things that are finished are dead. With our own poet (Mrs. Piatt) we see "a waste of grave-dust, stamped with crown and crest," and we are content to be still growing. Whatever the inconveniences of our paradoxes and crudities in language, and there are many, they are not morbid symptoms.

Order and uniformity in language are desirable qualities; we should and do seek them ever. We may have them when we are willing to pay the price, but the price is one which Americans are unwilling to pay. Its name is aristocracy. We believe in the principle of civilian control. If we were willing to hand over our language to some imperial council or royal academy we might have in it the same system and efficiency that, for example, the Germans have, which is all that is humanly possible, a fixed standard of correctness, follow it who may. But we Americans are apt to resent even the implication of aristocracy implied in some of the objections often raised to our free and easy way of handling English. "The King's English" our critics sometimes call it, as if the king were defender of the language no less than of the faith; as if it were a possession of his which he had graciously lent his people for their use, not abuse. They in turn imply proprietary rights in it when they express anxiety for its fate page 67/ in our irreverent hands. And even among ourselves there is a small group who seem at times to claim special privilege. Professors, school-teachers, pedants, and many arbiters of taste, may now and then be caught in the act of commenting on language as if they owned it. Every man, be he king, peasant, or emperor, owns just so much of the language as he wields power over. . . . But the more one observes the ways of language the more is one inclined to believe that neither demagogue, pedagogue, king, critic, nor any law but its own has any measurable effect on it. Man-made laws affect it very much as engineering works affect the Mississippi River. If the engineers creep up when the river isn't looking and put in a sincere piece of work that harmonizes with natural forces, it may last for a time. Such work is very much like trying to "change a law of nature by Act of Congress," and so is any decree in regard to language. . . . Laws come and go, but language goes on forever. . . .

Now, if the matter were as simple as voting "yes" or "no" on a single proposition, we could understand it easily enough. A vote might not count more than a grain of sand in a ton, but at least each voter would know that he had contributed one millionth of one per cent. **page 68/** to a result, and would know within a lifetime what the result was. But how is it with language? We have a hundred million voters each voting every day and all day, and each voting for a different thing. If we think of a deliberative body of fifty men proceeding under parliamentary rules to some action, each wanting something slightly different from anything wanted by any of the others, we can easily imagine that not one, or at most not more than one, will be satisfied with the action of the whole body. Multiply the number by a million or two and remove all parliamentary rules, and you have a figure that might serve to show the status of the "science" of language. Language is a resultant we cannot hope to calculate, from a composition of forces so intricate we cannot trace it. . . . Attempts to modify language deliberately are like eugenics, which is faultless in theory, and works beautifully on guinea-pigs. . . . **page 69/**

from *The American Scholar*, Vol. XXI
Summer, 1952

Our National Mania for Correctness

Donald J. Lloyd

Every now and then the editors of the university presses let out a disgruntled bleat about the miserable writing done by scholars, even those who are expert in literary fields; and from time to time there are letters and editorials in our national reviews bewailing some current academic malpractice with the English language. At present, even PMLA (the Publications of the Modern Language Association), traditionally the repository of some of the worst writing done by researchers, is trying to herd its authors toward more lucid exposition. And at two recent meetings of the august Mediaeval Academy, one at Boston and one at Dumbarton Oaks, bitter remarks were passed about the failure of specialists in the Middle Ages to present their findings in some form palatable to the general reader, so that he can at least understand what they are writing about.

Even admitting that a really compelling style is the result of years of cultivation, much scholarly writing is certainly worse than it needs to be. But it is not alone in this. Generally speaking, the writing of literate Americans whose primary business is not writing but something else is pretty bad. It is muddy, backward, convoluted and self-strangled; it is only too obviously the product of a task approached unwillingly and accomplished without satisfaction or zeal. Except for the professionals among us, we Americans are hell on the English language. I am not in touch with the general run of British writing by non-professionals, but I suspect that it is nothing to make those islanders smug, either. page 283/

. . . Nevertheless, there is no question what makes our writing bad, or what we shall have to do to better it. We shall simply have to isolate and root out a monomania which now possesses us, which impedes all language study and inhibits all mastery of our native tongue — all mastery, that is, on paper; for as speakers of English, we Americans are loving and effective cultivators of our expression. I recall the gas station attendant who was filling my car. The gasoline foamed to the top of the tank, and he shut off the pump. "Whew!" I said, "that nearly went over." "When you see white-caps," he replied, "you better stop." "You better had," I said, lost in admiration. But if you had given him a pencil, he would have chewed the end off before he got one word on paper.

The demon which possesses us is our mania for correctness. It dominates our minds from the first grade to the graduate school; it is the first and often the only thing we think of when we think of our language. Our spelling must be "correct" — even if the words are ill-chosen; our "usage" must be "correct" — even though any possible substitute expression, however crude, would be perfectly clear; our punctuation must be "correct" — even though practices surge and change with the passing of years, and differ from book to book, periodical to periodical. Correct! That's what we've got to be, and the idea that we've got to be correct rests like a soggy blanket on our brains and our hands whenever we try to write. page 285/

. . . In our speech we have arrived, I think, at a decency of discourse which is conducive to effective expression. We listen, with a grave courteous attention, to massive patterns of speaking different from our own because they come from differences in dialect and social status; we listen without carping and without a mean contempt. Furthermore, we participate; we go with a speaker through halts and starts, over abysses of construction, filling in the lacunae without hesitation; we discount inadvertencies and disregard wrong words, and we arrive in genial good will with the speaker at his meaning. In this atmosphere, our speech has thrived, and the ordinary American is in conversation a confident, competent expressive being. In writing he is something else again.

No one flourishes in an atmosphere of repression. It is possible, of course, for a person with special aptitudes and a special drive to bull his way past the prohibitions and achieve an individual style. But with the negative attitude that attends all our writing, those whose main interest lies elsewhere are inhibited by fear of "error" and the nagging it stirs up from setting pen to paper, until the sight of a blank white page gives them the shakes. It is no wonder that their expression is halting and ineffective. They cannot fulfill the demands of a prissy propriety and trace the form of an idea at the same time. They thus arrive at adulthood victims of the steely eye of Mr. Sherwin Cody, whose bearded face stares at them from the countless ads for his correspondence school, demanding, "Do YOU make these mistakes in English?" The locutions he lists are not mistakes, and Mr. Cody knows they are not; but his readers do not know it, and they do not know that they don't matter anyway.

For usage doesn't matter. What matters is that we get done what   page 288/ we have to do, and get said what we have to say. Sufficient conformity is imposed upon us by the patterns of our language and by the general practices of its users so that we do not have to run the idea of conformity into the ground by carping about trivial erratics in expression. Why in this matter of language alone complete conformity should be considered a virtue — except to typists, printers and typesetters — it is difficult to see (unless, perhaps, we are using it as a covert and pusillanimous means of establishing our own superiority). In our other concerns in life, we prize individuality; why in this one matter we should depart from a principle that otherwise serves us well is a puzzle for fools and wise men to ponder, especially since there is no general agreement on what to conform to, and one man's correctness is another's error. Not until we come to our senses — teachers, editors, writers and readers together — and stop riding each other's backs, will the casual, brisk, colorful, amused, ironic and entertaining talk of Americans find its way into print. We should all be happy to see it there.
page 289/

from *The Atlantic Monthly*, Vol. CXCIX
May, 1957

What Is Good English?

Margaret Nicholson

2

...What is it that tells the English reader "this book was written by an American"? First, of course, as with us, the spelling. We wantonly omit hyphens when they are needed and insert them when they are unnecessary; we use a *z* when *s* is called for and discard the *u* in *-our* endings; we do not realize (or realise) that *worshiped* and *kidnaped,* without doubling the penultimate consonants, are not only wrong but invite flagrant mispronunciation. So let us forget the spelling. Wanting to have something more than a theoretical opinion, I asked some English friends how they identified a nonfiction book as American. "By its illiteracies," one of them retorted immediately. And what are the peculiarly American illiteracies? I insisted. Although it is rather unfair, since this was an informal, off-the-record conversation, I am going to give his list in the order in which it was presented.

Improper use of *will* for *shall,* first person future. This delighted me. It is true that the distinction between *will* and *shall* is less and less observed in America, even by good speakers and writers. Those of us who were brought up on traditional English still observe it instinctively; we are a minority. But is *will* for *shall* in this usage peculiarly American and indisputably an illiteracy? Sir Ernest Gowers, in his *ABC of Plain Words,* published in England for English writers in 1951, does not agree. He points out that "I will go" has always been the plain future for the Celts, that Americans have followed their practice, and that "the English have taken to imitating the Americans." "If we go by practice rather than precept," he continues, "we can no longer say dogmatically that 'I will go' for the plain future is wrong." Fowler would not like this. In his article on *will* (MEU) he says: "Of the English of the English *shall & will* are the shibboleth . . . and endow his speech with a delicate precision that could not be attained without it." Opposite views by two men to the manner born. Americans may choose whichever they will.

In back of for *behind.* "All Americans say it," according to my friends. Well a great many Americans do. Certainly it slips easily from the tongue of many who should know better. I do not remember having come across it in print, and I cannot believe that a serious writer would be guilty of it. I agree that it is an illiteracy. Of *back of* for *behind* (the *in* is completely otiose) Fowler says gently, "An American, not an English idiom." page 72/

The omission of the preposition in such phrases as "I'll see you Tuesday," "He works nights," "I'll write you as soon as I know." These are all standard American usage now; the Englishman, however, would say *on Tuesday, at night,* and *to you.* In recording *write you* when there is no direct object, *The Oxford English Dictionary* says, "freq. c.1790–c.1865" and gives several examples.

He aimed to (be) rather than *at (being).* Whatever the purists may say, this is now standard American usage, although it is no longer condoned in England. OED lists it as obsolete, *Webster's Collegiate* without qualification, and ACD as "U.S.," contrasting it with the English *at* plus the gerund.

Different than instead of *different from.* How long this battle has been going on! It was in full swing in my own schooldays, and quite recently when I was discussing Americanisms with a college professor she exclaimed in horror, "I hope you're not going to allow *different than!*" Allow it? We have it, whether we like it or not. Again I turn for comfort to OED: "The usual construction is now with *from.* . . . The construction with *than* is found in Fuller, Addison, Steele, DeFoe,

Richardson, Goldsmith, Miss Burney, Coleridge, Southey, De Quincey, Carlyle, Thackeray, Newman, Trench, and Dasent, among others" — the others, I am afraid, including two thirds of the American public.

So much for peculiarly American illiteracies. We have them, yes. But I was happy that my friend selected the examples he did.

Apart from so-called illiteracies, there are some words that have different meanings on the two sides of the Atlantic. For example, *faculty* is used on the *campuses* (so used only in America) of both English and American colleges, but as applied to the whole body of teachers and perhaps administrative officers (*A faculty meeting was called for Wednesday night*) it is "U.S. only." *Sabbatical* is used in England in its religious sense but not for an academic *sabbatical leave.* *The Humane Society* in England rescues the drowning and has nothing to do with the prevention of cruelty to animals.

Differences of this kind can be misleading, and it is well not to have too sanguine an acceptance of dictionary definitions. Even in the most recent edition of *The Concise Oxford Dictionary,* which helpfully uses an asterisk to indicate words and meanings "chiefly or originally American," one discovers some surprising things. "*Faucet* (chiefly U.S.), tap for a barrel." "*Filibuster . . .* * obstructionist in legislative assembly." "*Barn-dance* (orig. U.S.), dance in which partners advance side by side & then dance a schottische step." "*Bat,* v. (U.S. & dial.), to wink (*never batted an eyelid = did not sleep a wink*)." "*Beauty Parlour* (orig. U.S.), establishment in which the art or trade of face massage, face lifting, applying cosmetics, &c. is carried on." A *bouncer,* U.S. slang, is a *chucker out. Call down,* U.S. colloq., means *challenge.*

There are of course many words that we — and the British — now use without being conscious of the fact that they are Americanisms: a *blanket* ruling, a blood *donor,* the Red Cross *drive,* to be *through* one's work, to *grill* the prisoner, to meet the *deadline.* Most of these were at one time slang or colloquial, but are now standard, at least in informal use.

Understandably it is in slang and colloquialisms that the differences between British and American are greatest and most apparent. Even in one country there is difference in regional, occupational, and social slang. If slang has color, if it expresses some idea or feeling with an economy not found in standard English, it may pass its own boundaries and even become part of the permanent language. No one thinks now of *mob, bus,* or *cab* as slang. It is my belief that *gangster, hold-up,* and *hoodlum* are also in the language to stay (although it is regrettable that they reflect so unsavory an element of American life). The R.A.F. *gremlins* are as much at home in the United States as they are in England and may live to rival pixies and elves. Americans *grouse* (British slang) about their troubles and the British have little sympathy with *grouches* (U.S. slang).

Fowler says, speak as your neighbor speaks. True, the advice comes from his article on pronunciation, but it is as applicable to the use of English-English and American-English idiom. Personally I am unable to go the whole way and concede that if a large enough number of my neighbors say or write a thing in a given way, that way is right — or at least not until enough time has elapsed to give its blessing to the usage in question. To me *adviser* is so spelled, no matter how many times I see *advisor* in print, even in scholarly books. I prefer *John's going to Boston amazed me* to *John going to Boston* . . . even though I am assured that the gerund in America is dead. Speak as your neighbor speaks — but today our neighbor is the English-speaking world. If we have an idea to give to our neighbor, whether it is a commercial product or a global (U.S. vogue word) philosophy, we are inefficient if we allow disputed constructions or local peculiarities in our language to distract his attention. English-English and American-English are coming closer together, not growing farther apart. Two world wars, our publications, motion pictures, radio, television, and even the UN are seeing to that.

My feeling is that good English is good English, whatever the nationality of the writer. In every community there are local meanings, terms, and constructions, arising from the circumstances and environment of that particular locality. Some of these should be treasured, some should be eschewed in formal writing. There is no essentially American-English or English-English. There are only not-too-important regional variations.　**page 73/**

from *The Atlantic Monthly*, Vol. CCV
March, 1960

Grammar for Today

Bergen Evans

. . . Scholars agree with Puttenham (1589) that a language is simply speech "fashioned to the common understanding and accepted by consent." They believe that the only "rules" that can be stated for a language are codified observations. They hold, that is, that language is the basis of grammar, not the other way round. They do not believe that any language can become "corrupted" by the linguistic habits of those who speak it. They do not believe that anyone who is a native speaker of a standard language will get into any linguistic trouble unless he is misled by snobbishness or timidity or vanity.

He may, of course, if his native language is English, speak a form of English that marks him as coming from a rural or an unread group. But if he doesn't mind being so marked, there's no reason why he should change. Johnson retained a Staffordshire burr in his speech all his life. And surely no one will deny that Robert Burn's rustic dialect was just as good as a form of speech as, and in his mouth infinitely better as a means of expression than, the "correct" English spoken by ten million of his southern contemporaries.

The trouble is that people are no longer willing to be rustic or provincial. They all want to speak like educated people, though they don't want to go to the trouble of becoming truly educated. They want to believe that a special form of socially acceptable and financially valuable speech can be mastered by following a few simple rules. And there is no lack of little books that offer to supply the rules and promise "correctness" if the rules are adhered to. But, of course, these offers are specious because you don't speak like an educated person unless you are an educated person, and the little books, if taken seriously, will not only leave the lack of education showing but will expose the pitiful yearning and the basic vulgarity as well, in such sentences as "Whom are you talking about?"

As a matter of fact, the educated man uses at least three languages. With his family and close friends, on the ordinary, unimportant occasions of daily life, he speaks, much of the time, a monosyllabic sort of shorthand. On more important occasions and when dealing with strangers in his official or business relations, he has a more formal speech, more complete, less allusive, politely qualified, wisely reserved. In addition he has some acquaintance with the literary speech of his language. He understands this when he reads it, and often enjoys it, but he hesitates to use it.   page 81/   In times of emotional stress hot fragments of it may come out of him like lava, and in times of feigned emotion, as when giving a commencement address, cold, greasy gobbets of it will ooze forth.

The linguist differs from the amateur grammarian in recognizing all of these variations and gradations in the language. And he differs from the snob in doubting that the speech of any one small group among the language's more than 300 million daily users constitutes a model for all the rest to imitate.

The methods of the modern linguist can be illustrated by the question of the grammatical number of *none*. Is it singular or plural? Should one say "None of them is ready" or "None of them are ready"?

The prescriptive grammarians are emphatic that it should be singular. The Latinists point out that *nemo*, the Latin equivalent, is singular. The logicians triumphantly point out that *none* can't be more than one and hence can't be plural.

The linguist knows that he hears "None of them are ready" every day, from people of all social positions, geographical areas, and degrees of education. He also hears "None is." Furthermore, literature informs him that both forms were used in the past. From Malory (1450) to Milton (1650) he finds that *none* was treated as a singular three times for every once that it was treated as a plural. That is, up to three hundred years ago men usually said *None is*. From Milton to 1917, *none* was used as a plural seven times for every four times it was used as a singular. That is, in the past three hundred years men often said *None is*, but they said *None are* almost twice as often. Since 1917, however, there has been a noticeable increase in the use of the plural, so much so that today *None are* is the preferred form.

The descriptive grammarian, therefore, says that while *None is* may still be used, it is becoming increasingly peculiar. This, of course, will not be as useful to one who wants to be cultured in a hurry as a short, emphatic permission or prohibition. But it has the advantage of describing English as it is spoken and written here and now and not as it ought to be spoken in some Cloud-Cuckoo-Land.

The descriptive grammarian believes that a child should be taught English, but he would like to see the child taught the English actually used by his educated contemporaries, not some pedantic, theoretical English designed chiefly to mark the imagined superiority of the designer.

He believes that a child should be taught the parts of speech, for example. But the child should be told the truth — that these are functions of use, not some quality immutably inherent in this or that word. Anyone, for instance, who tells a child — or anyone else — that *like* is used in English only as a preposition has grossly misinformed him. And anyone who complains that its use as a conjunction is a corruption introduced by Winston cigarettes ought, in all fairness, to explain how Shakespeare, Keats, and the translators of the Authorized Version of the Bible came to be in the employ of the R. J. Reynolds Tobacco Company.

Whether formal grammar can be taught to advantage before the senior year of high school is doubtful; most studies — and many have been made — indicate that it can't. But when it is taught, it should be the grammar of today's English, not the obsolete grammar of yesterday's prescriptive grammarians. By that grammar, for instance, *please* in the sentence "Please reply" is the verb and *reply* its object. But by modern meaning *reply* is the verb, in the imperative, and *please* is merely a qualifying word meaning "no discourtesy intended," a mollifying or de-imperatival adverb, or whatever you will, but not the verb.

This is a long way from saying "Anything goes," which is the charge that, with all the idiot repetition of a needle stuck in a groove, the uninformed ceaselessly chant against modern grammarians. But to assert that usage is the sole determinant in grammar, pronunciation, and meaning is *not* to say that anything goes. Custom is illogical and unreasonable, but it is also tyrannical. The least deviation from its dictates is usually punished with severity. And because this is so, children should be taught what the current and local customs in English are. They should not be taught that we speak a bastard Latin or a vocalized logic. And they should certainly be disabused of the stultifying illusion that after God had given Moses the Commandments He called him back and pressed on him a copy of Woolley's *Handbook of English Grammar*.

The grammarian does not see it as his function to "raise the standards" set by Franklin, Lincoln, Melville, Mark Twain, and hundreds of millions of other Americans. He is content to record what they said and say.

Insofar as he serves as a teacher, it is his business to point out the limits of the permissible, to indicate the confines within which the writer may exercise his choice, to report that which custom and practice have made acceptable. It is certainly not the business of the grammarian to impose his personal taste as the only norm of good English, to set forth his prejudices as the ideal standard which everyone should copy. That would be fatal. No one person's standards are broad enough for that.   **page 82/**

from *American Association of University Professors Bulletin*, Vol. XXXVIII
Autumn, 1952

Whose Good English?

Louis B. Salomon

I think it's about time to warn the English-speaking public — in this country, anyway — that there's a growing conspiracy to give their language back to them, lock, stock, and barrel. The conspirators are, of all people, professional experts, teachers of English: members of that priesthood whom the public has long regarded as the custodians if not outright owners of the crown jewels and holy things of the King's English. And now some of them want to dump the whole glittering treasure into the public's lap, saying, "Here, take it; it's been yours all along. Don't ask *us* what to do with it. We only work here."

In case you don't even know this is going on, let me explain what has happened. In place of the old-fashioned grammarian who treated English as if it were a dead language, with a neat, logical code of laws, modern scholars and workers on the educational production-line lean more to the view that a language is made (and continually altered) by the people who use it — that it has no *a priori* rules whatever but only customs and usages which can be observed and tabulated like preferences in brands of cigarettes. For example, it's meaningless to say that *Whom do you want?* is right and *Who do you want?* is wrong; we should say only that among well-educated people 62% (or whatever) at the present time say *Whom* to 38% who say *Who*, and that therefore in such a sentence *Whom* is *standard* English. If we find that among people of moderate education *Who* makes the grade 90% of the time and among semi-illiterates 100%, these are usable statistics but not value judgments.

Thus, every time you bawl out a taxi-driver or deliver an afterdinner speech your manner of expression automatically becomes part of the way English is spoken and understood by people of your cultural level, and whether your locutions are used by the page 442/ majority or not is a purely statistical question. Whether you pen sophisticated epigrams for little magazines or scrawl the simplest obscenities on washroom walls, you are contributing your own little bits of building-stone to that tremendous pyramid of written communication which all the English teachers in the country can only try, at best, to shore up where it shows signs of weakness or strain. A sentence communicates an idea or starts a revolution not because a grammarian says it's correct but because for the eyes and ears of its audience it *is* correct by the surest test of all: it works.

II

So that's why some of the vigilantes who used to waylay your themes to flog each dangling participle and lynch every run-on sentence now seem to be looking for a chance to lay the language on your doorstep like a foundling and run like hell before you can catch them and ask them how to rear the brat. They're convinced that it's healthy, that it will grow up very well-adjusted provided it's never spanked or threatened or scrubbed or fussed over. They're perfectly willing to furnish you with its past history, and even help you keep records on its day-to-day development, but they'll only tell you what it has done, not what it should or should not do. The English grammar textbook of the future may approach its subject in the same spirit in which the Kinsey report tackled sex.

Now, in many respects this is a very fine thing, because there obviously is a great deal of flummery in the kind of language "rules" that for generations have been crammed down the throats of docile or perhaps just apathetic students all the way from grade school through college; and nobody should be asked to waste time studying mummified language forms which he never has used and never will use — which, furthermore, aren't even used by most of the teachers themselves outside the classroom. The only tangible result of all the attempts to teach a language of logical rules instead of real practice has been to make a lot of people self-conscious, like a little boy receiving a prize Bible for Sunday school attendance. It took the National Council of Teachers of English a long time to page 443/ get around to endorsing *It is me,* and even now a good many people find it so hard to believe that the expression they've always used is quite proper, that they gulp down their Adam's apple and bring out *It is I,* and then, by their own brand of analogy, of course, go proudly on to *They invited Mary and I for the week-end.* English teachers undoubtedly have a lot to answer for (including the half-educated conviction that this sentence would read more elegantly: "English teachers have a lot for which to answer").

And yet, despite the clear benefits of jettisoning such deadweight as the formal distinction between *shall* and *will,* the new trend if carried to extremes raises some questions of more than merely academic interest. For example, what if the public doesn't *want* to be crowned as the final arbiter of language use and abuse? I'm an English teacher, have been for twenty-five years, and I know how many people (not students) have asked me, "Is it right to say so-and-so?" and how many have been not merely unsatisfied but indignant when I've answered that usage rules in such matters, that if enough people say it it's right and if enough people avoid it it's wrong. They look at me as they'd look at a doctor who said, when they took their grippe to him: "My dear fellow, at any given time 51% of the population has virus infections of one sort or another. What do you want to do, be abnormal?" Most of the public, needless to say, will go on speaking and writing English in their accustomed fashion no matter what the pedagogues do or say about it, but that doesn't mean that there's no demand for a priestly caste to glorify and interpret the Tables of the Law. A lot of church-goers give the Ten Commandments quite a beating at home and in the market-place, but the anti-clerical movement has never got very far in this country.

People who abandon babies on your doorstep seldom ask in advance whether you want the gift or not. Maybe you're a dear old thing who's been pining for someone to love and cherish; maybe you're a flint-hearted wretch who'll be delighted to feed a prospective slave; but if you're an average sort of person you may hotfoot it to the nearest police station to get rid of the responsibility as fast as possible. There are institutions, you'll say, where my taxes support experts for the very purpose of handling these cases as they should be handled; why should *I* have to make decisions? page 444/ So you'd better ask yourself whether you want to be told about your language what the advertisers tell you about canned beans and TV sets and broadloom carpeting: "You are the Boss in this Land of Brands."

III

It's noteworthy that the more advanced proponents of the hands-off-the-language school tend to soft-pedal the title of English teacher and prefer to style themselves students of linguistics. Now, linguistics, or the study of the way language is actually used at any given time, is undoubtedly a useful branch of investigation, which can be pursued as scientifically as biochemistry or atomic physics. There's plenty of reason for objective and continued study of all varieties of verbal communication: the argot of con men, the circumlocution of government documents, the expressive flow of good literary prose, the clichés of business correspondence, the terse vigor of street-corner brawling. I just want to point out the danger of falling into the big scientific fallacy of our time: the fallacy of believing that the scientist's sole responsibility lies in amassing factual information. The greatest of the atomic scientists, like Einstein and Oppenheimer, have blasted this view, but it remains tempting — far too tempting — to all who want, for whatever reasons, to evade or abdicate responsibility for leadership. An even more dangerous temptation is to confuse the findings of pure scientific research with standards of value, a confusion leading to the doctrine that whatever is is right. page 445/ . . . .

V

As I said before, I hold no brief for the embalming of old useless forms. The taboo against *like* as a conjunction, for instance, is being subjected to increasing pressure among the groups who set the tone for standard English, and if the day should come when even English teachers write *He sings like his brother does,* I for one don't feel that the language will have suffered any great loss. Like (not as) most of my colleagues, I've been fighting a rear-guard action for many years in defense of *as* and *as if,* but I'm afraid I've only succeeded in launching a boomerang which sometimes comes whizzing back in such an unnatural shape as *He looks as his father* — obviously a first cousin of *They invited Mary and I.*

Where the public, then, is busily trying to bury a form that's page 448/ outlived its usefulness if it ever had any, I'm all for pitching in and helping. But first let's make sure whether the corpse is really dead or whether it might be revived and, if so, made into a useful citizen. When a lifeguard at the beach rescues a waterlogged bather he doesn't eschew artificial respiration just because most of the onlookers shake their heads and say, "Poor fellow, he's a goner!"

I can't see any gain for anybody in reducing English teaching to the status of a spectator sport. My colleagues who are working in that direction may, I'm afraid, be cutting their own throats, because the more effectively they manage to sell the public the idea that whatever passes current is right, the less reason the public will find for supporting them. How many dollars will a congregation drop into the collection-box for a preacher whose sole text is a running analysis of the percentage of the population that doesn't attend church?

Conceivably the public may not care whether English teachers eat or not, but if there is any sentiment in favor of feeding them I'm willing to bet that the idea is to keep them alive as English teachers, that is, as a kind of traffic cop to tell the average person when to stop and when to move on, where he may park and where he may not. If English teachers don't want to be traffic cops — if they just want to stand on the corner and count the cars that try to beat the red light — then they might as well turn in their badges. Because sooner or later the taxpayers will (a) begin to wonder why the accident rate keeps going up, and (b) discover that a machine with an electric eye can do the counting more cheaply and more efficiently.   page 449/

from *The Saturday Evening Post*, Vol. CCXXIX
September 22, 1956

An Old-School-Type Grammarian Gives Up the Struggle

Bruce Bliven

This is to serve notice on the world that I quit. I resign. I give up the crusade.

For forty years I worked on the copy desks of newspapers and magazines, trying to straighten out the grammar of the great American public, and, in particular, six of the most common faults. My success has been about that of most reformers. From the instant I began my efforts, things have been getting steadily worse and worse.

As every copyreader knows, six of the most common faults are these:

Using "data" as a singular noun. ("The data is readily available.")

Using "contact" as a verb. ("I'll contact you tomorrow.")
Confusing "like" and "as." ("Just go on acting like you did before.")
Comparing "unique." ("His collection of coins is rather unique.")
Using "providing" for "provided." ("He will come providing he is able.")
Using "literally" for "figuratively." ("I was literally burned up at what he said.")

I am no longer on any copy desk, but old habits die hard. I find that I go on editing printed copies of newspapers and magazines furiously, and then throwing them into the wastebasket, which is not a very effective plan of operation. I also sit in front of my television set shouting at the tiny figures on it: "No, no, you dope! 'Like' is a preposition. The conjunction is 'as, as, as'!" . . . I can't understand why my wife insisted on having this psychiatrist to dinner, a man I hardly know, or why he kept asking me those extremely personal questions.

Now I am resigning from my crusade, not merely because of my blood pressure — as to which the doctor tells me, "When it breaks 200, sell" — but for a more logical reason. It is perfectly clear that the American people in their collective unconscious wisdom are changing the language. They have every right to do it. I can't stop it. This has been going on as long as there has been a language, with fuss-budgets like me being dragged, kicking and screaming, at the tail of the procession. Another few years and even the purists will happily use the expressions I find so painful today.

When that day comes, just contact me, like I'm asking you now to do. I'll then look in my most unique files for the data which is there confirming my prophecy. That is, of course, providing I am not literally frozen with horror at the way things are going. **page 10/**

APPENDIX

QUOTABLE QUOTES

We have really everything in common with America nowadays except, of course, language. — Oscar Wilde, *The Canterville Ghost*, 1888

The greatest barrier between the English and the Americans is that they speak the same language. — Oscar Wilde, from Notes on a Tour of the United States, 1883

I have frequently remarked that the Americans, who generally treat of business in clear, plain language, devoid of all ornament, and so extremely simple as to be often coarse, are apt to become inflated as soon as they attempt a more poetical diction. They then vent their pomposity from one end of a harangue to the other, and to hear them lavish imagery on every occasion, one might fancy that they never spoke of anything with simplicity. — Alexis de Tocqueville, *Democracy in America*

Life is our dictionary. Years are well spent in country labors; in town, — in the insight into trades and manufactures; in frank intercourse with many men and women; in science; in art; to the one end of mastering in all their facts a language by which to illustrate and embody our perceptions. I learn immediately from any speaker how much he has already lived, through the poverty or the splendor of his speech. Life lies behind us as the quarry from whence we get tiles and copestones for the masonry of to-day. This is the way to learn grammar. Colleges and books only copy the language which the field and the work-yard made. — Ralph Waldo Emerson, *The American Scholar*

The new circumstances under which we are placed call for new words, new phrases, and for the transfer of old words to new objects. An American dialect will therefore be formed. — Thomas Jefferson, letter to John Waldo, 1813

When we want to freshen our speech, we borrow from American — *poppycock, rambunctious, flip-flop, booster, good mixer.* All the expressive, ugly, vigorous slang which creeps into use among us, first in talk, later in writing, comes from across the Atlantic. — Virginia Woolf, *Saturday Review of Literature*, August 1, 1925

Having inherited, borrowed or stolen a beautiful language, they [the Americans] wilfully and of set purpose degrade, distort and misspell it apparently for the sole purpose of saving money in type-setting. — T. W. H. Crosland, *The Abounding American*, 1907

Language is always a mirror of the life of a people. Every branch of industry, every new way of thinking, every change in politics is fully represented by a new word or a peculiar phrase. — Schele De Vere, *Americanisms,* 1872

If we had a complete history of all the words which America has preserved, invented, or modified, we should possess the most revealing history conceivable of the American people. — Robert L. Ramsay, *A Mark Twain Lexicon,* 1938

Language does not exist in isolation from the culture of which it forms the chief vehicle. One really acquires a language only insofar as he acquires a culture. — Grace De Laguna, in *Human Biology,* December, 1929

MIDWAY SIGNS LIMEY PROF TO DOPE YANK TALK — Headline in *The Chicago Tribune,* October 18, 1924, on the occasion of the arrival of Sir William Craigie in the United States to begin work on *A Dictionary of American English.*

Mencken's Law: Whenever A annoys or injures B on the pretense of saving or improving X, A is a scoundrel. — H. L. Mencken

The American language is the American language and the English language is the English language. The only way to preserve the purity of the English language is to present a steadily hostile resistance to every American innovation. America is the only dangerous enemy. She must develop her own language and allow us to develop ours. — *The New Statesman,* June 25, 1927

Language is part of our social heritage, slowly and painfully built up. We can and should improve it, but it is not ours to destroy. Just how the damage is ever going to be mended is a problem which sooner or later we must face, if the finest values of our civilization are to be permanently preserved. — Louis Foley, "The Modern Crime of Linguacide," *School and Society,* May 5, 1951

When we Americans are done with the English language it will look as if it had been run over by a musical comedy. — Mr. Dooley

The official language of the state of Illinois shall be known hereafter as the American language, and not as the English language. — *Acts of Legislature,* State of Illinois, Chapter 127, Section 178, 1923

I know a lot of people who ain't eatin' because they ain't sayin' ain't. — Will Rogers

There is a Gresham's law in language as in economics. Bad currency once admitted will tend to drive the good out of circulation. The bilge of Hollywood will sink the language of Churchill and Lincoln. — Lord Conesford, "You Americans are Murdering the Language," *Saturday Evening Post,* July 13, 1957

A lot of English writers are so dazzled by the vernacular crackle of American-English that they don't hear other things. They don't hear — what worries a good many Americans when they get to work on discursive prose — that in a good many ways American-English is a significantly more abstract language than ours is. We say: "I want to book a seat." You say: "I want to make a reservation." That is part of common speech and works itself into the discursive prose. There is a great richness, sparkle, and invention in many of the American vernaculars, but the thought frame is often not as direct as in English-English. For a writer's purposes, the gains and losses linguistically just about cancel out. — C. P. Snow, "Which Side of the Atlantic?" *Harper's Magazine,* October, 1959

Let us believe it, then, once for all, that there is no hope for us in these smooth, pleasing writers that know their powers. Without malice, but to speak the plain fact, they but furnish an appendix to Goldsmith, and other English authors. And we want no American Goldsmiths, nay, we want no American Miltons. It were the vilest thing you could say of a true American author, that he were an American Tompkins. Call him an American and have done, for you cannot say a nobler thing of him. But it is not meant that all American writers should studiously cleave to nationality in their writings; only this, no American writer should write like an Englishman or a Frenchman; let him write like a man, for then he will be sure to write like an American. — Herman Melville, "Hawthorne and His Mosses," *The Literary World,* August 17, 1850

Wherever there is a touch of Virginia left, there is the United States language. The United States language is Virginia with the *r* put back into it. — Vachel Lindsay, "The Real American Language," *The American Mercury,* March, 1928

The common faults of American language are an ambition of effect, a want of simplicity, and a turgid abuse of terms. To these may be added ambiguity of expression. Many pervasions of significations also exist, and a formality of speech, which, while it renders conversation ungraceful, and destroys its playfulness, seriously weakens the power of the language, by applying to ordinary ideas, words that are suited only to themes of gravity and dignity. . . .

The love of turgid expressions is gaining ground, and ought to be corrected. One of the most certain evidences of a man of high breeding, is his simplicity of speech, a simplicity that is equally removed from vulgarity and exaggeration. He calls a spade, a "spade." His enunciation, while clear, deliberate and dignified, is totally without strut, showing his familiarity with the world, and, in some degree, reflecting the qualities of his mind, which is polished without being addicted to sentimentalism, or any other bloated feeling. . . .

All cannot reach the highest standard in such matters, for it depends on early habit, and particularly on early associations. . . . Simplicity should be the first aim, after one is removed from vulgarity, and let the finer shades of accomplishment be acquired as they can be attained. In no case, however, can one who aims at turgid language, exaggerated sentiment, or pedantic utterance, lay claim to be either a man or a woman of the world. — James Fenimore Cooper, *The American Democrat,* 1838

The average healthy-minded American has always regarded British speech with amusement. He doesn't deny the right of the British to speak in any manner they choose, even though he may brand that particular manner as having a lavender tinge. . . . Please do not read an anti-British meaning into this discussion. I am neither an Anglophobe nor an Anglophile. I am a simple American. I love my

country, its distinctive American culture, its melting-pot people, and, especially,
its ingenious, picturesque, delicately expressive, and non-British language. . . .
by holding fast to the principle that American ways and American speech are
best for Americans, we of the United States have fashioned and have given to
the world the richest, the most expressive, and the most widely spoken tongue
ever devised by man — THE AMERICAN LANGUAGE. — Frank Colby, *The
Practical Handbook of Better English*, 1944

CHARACTERISTIC AMERICAN-BRITISH EQUIVALENTS

AMERICAN	BRITISH
Household terms	
absorbent cotton	cotton wool
ash can	dust bin; ash bin
baby carriage;	perambulator; pram;
baby buggy	baby coach
baseboard	skirting
bucket	pail
bureau	chest of drawers
can	tin
cheesecloth	butter muslin
closet	cupboard
clothespin	clothespeg
comforter	eiderdown
denatured alcohol	methylated spirits
dipper	pannekin
dishpan	washer
dish towel	dish cloth
drape	curtain
dumbwaiter	service lift
extension wire	flex
eye glasses	spectacles
faucet	tap
flashlight	torch
garbage can	dust bin
hallway	passage
hope chest	bottom drawer
junk	rubbish
kerosene	paraffin
living room	sitting room
napkin	serviette
pantry	larder
paraffin	white wax
pillowcase	pillowber
pitcher	jug
scratch pad	scribbling block
shade	blind
stairway	staircase
toilet	lavatory; water closet
transom	fanlight
washbowl	washbasin
wash rag	face cloth
water heater	geyser

Eating and drinking	
ale	bitters; stout, porter, etc.
beer	lager
beet	beet-root
biscuit	scone or tea cake
broiled (meat)	grilled
café	tea room
candy	sweets
cone (ice cream)	cornet
corn	maize; Indian corn
cornmeal	Indian meal
cornstarch	cornflour
cracker	biscuit
dessert	sweet course
dining car	restaurant car
French-fried pota-	chips
toes	
ginger snaps	ginger-nut
hash	shepherd's pie
highball	whiskey and soda
ice cream	ice
layer cake	jam sandwich
menu	tariff
molasses	treacle
oatmeal	porridge
peanut	monkey nut
picnic	beanfest
potato chips	crisps
rare (meat)	underdone
roast	joint
rutabaga	Swede
scallion	spring onion
scrambled eggs	buttered eggs
seafood	fish
sherbet	ice
silverware	silver-plate
smoked herring	kipper
soda biscuit	cream cracker
soft drinks	minerals
squash	vegetable marrow
straight (drink)	neat
string bean	French bean
sugar bowl	sugar basin

Eating and Drinking (cont'd)

supper	tea
taffy	toffee
tavern	inn
tenderloin (beef)	undercut or fillet

Clothing terms

bathrobe	dressing gown
business suit	lounge suit
cane	walking stick
collar button	stud
corset	stays
custom-made	bespoke; made to measure
derby	bowler
doll-up	dress-up to the nines
garters	sock-suspenders
laprobe	rug
overcoat	great coat
overshoes	galoshes
oxfords	walking shoes
pants	trousers
raincoat	waterproof; mackintosh; mac
ready-to-wear	ready-made
run (stocking)	ladder
shirt	blouse
slacks	bags
shoestring	bootlace; shoelace
straw hat	boater
suspenders	braces; galluses
sweater	pull-over
undershirt	vest
union suit	combination
vest	waistcoat

Recreational terms

bingo	house or housey-housey
bowling alley	skittle alley
carnival	fun fair
carom (billiards)	cannon
carousel; merry-go-round	roundabout; merry-go-round
checkers	draughts
commutation ticket	season ticket
deck (cards)	pack
diamond (baseball)	field
dime novel	penny dreadful; shilling shocker
game (football)	match
jumping rope	skipping rope
poolroom	billiards saloon
race track	race course
roller coaster	switchback railway; scenic railway
solitaire (cards)	patience
tenpins	nine-pins
vacation	holiday

Housing terms

annex	annexe
apartment	flat
apartment hotel	service flats
apartment house	block of flats
building	house
elevator	lift
first floor	ground floor
freight elevator	hoist
flop house	doss house
frame house	wooden house
hospital	nurse's home
powder room	ladies' cloakroom
second floor	first floor
stairway	staircase
yard	small garden

Business and Professional terms

barber	hairdresser
bartender	barman; potman; barmaid
bell boy	page
deliveryman	roundsman
druggist	chemist
farm hand	agricultural laborer
fish dealer	fish monger
floorwalker	shopwalker
fruitseller	fruiterer
garbage man	dustman
hardware dealer	ironmonger
hog raiser	pig dealer
holdup man	raider
janitor	caretaker; porter
lawyer	barrister
life-guard	life-saver
longshoreman	docker
operator	machine minder
magician	conjuror
pin boy (bowling)	thrower-up
porch climber	cat burglar
president	chairman
realtor	estate agent
saloon keeper	publican
shoe clerk	bootmaker's assistant
stenographer	shorthand writer

Government and Legal terms

administration	ministry
administrator	administer
admit to the bar	call to the bar
appropriation	vote
assignment	appointment or commission
brief case	portfolio
calendar	cause list
cop	bobby
county	shire
delegation	deputation
district	division

Government and Legal Terms (cont'd)

fusion	coalition
general delivery (mail)	poste restante
jail	gaol
legal holiday	bank holiday
ordinance	by-law
parole	ticket of leave
patrolman	constable
penitentiary	prison
run (for office)	stand
speed cop	mobile police
table	postpone
taxes	rates
warden	governor
weather bureau	meteorological office
witness stand	witness box

Monetary terms

bill	note
billion (1,000,000,-000)	billion (1,000,000-000,000)
billion	milliard
check	cheque
dime	six pence; half shilling
dues	subscription
nickel	three pence
penny	half penny
roll of bills	sheaf of notes
rubber check	stummer cheque
stub	counterfoil
trade	negotiate

Educational terms

AB (degree)	BA
alumnus	graduate; old boy
AM (degree)	MA
bench	form
bulletin board	notice board
campus	meadow; field; quad; school
catalogue	calendar
commencement	speech day; prize day; encaenia
date	appointment; engagement
eraser	Indian rubber
expelled	sent down
extension	extra-mural studies
faculty	staff
fraternal order	friendly society
grade	form; standard; class
letter man	blue
principal	headmaster
private school; prep school	public school
public school	council school
recess	break

recitation	hearing of lesson
scholarship	studentship
schoolma'am	school mistress
student	school boy or girl
win a letter	win a cap

Journalistic terms

ad	advert
clipping	cutting
clipping bureau	press cutting agency
editorial	leading article
news dealer	news agent
newsstand	kiosk

Theatrical terms

aisle	gangway
headliner	topliner
intermission	interval
line	queue
moving pictures	cinema
movies	flicks
orchestra seats	stalls
reservations	bookings
ticket office	booking office
vaudeville	variety
vaudeville theatre	music hall

Mail and Communication

long distance (telephone)	trunk
mail	post
postcard	postal card
postpaid	post free
special delivery	express delivery

Conveyances

airplane	aeroplane
automobile	motor car
subway	underground railway; tube
transport (ship)	troop ship
trolley	tram
truck line	road haulier

Roads and Passageways

banked (road)	super-elevated
boulevard	arterial road; trunk road
corner	turning
detour	road diversion; loopway
dirt road	unpaved road
dock	wharf
driveway	drive
grade	gradient
main street	high street
shoulder (road)	verges
viaduct	overpass

Automobile terms

battery	accumulator
bumper	buffer
fender	wing; mudguard
filling station	petrol pump
gasoline	petrol
gear shift	gear lever
generator	dynamo
hood	bonnet
horn	hooter
low gear	first speed
motorman	driver
muffler	silencer
oil pan	sump
parking lot	car park
puncture	flat
roadster	two-seater
rumble seat	dickey
sedan	saloon car
spark plug	sparking plug
taxi	hack
tie up (traffic)	hold-up
tire	tyre
top	hood
truck	lorry
van	waggon
windshield	wind screen
wrench	spanner

Railroad terms

all aboard	hurry along now
baggage	luggage
baggage car	luggage van
box car	covered waggon
brakeman	brakesman
caboose	brake-van
call boy	knocker-up
car	carriage; coach
check baggage	register
conductor	guard
cowcatcher	pilot; plough
crossties	sleepers
cut	cutting
dining car	restaurant car
engineer	engine driver
express company	carrier; forwarding agency
fireman	stoker
freight car	goods waggon
gondola	mineral waggon
grade crossing	level crossing

information bureau	inquiry office
limited	express
mail car	postal van
one-way ticket	single ticket
parlor car	saloon carriage
railroad	railway
roundhouse	running shed
round trip	return trip
schedule	time table
stopover	break one's journey
switch	shunt
ticket seller	booking clerk
track	line
union station	joint station

Miscellaneous terms

across from	opposite
affiliate	fraternize
almost	scarcely
aluminum	aluminium
aside from	apart from
billboard	hoarding poster
chicken yard	fowl run
cigarette butt	cigarette end
clapboard	shiplap
coal-oil	paraffin
crew cut	close crop
deadline	time limit
dicker	haggle
diction	elocution
downtown	the city
draft	conscription
fall	autumn
fire cracker	squib
fog	mist
from the ground up	down to its last detail
full time	full out
hot air	mere vaporing
OK	all right
pen point	nib
period (punctuation)	full stop
pound (unit of weight)	stone (equal to 11 lbs.)
pry	prize
sideburns	side whiskers
sidewalk	pavement; footway
shotgun	fowling piece
slingshot	catapult
snicker	snigger
streamlined	swept out
that's right	hear! hear!
Z (zee)	zed

SOME AMERICANISMS
AND THE WRITERS WHO FIRST RECORDED THEM

Word or Expression	*Author*	*Earliest date*
almighty dollar	Washington Irving	1836
Americana	Herman Melville	c.1886
Americanism	John Witherspoon	1781
Americanize	John Jay	1797
Babbitt	Sinclair Lewis	1922
belittle	Thomas Jefferson	1781–2
betsey (a gun)	David Crockett	1836
blue-nosed	Washington Irving	1819
blurb	Gelett Burgess	1907
booboisie	H. L. Mencken	1922
booziness	Nathaniel Hawthorne	1863
bromide	Gelett Burgess	1906
button pear	Samuel Sewell	1687
campus	John Witherspoon	1774
cold war	Walter Lippmann	1947
cybernetics	Norbert Weiner	1948
debunk	William E. Woodward	1923
demoralize	Noah Webster	1794
diddle	A. B. Longstreet	1835
do-funny	Frank Norris	1901
doll (a fop)	Ralph Waldo Emerson	1841
dummy	James Fenimore Cooper	1823
dust cloud	John Greenleaf Whittier	1849
fraternize (to agree)	J. W. Wilbarger	1889
galoot	Artemus Ward	1866
gang (political sense)	John Quincy Adams	1833
glad hand	George Ade	1896
genocide	Raphael Lenkin	1944
globaloney	Clare Booth Luce	1943
gobbledegook	Maury Maverick	1944
goner	Henry David Thoreau	1857
goop	Gelett Burgess	1900
gospel mill	Mark Twain	1872
Gulf Stream	Benjamin Franklin	1769
highbrow	Will Irwin	1905
home-made	James Fenimore Cooper	1823
honky tonk	Carl Sandburg	1927
Hub (Boston)	Oliver Wendell Holmes	1858

Word or Expression	Author	Earliest date
Indian leave	Washington Irving	1835
Indian trader (gun)	A. B. Longstreet	1835
inside man	Theodore Dreiser	1912
ivory tower	Henry James	1917
kid glove (verb)	Oliver Wendell Holmes	1858
killniferously	A. B. Longstreet	1835
kinspirit	Christopher Morley	1923
knock down/drag out	James Fenimore Cooper	1827
lap tea	James Russell Lowell	1890
lipograph (kiss)	Herman Melville	1852
logrolling (political sense)	David Crockett	1835
lowbrow	Will Irwin	1905
memorandize	Walt Whitman	1892
millionocracy	Oliver Wendell Holmes	1861
milquetoast	H. T. Webster	c.1910
moccasin	Capt. John Smith	1612
momism	Philip Wylie	1942
monocrat (partisan of monarchy)	Thomas Jefferson	1792
moron	Henry H. Goddard	1910
moola (money)	John O'Hara	1939
mother country	William Bradford	1617
multimillionaire	Oliver Wendell Holmes	1858
new deal (political sense)	Andrew Jackson	1834
new rich	William Dean Howells	1884
omniverbivorous	Oliver Wendell Holmes	1858
Okie	John Steinbeck	1939
panhandler	George Ade	1899
petting	Sinclair Lewis	1922
peppy	Sinclair Lewis	1922
rich-widowitis	Sinclair Lewis	1924
ripsnorter	David Crockett	1840
robber baron	D. G. Phillips	1905
scaly	George Washington	1786
shebang	Walt Whitman	1862
side-kick	O. Henry	1904
silk-stocking gentry	Thomas Jefferson	1812
skiddoo	Tad Dorgan	1904
spandangalous	Herman Melville	1849
spec (abbr. speculation)	John Adams	1794
square deal	Mark Twain	1883
squinch	A. B. Longstreet	1835

Word or Expression	Author	Earliest date
stuffed shirt	Willa Cather	1913
swimming hole	George Washington Harris	1867
tight wad	George Ade	1900
timothy (grass)	Benjamin Franklin	1747
underground railroad	Harriet Beecher Stowe	1852

QUESTIONS AND EXERCISES

Section 1

1. In the several essays in this section, the word *language* is used in varying senses. Part of the difference of opinion of the authors is actually a semantic problem. Define *language* as it is employed by the several authors. Does your dictionary include all of these meanings for the word?

2. Ivor Brown suggests that language employed for one purpose may not be appropriate for another. This theory of usage is usually called "the doctrine of appropriateness." How does it condone the use of slang and colloquial expressions? Write a paragraph in which you translate a sample of formal discourse into informal American English.

3. In what respects do John Erskine and Mark Twain agree regarding the difference between British and American English? In what respects do they disagree? Which position do you consider the more defensible?

4. J. St. Loe Strachey mentions America's linguistic conservatism. What is the basis for this appraisal of America's attitude toward language?

5. Mark Twain gives both British and American meanings for the word *directly*. Find this word in Melville's *Moby Dick*, Chapter III, paragraph 9, and determine whether it is used in the British or American sense. Check the *Dictionary of American English* and *Dictionary of Americanisms* to ascertain if this was the earliest use of this word in American literature.

6. Mr. Erskine says "It's the language we speak that counts, in life and in literature." Write a paper in which you either defend or refute this thesis.

7. Explain why a language must change in order to remain alive.

8. In the expression "the exception proves the rule," employed by Strachey, *prove* has a now obsolete meaning. Find that meaning in the *Oxford English Dictionary* and note how the language has changed since the expression first entered the language. What other author in this collection employs the same expression? Does he use it in the old sense?

9. How might you take issue with Strachey's basic argument?

10. Look up the discussion of a British glossary for Sinclair Lewis' slang in *Babbitt*, in *Society for Pure English Tracts*, Vol. III, pp. 118ff. or in H. L. Mencken's *The American Language*, pp. 263 (note), and decide whether or not Ivor Brown's position regarding the intelligibility of American slang is defensible.

11. Check in two or three handbooks of English usage the use of *an* before words starting with the letter *h*, mentioned by Mark Twain. Can you find an example in American writing that offends Mark Twain's rule of thumb?

12. Make a list of various American meanings for the word *clever*.

Section 2

1. Read Winston Churchill's account of Anglo-American misunderstanding in *The Second World War* (London: Cassell and Co., Ltd., 1950), p. 609, and evaluate Mr. Quirk's affirmation that most stories of such misunderstandings are pure invention.

2. Considering Mr. Quirk's belief that many so-called divergences in American and British usage are mere variants which may be employed interchangeably, refer to the list of American and British equivalents in the appendix to this volume and list so-called Briticisms that you find commonly used in America.

3. Criticize Claude de Crespigny's statement that "the only safe and sane way for travelers to avoid misunderstandings is to practice the principle of the purist."

4. In what respect do Robert C. Holliday and Claude de Crespigny agree as to the reason for differences between American and British English?

5. Which of the influences affecting American English mentioned by John Clark, in this section, are discussed by Timothy Dwight and James Fenimore Cooper elsewhere in this volume?

6. By using the list of American-British equivalents in the Appendix, demonstrate Mr. Quirk's position that the terms are interchangeable in England and America.

7. By referring to a good dictionary, explain the difference between the British and American meanings of *lady*.

8. List as many "standard" words as you can that have different meanings in England than they have in America.

9. Find a number of expressions which in your opinion are slang expressions and notice how they are classified in your college dictionary.

10. Make an outline of John W. Clark's essay on "The Characteristics of American English."

11. Compare the tone of George Ade's fable with Mark Twain's discussion of American English in the previous section. What do you think each author is arguing for?

Section 3

1. Analyze the various arguments of the authors in this section and construct an outline of both the affirmative and negative positions. Which of the six essays do you think defends the best thesis? Why?

2. Most writers commenting on the value of slang, emphasize its impermanence. Stephen Leacock is one of these. Check the listing of slang phrases in De Vere's *Americanisms* (1872), and notice how many of them are still current in much the same sense as they were nearly a century ago.

3. How does Timothy Dwight defend America's inventiveness with words? What additional examples can you add to his list?

4. Dwight takes issue with the approved pronunciations in Webster's dictionary. What modern dictionary would better satisfy Dwight's plea for recognition of standard pronunciation?

5. Study the suggestions for improving the state of English in America as presented in the final paragraph of the essay from *The Dial*. On what assumption is this argument based? Do you find the assumption sound? What program for improving the nation's language would you propose?

6. Analyze the arguments of two of the essays in this section, one pro-American and one anti-American. Which do you think presents the better argument? Which is guilty of special pleading?

Section 4

1. Referring to Mencken's essay, explain why you agree or disagree with Noah Webster's assertion that "his countrymen had not only a right to adopt new words, but were obliged to modify the language to suit the novelty of circumstances in which they were placed."

2. Both John Adams and Noah Webster were "linguistic patriots." In what respects were their ideas in respect to the future of the English language in America similar? In what respects different?

3. "Language by Legislation" was written more than 100 years after "Resolutions Regarding the American Language." Can you detect any radical changes in the styles of writing?

4. What are the salient characteristics of American English as expressed by the writers in this section?

5. Why must a language change from time to time if it is to remain "healthy"? Adams calls Latin a "dead language." What does he mean? What is a living language? How does it stay alive?

6. Write a paper in which you show how accurate John Adams' prediction was that English would become a universal language. Read in this connection "English on the Weighing Scales," in *The Story of English* by Mario Pei, pp. 296–309.

Section 5

1. Two of the essays in this section were written by Englishmen. What evidence of this do you find in the writing, composition, spelling, vocabulary, etc., exhibited in the essays?

2. To what extent are De Tocqueville's criticisms of American writing valid today? Find samples of current prose to support your answer.

3. Using evidence from all three of the authors in this section, support Emerson's thesis that "we infer the spirit of the nation in great measure from the language."

4. Support the theory, with whatever linguistic evidence you can find, that America is a classless society.

5. Charles Whibley noted the difference between the written and spoken word in America. Has time increased or decreased this difference? Support your answer.

6. De Tocqueville argues for a doctrine of clarity in language. Compare his idea with that expressed by Ben Ray Redman in "Words, Words, Words," in *The Saturday Review of Literature* 40:22 (March 2, 1957).

7. What two kinds of American expressions does Whibley single out for discussion? Find examples of both of these kinds of expression in Melville's *Moby Dick*.

8. Read Charles Dickens' criticism of the American Language in *American Notes* and *Martin Chuzzlewit* and write a paper in which you summarize his points of attack.

Section 6

1. John Witherspoon says he coined the word *Americanism*. Check the American and British dictionaries on historical principles, and ascertain if he is credited with its introduction into literature. With respect to the various meanings of this word, show how the connotation of a word may change from one period of time to another.

2. Write a definition for *Americanism* which incorporates ideas of all the authors in this section. Make a list of criteria by which an Americanism can be identified.

3. Which of the words to which Dr. Witherspoon objected are considered standard English today? Check the status of these words in at least two college dictionaries.

4. Select a passage from eighteenth or nineteenth-century American writing and see if you can find an Americanism that has evaded the dictionaries on historical principles.

5. In his discussion of "Fellow Countrymen," Dr. Witherspoon uses the expression "may be daily seen." Check in Margaret Nicholson's *Dictionary of American-English Usage* under "split infinitives" and determine whether or not this usage is allowed.

6. What is the definition of *nice* as employed by Witherspoon in the second to the last paragraph of his paper?

7. What is the essential difference between the ideas of Lounsbury and John S. Farmer on what constitutes an Americanism?

Section 7

1. With Hans Kurath's *Word Geography of the Eastern United States* at hand, check seven or eight familiar names for things in your experience, and determine on the basis of your selections what part of the eastern seaboard your parents probably migrated from.

2. Compare Frederic G. Cassidy's ideas about the frontier with Frederick Jackson Turner's thesis in "The Significance of the Frontier in American History." Explain the apparent similarities or differences in the arguments.

3. Compare Thomas Nichols' classifications of dialect with those of Otis Skinner and of Edward Eggleston. How do these classifications compare with Kurath's findings?

4. How scientific is Kurath's discussion of levels of usage? What is the basis for the three classes?

5. Compare the characteristics of American language outlined by Schele de Vere with those discussed by H. L. Mencken. What new light does Mencken add to De Vere's analysis?

6. List a number of words that have acquired a pejorative connotation in America that in other countries, especially in England, are neutral words.

7. Write a report on the etymology of one of the following words: *scrounge, lynch, doughboy, gobbledegook, motel.*

8. What does Otis Skinner mean by "Main Street" in his essay? How does this compare with Sinclair Lewis' definition as he employed the word in his novel of the same name?

Section 8

1. Analyze the language of the letter by Edward Winslow and specify the principal differences between the language of the colonists and of modern Americans.

2. Find examples of "tall talk" in several American public addresses. The speeches of Daniel Webster and Thomas Benton should offer examples.

3. What are the sources of Scotty's vocabulary in Mark Twain's "Buck Fanshaw's Funeral"? Which expressions are still current in America?

4. What evidence of "tall talk" or booster language do you find in Mark Twain's story?

5. Find examples of exaggeration in American fiction, such as Melville's *Moby Dick* and Sinclair Lewis' *Babbitt.*

6. What differences do you find in the dialects employed in the selections from Harris, Hall, and Mark Twain?

7. Write a story in which you employ the characteristic speech patterns of some section of the United States.

8. Who among current American writers do you consider masters of the American idiom? Explain.

Section 9

1. What does Walt Whitman mean by "protestantism in speech," in the second paragraph of "Slang in America"?

2. Notice Whitman's discussion of extension of word meanings, in the third paragraph of "Slang in America." Make a list of common words which have meanings quite removed from their original significations.

3. What is the democratic principle that operates in language to which people who use a language are more or less oblivious?

4. In the last paragraph of "Slang in America," Whitman mentions two analogies by which to describe the nature of language. How many other analogies can you find throughout the readings in this volume? Which do you find most effective as explanation of how language operates?

5. Judging by their discussions of slang, what is the essential difference between the philosophies of Walt Whitman and Oliver Wendell Holmes?

6. Compare Sinclair Lewis' use of *sagashitiferousness* (*Babbitt*, p. 170) with Webster's use of *sagaciate* in "They Don't Speak Our Language." Are these words related?

7. Compare the various authors' ideas in this section regarding the place where slang probably originates.

8. What other sources of slang than the Congressional Record influence the national speech patterns?

9. Bring H. T. Webster's discussion of slang up to date by discussing several categories that did not exist in the 1930's.

10. Check several dictionaries on the status of words which you think may be slang expressions. What do your findings suggest? What precisely is the difference between a slang expression and a colloquialism?

11. Lexicographers and linguists have their own peculiar brand of "alphabet soup." Identify the following specimens: OED, DAE, DA, EDD, NED, SOED, ADD and ACD.

Section 10

1. Show how new words may be formed from familiar elements in as many ways as you can, supporting each method of word-formation with a number of examples.

2. How is the "tall talk" of the frontier still maintained in American English? Give examples.

3. Make a list of words that have been added to our vocabulary by any of the following methods: onomatopoeia, analogy, fusion of elements, abbreviation, acronyms, or pure invention.

4. What slang terms among politicians today may be added to the list presented by De Vere?

5. Find as many words as you can in the current news that have not yet found their way into the dictionary.

6. Select a specific occupational or avocational area and compile an extensive vocabulary list of the words commonly used by people in this activity.

7. What devices of word-formation do you find employed by commercial advertisers?

8. Allen Walker Read once remarked that a history of American opposition movements could be written from the treatment of the prefix *anti-* in the *Dictionary of American English*. Write a paper on some aspect of American life by organizing your ideas around significant words which appear in *The Dictionary of American English* or Mathews' *Dictionary of Americanisms*.

Section 11

1. Explain the doctrine of appropriateness in matters of usage mentioned by Walter Barnes in his essay in this section.

2. Compare James Russell Lowell's attitude toward a living language with Emerson's ideas as expounded in "The American Scholar."

3. Compare Margaret Nicholson and Evans and Evans on several examples of disputed usage. Find contexts in the writings of current American authors to support either point of view.

4. List all of the so-called "errors" in the last paragraph of Bruce Bliven's editorial. Look these usages up in two handbooks of grammar and composition, and determine to what extent they are considered acceptable.

5. Using Lesslie Hall's *English Usage* as a model, find as many examples as you can of "grammatical errors" in the writings of eminent American writers.

6. Find examples in current literature of what Lowell calls truly masculine English.

7. Read Norman Lewis' "How Correct Must Correct English Be?" in *Harper's Magazine*, 198:68–74 (March, 1949). Check his nineteen usages in Nicholson's *Dictionary of American-English Usage* and in Evans and Evans *Dictionary of Contemporary American Usage*. How many of these usages are frowned on by both authorities?

8. What in your opinion should be the criterion of correctness or appropriateness in matters of language usage? Defend your position.

TOPICS FOR LONGER PAPERS

1. Shakespeare's Language and American English
2. Conservatism and Liberalism in the American Language
3. The Differences between Written and Spoken American
4. The Semantics of "American" Language
5. The Social Acceptability of Speech Patterns
6. Real versus Fictitious Differences between British and American English
7. Social and Psychological Significance of Language Patterns
8. Same Words and Different Meanings
9. Linguistic Determinism in America
10. British and American Styles of Writing
11. Americanisms in the Writings of Emerson, Poe, Melville, Runyan, Sandburg, Sinclair Lewis, Mark Twain, James Thurber, James Ferril, Bret Harte, etc.

12. The Democratic Principle in Language
13. Social Status of Language Habits
14. Specific Characteristics of American English
15. The Language of Advertising
16. New Trends in the American Language
17. How Language Records the History of a People
18. Individuality versus Conformity in Speech
19. American and British Spelling
20. How Dictionaries are Made
21. Why Dictionaries Must Be Revised
22. The American Dialects
23. Problems of Communication between Britons and Americans
24. An American Academy of Linguistics
25. The Nature of Slang
26. The Fusion of Tongues in America
27. A Standard American Language
28. Forces Making for Language Uniformity
29. The Sins of Americans in Linguistic Matters
30. American as an International Language
31. Effects of Movies, TV, Radio on Language
32. The Future of American English
33. Linguistic Conformity in the United States
34. Government Control of Language
35. The Language of Boosterism
36. Tall Talk and Public Address
37. Why Languages Change
38. Levels of Usage in a Classless Society
39. Effects of Linguistic Uniformity on the Spirit of a Nation
40. The Doctrine of Usage
41. The Influence of Printing on Language
42. Factors Which Influence American English
43. Theories Regarding the Divergence of British and American English
44. Dissemination of Speech Patterns
45. The Language of Sport
46. The Evanescence of Slang
47. Technology and the American Language
48. Nautical Terms in American English
49. American Borrowings from Other Countries
50. How Place Names Record the History of a Country
51. Folk Etymology in American English
52. Toward Simplified Spelling
53. The Problem of Ambiguity in American Speech
54. The American Language and Manifest Destiny
55. Social Status of Slang in America
56. Economy of Expression: a Problem of Word Choice
57. Euphemistic Expressions: a Form of Dishonesty
58. Changing Styles in American Writing
59. Formality versus Informality in American Speech
60. Linguistic Authoritarianism versus Laissez Faire

SELECTED BIBLIOGRAPHY

AMERICAN ENGLISH

"Americanisms," *The Nation*, 131:572 (November 26, 1930).

"American English," *The Outlook*, 89:236 (May 30, 1908).

"American English," *Harper's Weekly*, 56:25 (July 20, 1912).

"American Words," *Saturday Review of Literature*, 13:8 (January 18, 1936).

"The American Language," *Review of Reviews*, 20:589–91 (November, 1899).

"The American Language," *The Living Age*, 254:123–25 (July 13, 1907).

"The American Language Again," *The Nation*, 84:28–29 (January 10, 1907).

"At Last! An American Language," *The Literary Digest*, 53:848–50 (September 30, 1916).

Bourke, Joseph, "Do You Speak American?" *Catholic World*, 155:448–53 (July, 1942).

"A Briton Concedes Our Language," *The Literary Digest* 73:36–37 (May 6, 1922).

Carey, Gordon V., *American Into English*, London: William Heinemann, Ltd., 1953.

Colton, Arthur, "Gains and Losses in Language," *Harper's*, 140:707–09 (April, 1920).

Cousins, Norman, "The Living Language," *Saturday Review*, 35:22 (September 27, 1952).

Craigie, William A., *The Growth of American English*, Parts I and II, Society for Pure English, Tracts LVI and LVII, Oxford: Clarendon Press, 1940.

————, *The Study of American English*, Society for Pure English, Tract XXVII, pp. 199–219, Oxford: Clarendon Press, 1927.

Eliason, Norman E., "American English in Europe," *American Speech*, 32:163–69 (October, 1957).

Feather, William, "Anglicizing Americanisms," *American Speech*, 1:269–70 (February, 1926).

Foley, Louis, "Good Old American," *Education*, 61:288–93 (January, 1941).

Hamilton, Agnes, "The American Brogue," *Ladies' Home Journal*, 20:46 (May, 1903).

Hartt, Irene Widdemer, "Americanisms," *Education*, 13:367–74 (February, 1893).

Horwill, H. W., *American Variations*, Society for Pure English, Tract XLV, Oxford: Clarendon Press, 1934.

"How Yankee Chatter Clicks in Dear Old London," *The Literary Digest*, 109:35 (May 30, 1931).

Howard, Leon, "A Historical Note on American English, *American Speech*, 2:497–99 (September, 1927).

Johnson, Falk, "The History of Some 'Dirty' Words," *The American Mercury*, 71:538–45 (November, 1950).

Johnson, Jotham, "The Changing American Language," *Scientific American*, 193:78–83 (August, 1955).

Krapp, George P., *The English Language in America*, 2 vols., New York: The Century Co., 1925.

Lewis, "Our Changing Language," *Ladies' Home Journal*, 57:12 (March, 1940).

Lynd, Robert, "The King's English and The Prince's American," *The Living Age*, 334:549–51 (March 15, 1928).

Mallery, Richard D., *Our American Language*, Garden City: Halcyon House, 1947.

Malone, Kemp, "American and Anglo-Saxon," *American Speech*, 1:371–77 (April, 1926).

Marckwardt, Albert H., *American English*, New York: Oxford University Press, 1958.

Marshall, Archibald, "American Speech and English Language," *North American Review*, 214:628–35 (November, 1921).

Massey, B. W. A., "Divergence of American from English," *American Speech*, 6:1–9 (October, 1930).

Mathews, Mitford M., *The Beginnings of American English*, Chicago: University of Chicago Press, 1931.

Matthews, Brander, "American English and British English," *Scribner's*, 68:621–26 (November, 1920).

——, "Briticisms and Americanisms," *Harper's*, 83:215–22 (July, 1891).

McFee, William, "Mencken and Mencken, or The Gift of Tongues," *Bookman*, 54:361–63 (December, 1921).

McLean, Margaret P., *Good American Speech*, New York: E. P. Dutton & Co., 1941.

Mencken, Henry L., *The American Language*, 4th edition, New York: Alfred A. Knopf Co., 1936. *Supplement I*, 1945; *Supplement II*, 1948.

Moore, H. E., "The American Language," *The Living Age*, 327:416–20 (November 21, 1925).

Partridge, Eric and Clark, John W., *British and American Since 1900*, New York, Philosophical Library, 1951.

Phipson, Evacustes A., "British vs. American English," *Dialect Notes*, 1:428–37 (December, 1896).

——, "Americanisms," *Spectator*, 73:405 (September 29, 1894).

Pitts, Alice, "You Think You Speak English?" *Christian Science Monitor*, September 10, 1949, p. 12.

Pyles, Thomas, *Words and Ways of American English*, New York: Random House, Inc., 1952.

"Some So-called Americanisms," *The Living Age*, 204:438–43 (February 16, 1895).

Tucker, Gilbert M., *American English*, New York: Alfred A. Knopf Co., 1921.

Tucker, Thomas G., "British English and American English," *Scribner's*, 70:730–36 (December, 1921).

Weber, Carl J., "Do We Speak English?" *North American Review*, 207:91–101 (January, 1918).

Wild, Jacob Henry, *Glimpses of the American Language and Civilization*, Bern: A. Francke, 1945.

Wilder, Thornton, "Toward an American Language," *Atlantic Monthly*, 190:31–37 (July, 1952).

DICTIONARIES AND GLOSSARIES

Adams, Ramon F., *Western Words: A Dictionary of the Range, Cow Camp and Trail*, Norman: University of Oklahoma Press, 1945.

Ashley, Clifford W., "Glossary of Whaling Terms," in *The Yankee Whaler*, Boston: Houghton Mifflin Co., 1938.

Barrére, Albert, and Leland, Charles G., *Dictionary of Slang, Jargon and Cant*, 2 vols., 2nd edition, London: Bell, 1897.

Bartlett, John Russell, *Dictionary of Americanisms*, Boston: Little, Brown & Co., 1859, 1877.

Berry, Lester V., and Van Den Bark, Melvin, *The American Thesaurus of Slang*, New York: Thomas Y. Crowell Co., 1943.

The Century Dictionary and Cyclopedia, 12 vols., New York: The Century Company, 1911.

Colcord, Joanna Carver, *Sea Language Comes Ashore,* New York: Cornell Maritime Press, 1945.

Craigie, William A., and Hulbert, James R., *Dictionary of American English on Historical Principles,* Chicago: University of Chicago Press, 1936–1944.

Criswell, Elijah, "Lewis and Clark: Linguistic Pioneers," *University of Missouri Studies,* Vol. XV, No. 2 (April 1, 1940).

Farmer, John S., *Americanisms Old and New: A Dictionary of Words, Phrases and Colloquialisms Peculiar to the United States, British America, the West Indies, etc.,* 2 vols., London: Thomas Poulter & Sons, 1889.

Funk, Issac K., and others, *A New Standard Dictionary of the English Language,* New York: Funk and Wagnalls Co., 1929.

Halliwell, James O., *Dictionary of Archaic and Provincial Words, etc.,* 7th ed., London: Routledge, 1924.

Herman, Lewis Helmar, and Herman, Marguerite S., *Manual of American Dialects,* Chicago and New York: Ziff-Davis Publishing Co., 1947.

Hogan, Homer, *Dictionary of American Synonyms,* New York: Philosophical Library, 1956.

Hotten, J. C., *The Slang Dictionary,* London: Chatto and Windus, 1873.

Kenyon, John S. and Knott, Thomas A., *Pronouncing Dictionary of American English,* Springfield, Massachusetts: G. and C. Merriam Co., 1944.

Krapp, George P., *The Pronunciation of Standard English in America,* New York: Oxford University Press, 1919.

Kurath, Hans, and associates, *A Linguistic Atlas of the United States and Canada,* Providence: Brown University Press, 1939–1941.

———, *A Word Geography of the Eastern United States,* Ann Arbor: University of Michigan Press, 1949.

Little, William, Fowler, H. W., and Coulson, J., *A Shorter Oxford English Dictionary on Historical Principles,* revised and enlarged by C. T. Onions, 2 vols., Oxford: Clarendon Press, 1933.

Maitland, James, *American Slang Dictionary,* Chicago: R. J. Kittredge & Co., 1891.

Mathews, Mitford M., *Dictionary of Americanisms on Historical Principles,* Chicago: University of Chicago Press, 1951.

Murray, J. A. H., and others, *A New English Dictionary on Historical Principles,* 12 vols., Oxford: Clarendon Press, 1884–1928. *Supplement,* 1933.

O'Leary, Frank, *Dictionary of American Underworld Lingo,* New York: Twayne, 1951.

Partridge, Eric, *Dictionary of Slang and Unconventional English,* London: Routledge and Kegan Paul, 1949.

Ramsay, Robert L., and Emberson, Frances Guthrie, "A Mark Twain Lexicon," *University of Missouri Studies,* Vol. XIII (January 1, 1938).

Scott, George Ryley, *Swan's Anglo-American Dictionary,* New York: Library Publishers, 1950.

Thornton, R. H., *An American Glossary,* 2 vols., Philadelphia: Lippincott, 1912. Volume 3 in *Dialect Notes,* Vol. VI (1931–1939), Madison, Wisconsin: American Dialect Society, 1939.

Waldhorn, Arthur, *Concise Dictionary of the American Language,* New York: Philosophical Library, 1956.

Wentworth, Harold, *American Dialect Dictionary,* New York: Thomas Y. Crowell & Co., 1944.

———, and Flexner, Stuart Berg, *Dictionary of American Slang,* New York: Thomas Y. Crowell Co., 1960.

Webster, Noah, *An American Dictionary of the English Language*, New Haven: The
     Author, 1841; New York: S. Converse, 1828.
Webster's New International Dictionary, 2nd edition, Springfield, Massachusetts; G. and
     C. Merriam Co., 1934.
Webster's New World Dictionary of the American Language, Cleveland and New York:
     World Publishing Company, 1951.
Wyld, Henry C., *Universal Dictionary of the English Language*, London: Routledge,
     1932.

REGIONAL VARIETIES OF AMERICAN

Alexander, Henry, "The Language of the Salem Witchcraft Trials," *American Speech*,
     3:390–400 (June, 1928).
Allan, Philip F., "A Sample of New Hampshire Dialect," *Publications of the American
     Dialect Society*, No. 15 (April, 1951), pp. 65–68.
Ayers, Lucille, and others, "Expressions from Rural Florida," *Publications of the
     American Dialect Society*, No. 14 (November, 1950), pp. 81.
Babcock, C. Merton, "The Social Significance of the Language of the American
     Frontier," *American Speech*, 24:256–63 (December, 1949).
Berry, Lester V., "Southern Mountain Dialect," *American Speech*, 15:45–54 (February,
     1940).
Bradley, F. W., "A Word-list from South Carolina," *Publications of the American
     Dialect Society*, No. 14 (November, 1950), pp. 1–73 and No. 21 (April, 1954),
     pp. 16–41.
Buckner, Mary Dale, "Ranch Diction of the Texas Panhandle," *American Speech*,
     8:25–32 (February, 1933).
Buxbaum, Katherine, "Mark Twain and the American Dialect," *American Speech*,
     2:233–236 (February, 1927).
Dalton, A. P., "A Word-list from Southern Kentucky," *Publications of the American
     Dialect Society*, No. 13 (April, 1950), pp. 22–23.
Davison, Zeta C., "A Word-list from the Appalachians and the Piedmont Area of North
     Carolina," *Publications of the American Dialect Society*, No. 19 (April, 1953),
     pp. 8–14.
Eliason, Norman Ellsworth, *Tarheel Talk: An Historical Study of the English Language
     of North Carolina*, Chapel Hill: University of North Carolina Press, 1956.
Farr, T. J., "The Language of the Tennessee Mountain Region," *American Speech*,
     14:89–92 (April, 1939).
Greet, W. Cabell, "A Standard American Language," *New Republic*, 95:68–70 (May 25,
     1938).
Halsey, Ashley, Jr., "Do You Speak American?" *Saturday Evening Post*, 222:17
     (June 10, 1950).
Hogan, Charles H., "A Yankee Comments on Texas Speech," *American Speech*, 20:81–84
     (April, 1945).
Hubbell, Allen F., *The Pronunciation of English in New York City*, New York: King's
     Crown Press, 1950.
Hughes, Herbert L., "A Word-list from Louisiana," *Publications of the American
     Dialect Society*, No. 15 (April, 1951), pp. 69–71.
Hurston, Zora Neale, "Story in Harlem Slang," *The American Mercury*, 55:84–96
     (July, 1942).
Hutson, Arthur E., "Gaelic Loan-words in American," *American Speech*, 22:18–23
     (February, 1947).

Johnson, Falk, "How We Got Our Dialects," *The American Mercury*, 64:66–70 (January, 1947).

Kimmerle, Marjorie, and Gibby, Patricia Martin, "A Word-list from Colorado," *Publications of the American Dialect Society*, No. 11 (April, 1949), pp. 16–27.

Lindsay, Vachel, "The Real American Language," *The American Mercury*, 13:257–265 (March, 1928).

Lovell, Charles J., "The Background of Mark Twain's Vocabulary," *American Speech*, 22:88–98 (February, 1947).

Macy, William F., *The Nantucket Scrap-basket*, Boston and New York: Houghton Mifflin Co., 1930.

Matthews, William, "Early New England Words," *American Speech*, 15:225–31 (October, 1940).

Maxfield, E. K., "The Speech of Southwestern Pennsylvania," *American Speech*, 7:18–20 (October, 1931).

————, "Maine Dialect," *American Speech*, 2:76–83 (November, 1926).

Mathews, Mitford M., *Some Sources of Southernisms*, University, Alabama: University of Alabama Press, 1948.

McAtee, W. L., "Gleanings from the Dialect of Grant County, Indiana," *Publications of the American Dialect Society*, No. 15 (April, 1951), pp. 51–64.

McDavid, Raven I., Jr., "The Way We Talk," *New York Times Magazine*, April 23, 1950, pp. 44; 46; 47; 49.

McDavid, Raven I., and McDavid, Virginia Glenn, "The Relationship of the Speech of American Negroes to the Speech of the Whites," *American Speech*, 26:4–17 (February, 1951).

Moore, Helen L., "The Lingo of the Mining Camp," *American Speech*, 2:86–88 (November, 1926).

Morrison, Hugh, "New Yorkers Can't Speak English," *The American Mercury*, 45:42–46 (September, 1938).

Mullen, Kate, "Westernisms," *American Speech*, 1:149–153 (December, 1925).

Orbeck, Anders, *Early New England Pronunciation as reflected in Some Seventeenth-Century Town Records*, Ann Arbor: University of Michigan Press, 1927.

Page, Eugene R., "English in the Pennsylvania German Area," *American Speech*, 12:203–206 (October, 1937).

Read, Allen Walker, "Nantucketisms of 1848," *American Speech*, 10:38–42 (February, 1935).

Strainchamps, Ethel, "How to Talk Ozark," *Harper's*, 215:82–83 (July, 1957).

Thompson, William F., "Frontier Tall Talk," *American Speech*, 9:187–99 (October, 1934).

Tidwell, James Nathan, "A Word-list from West Texas," *Publications of the American Dialect Society*, No. 11 (April, 1949), pp. 3–15.

Tucker, R. Whitney, "Notes on the Philadelphia Dialect," *American Speech*, 19:37–42 (February, 1944).

Vance, Randolph, and Wilson, George P., *Down in the Holler; A Gallery of Ozark Speech*, Norman: University of Oklahoma Press, 1953.

Veltman, Peter, "Dutch Survivals in Holland, Michigan," *American Speech*, 15:80–83 (February, 1940).

Vogel, Joseph, "Backwoodsman Talk," *American Speech*, 2:39–41 (October, 1926).

Warner, James H., "A Word-list from Southeast Arkansas," *American Speech*, 13:3–7 (February, 1938).

White, E. B., "Maine Speech," in *One Man's Meat*, pp. 234–236, New York: Harper & Brothers, 1940.

Wise, C. M., "Southern American Dialect," *American Speech*, 8:37–43 (April, 1933).

Wood, Gordon R., "A List of Words from Tennessee," *Publications of the American Dialect Society*, No. 29 (April, 1958), pp. 3–18.

Woodward, C. M., "A Word-list from Virginia and North Carolina," *Publications of the American Dialect Society*, No. 6 (November, 1946), pp. 1–46.

Woofter, Carey, "Dialect Words and Phrases from West Central West Virginia," *American Speech*, 2:347–67 (May, 1927).

THE AMERICAN SLANGUAGE

Alderson, William L., "Carnie Talk from the West Coast," *American Speech*, 28:112–19 (May, 1953).

Anson, Lyman, and Funkhouser, Clifford, "The Rails Have a Word for It," *Saturday Evening Post*, 214:27 (June 13, 1942).

Arnold, Jane W., "The Language of Delinquent Boys," *American Speech*, 22:120–23 (April, 1947).

Bender, James F., "Lingo of the Big Top," *New York Times Magazine*, April 8, 1945, p. 20.

Bernstein, Theodore M., "Now It's 'Watch Your Slanguage,'" *New York Times Magazine*, February 28, 1960, pp. 31; 94.

Boone, Lalia Phipps, "Patterns of Innovation in the Language of the Oil Fields," *American Speech*, 24:31–37 (February, 1949).

Brown, Barbara, "The Great American Slanguage," *The Outlook*, 156:417; 435 (November 12, 1930).

Clark, J. W., "Lumberjack Lingo," *American Speech*, 7:47–53 (October, 1931).

Cummings, G. Clark, "The Language of Horse Racing," *American Speech*, 30:17–29 (February, 1955).

Davidson, Levette J., "Sugar Beet Language," *American Speech*, 6:10–15 (October, 1930).

De Lannoy, William C., and Masterson, Elizabeth, "Teen-age Hophead Jargon," *American Speech*, 27:23–31 (February, 1952).

Engler, Leo F., "A Glossary of United States Air Force Slang," *American Speech*, 30:115–20 (May, 1955).

Frazier, Marshall W., "Truck Driver's Language," *American Speech*, 30:91–94 (May, 1955).

"Glossary of Army Slang," Public Relations Division, U.S. Army, *American Speech*, 16:163–69 (October, 1941).

Gold, Robert S., "The Vernacular of the Jazz World," *American Speech*, 32:271–82 (December, 1957).

Hogan, Lt. Col. Pendleton, "Pentagonese," *Collier's*, 128:32–33; 67 (November 24, 1951).

Horne, Elliot, "For Cool Cats and Far-out Chicks," *New York Times Magazine*, August 18, 1957, p. 26.

Hughes, Dorothy, "The Language of the Fashion Sheet," *American Speech*, 10:191–94 (October, 1935).

Irwin, Godfred, *American Tramp and Underworld Slang*, London: Eric Partridge, Ltd, at the Scholartis Press, 1931.

"Language of Business," *Fortune*, 42:113–117ff. (November, 1950).

Mansell, Don, and Hall, Joseph S., "Hot Rod Terms in the Pasadena Area," *American Speech*, 29:89–104 (May, 1954).

Martin, Douglas S., "Business Jargon and the American Language," *Living Age*, 282:373–75 (August 8, 1914).

Maurer, David W., "The Argot of the Moonshiner," *American Speech*, 24:3–13 (February, 1949).

———, "The Argot of the Underworld," *American Speech*, 7:99–118 (December, 1931).

———, "The Argot of the Underworld Narcotic Addict," *American Speech*, 11:116–27 (April, 1936).

———, "Carnival Cant: A Glossary of Circus and Carnival Slang," *American Speech*, 6:327–37 (June, 1931).

———, "Whiz Mob: A Correlation of the Technical Argot of Pickpockets with their Behavior Patterns," *Publications of the American Dialect Society*, No. 24 (November, 1955), pp. 1–199, and No. 31 (April, 1959), pp. 14–30.

Mencken, H. L., "What the People of American Towns Call Themselves," *American Speech*, 23:162–84 (October–December, 1948).

———, "Names for Americans," *American Speech*, 22:241–256 (December, 1947).

Millstein, Gilbert, "Guys and Dolls Lexicon," *New York Times Magazine*, February 17, 1952, p. 20.

Montgomery, H. C., and Cottrell, W. F., "A Glossary of Railroad Terms," *American Speech*, 18:161–170 (October, 1943).

Morgan, Bayard Quincy, "Space in Speech," *American Speech*, 22:178–187 (October, 1947).

Moss, Arnold, "Jewels from a Box Office: The Language of Show Business," *American Speech*, 11:219–222 (October, 1936).

Motherwell, Hiram, "The Language of Lobster Alley," *Bookman*, 72:396–99 (December, 1930).

Musser, Benjamin Francis, "A Study in American Slang," *Catholic World*, 117:471–76 (July, 1923).

"My Mother's Slang," *Scribner's*, 68:246–48 (August, 1920).

Nieberg, George Frederic, "The American Slanguage," *The Forum*, 84:371–76 (December, 1930).

Norman, Arthur, M. Z., "Army Speech and the Future of American English," *American Speech*, 31:107–112 (May, 1956).

Oppenheimer, Reuben, "Legal Lingo," *American Speech*, 2:142–44 (December, 1926).

Ostrow, Albert A., "Service Men's Slang," *The American Mercury*, 57:552–56 (November, 1943).

"Our Strange New Language," *Literary Digest*, 53:708–10 (September 16, 1916).

Pond, Frederick R., "Language of the California Oil Fields," *American Speech*, 7:261–72 (April, 1932).

Pound, Olivia, "Educational Lingo," *American Speech*, 1:311–14 (March, 1926).

Ralph, Julian, "The Language of the Tenement Folk," *Harper's Weekly*, 41:90 (January 23, 1897).

Reynolds, Horace, "Slaunchwise and Catawampus," *Saturday Review of Literature*, 30:26–7 (August 23, 1947).

Rockwell, Harold E., "Headline Words," *American Speech*, 2:140–41 (December, 1926).

Saul, Vernon W., "The Vocabulary of Bums," *American Speech*, 4:337–346 (June, 1929).

Schauffler, Robert Haven, "Timesquarese," *Saturday Review of Literature*, 1:816–17 (June 13, 1925).

"Slang as a Democratic Agent," *Literary Digest,* 55:29 (July 21, 1917).

Shaw, Arnold, *The Lingo of Tin Pan Alley,* New York: Broadcast Music, 1949.

Sperber, Hans, and Tidwell, James N., "Words and Phrases in American Politics," *American Speech,* 25:91–110 (May, 1950), and 26:241–47 (December, 1951).

Taylor, A. Marjorie, *The Language of World War II,* New York: H. H. Wilson Co., 1948.

Tidwell, James N., "Political Words and Phrases: Card-playing Terms," *American Speech,* 33:21–28 (February, 1958).

Van Den Bark, Melvin, "Nebraska Pioneer English," *American Speech,* 6:237–52 (April, 1931), 7:1–17 (October, 1931), 7:161–71 (February, 1932).

Webb, H. Brook, "The Slang of Jazz," *American Speech,* 12:179–184 (October, 1937).

Whyte, William H., Jr., "The Language of Advertising," *Fortune,* 46:98–101 (September, 1952).

Wimberly, Lowry Charles, "American Political Cant," *American Speech,* 2:135–39 (December, 1926).

GUIDES TO USAGE

Aiken, Janet R., *Commonsense Grammar,* New York: Thomas Y. Crowell Co., 1936.

———, "Our Whimsical Grammarians," *Bookman,* 73:290–92 (May, 1931).

Babcock, C. Merton, "Never Use a Preposition to End a Sentence With," *ETC.: A Review of General Semantics,* 14:299–303 (Summer, 1957).

Barnard, Ellsworth, "Good Grammar Ain't Good Usage," *New York Times Magazine,* January 27, 1957, pp. 20; 32.

Barzun, Jacques, "How To Suffocate the English Language," *Saturday Review of Literature,* 26:3–4 (February 13, 1943).

———, "The Retort Circumstantial," *The American Scholar,* 20:289–93 (Summer, 1951).

Brown, Goold, *Grammar of English Grammars,* New York: William Wood & Co., 1851.

Bryant, Margaret M., *A Functional English Grammar,* Boston: D. C. Heath & Co., 1945.

———, and others, "Current English Forum," in successive issues of *College English.*

Conesford, Lord, "You Americans are Murdering the Language," *Saturday Evening Post,* 230:30; 71–3 (July 13, 1957).

De Voto, Bernard, "Grammarian's Funeral," *Saturday Review of Literature,* 16:8 (October 2, 1937).

———, "The Faculty Style," *Saturday Review of Literature,* 17:8 (December 18, 1937).

Evans, Bergen, and Evans, Cornelia, *A Dictionary of Contemporary American Usage,* New York: Random House, Inc., 1957.

Fadiman, Clifton, "Is there an Upper-class Language?" *Holiday,* 20:6–15 (October, 1956).

Foley, Louis, "The Modern Crime of Linguacide," *School and Society,* 73:273–75 (May 5, 1951).

Follett, Wilson, "Grammar Is Obsolete," *Atlantic Monthly,* 205:75–76 (February, 1960).

Fowler, Henry W., *A Dictionary of Modern English Usage,* London: Oxford University Press, 1947.

Fowler, H. W., and Fowler, F. G., *The King's English,* Oxford: Clarendon Press, 1931.

Fries, C. C., *American English Grammar,* English Monograph, No. 10, Chicago: National Council of Teachers of English, 1940.

Haber, Tom Burns, *A Writer's Handbook of American Usage,* New York and London: Longmans, Green & Co., 1942.

Hall, J. Lesslie, *English Usage,* Chicago: Scott, Foresman & Co., 1917.

Horwill, H. W., *A Dictionary of Modern American Usage*, New York: Oxford University Press, 1944.

Jespersen, Otto, *Modern English Grammar on Historical Principles*, Heidelberg: Winter, 1927–1949.

Kenyon, John S., "Cultural Levels and Functional Varieties of English," *College English*, 10:31–36 (October, 1948).

Leonard, Sterling Andrus, *Current English Usage*, English Monograph, No. 1, Chicago: National Council of Teachers of English, 1932.

Lewis, Norman, "How Correct Must Correct English Be?" *Harper's Magazine*, 198:68–74 (March, 1949).

Lloyd, Donald J., "Snobs, Slobs and the English Language," *The American Scholar*, 20:279–88 (Summer, 1951).

Lounsbury, Thomas R., *The Standard of Usage in English*, New York and London: Harper & Brothers, 1907.

Marckwardt, Albert H., "What Is Good English?" in *Talks* (published by Columbia Broadcasting System, Inc.), 1937.

———, and Walcott, Fred G., *Facts about Current English Usage*, English Monograph, No. 7, National Council of Teachers of English, New York: D. Appleton-Century Co., Inc., 1938.

Masson, Thomas L., "Speech, Common and Preferred," *Century Magazine*, 113:80–89 (December, 1926).

Maverick, Maury, "The Case Against 'Gobbledygook,'" *New York Times Magazine*, May 21, 1944, pp. 11; 35–36.

Nicholson, Margaret, *A Dictionary of American-English Usage* (based on Fowler's *Modern English Usage*), New York: Oxford University Press, 1957.

Pooley, Robert C., "Grammar and Usage in Textbooks on English," Bulletin No. 14, University of Wisconsin Bureau of Educational Research, Madison: University of Wisconsin Press, 1933.

Redman, Ben Ray, "Words, Words, Words," *Saturday Review*, 40:22 (March 2, 1957).

Scott, Fred N., *The Standard of American Speech and Other Papers*, Boston: Allyn and Bacon, 1926.

Withington, Robert, "Where Is Usage Bred?" *Commonweal*, 27:208–11 (December 17, 1937).